PRINCIPLES OF
QUANTUM
ARTIFICIAL
INTELLIGENCE

T0350052

PRINCIPLES OF
QUANTUM
ARTIFICIAL
INTELLIGENCE

Andreas Wichert

Instituto Superior Técnico - Universidade de Lisboa, Portugal

World Scientific

NEW JERSEY · LONDON · SINGAPORE · BEIJING · SHANGHAI · HONG KONG · TAIPEI · CHENNAI

Published by

World Scientific Publishing Co. Pte. Ltd.

5 Toh Tuck Link, Singapore 596224

USA office: 27 Warren Street, Suite 401-402, Hackensack, NJ 07601

UK office: 57 Shelton Street, Covent Garden, London WC2H 9HE

British Library Cataloguing-in-Publication Data
A catalogue record for this book is available from the British Library.

PRINCIPLES OF QUANTUM ARTIFICIAL INTELLIGENCE

ISBN 978-981-4566-74-2

Printed in Singapore

for André

Preface

Artificial intelligence and quantum computation divide the subject into many major areas. Each of these areas are now so extensive and huge, that a major understanding of the core concepts that unite them is extremely difficult. This book is about the core ideas of artificial intelligence and quantum computation. They are united in new subarea of artificial intelligence: "Quantum Artificial Intelligence".

The book is composed of two sections: the first is on classical computation and the second section is on quantum computation. In the first section, we introduce the basic principles of computation, representation and problem solving. In the second section, we introduce the principles of quantum computation and their relation to the core ideas of artificial intelligence, such as search and problem solving. We illustrate their use with several examples.

The notes on which the book is based evolved in the course "Information and Computation for Artificial Intelligence" in the years $2008 - 2012$ at Department of Computer Science and Engineering, Instituto Superior Técnico, Technical University of Lisbon. Thanks to Technical University of Lisbon for rewarding me a sabbatical leave in the 2012-2013 academic year, which has given me the time to finish this book. My research in recent years has benefited from many discussions with Ana Paiva, Luís Tarrataca, Ângelo Cardoso, João Sacramento and Catarina Moreira. Especially I would like to thank Luís Tarrataca and offer all of him deepest gratitude. The chapter about "Quantum Problem-Solving" is mainly based on his work. Finally, I would like to thank my loving wife *Manuela*, without her encouragement the book would be never finished.

Andreas Wichert

Contents

Chapter 1

Introduction

Symbolical artificial intelligence is a field of computer science that is highly related to quantum computation. At first glance, this statement appears to be a contradiction. However, the artificial intelligence framework, such as search and production system theory, allows an elegant description of a quantum computer model that is capable of quickly executing programs.

1.1 Artificial Intelligence

Artificial intelligence (AI) is a subfield of computer science that models the mechanisms of intelligent human behavior (intelligence). This approach is accomplished via simulation with the help of artificial artifacts, typically with computer programs on a machine that performs calculations. It should be noted that the machine does not need to be electronic. Indeed, Charles Babbage (1791-1871) sketched the first mechanical machine (a difference engine) for the calculation of certain values of polynomial functions [Hyman (1985)]. With the goal of mechanizing calculation steps, Babbage sketched the first model of a mechanical universal computer and called it an analytical engine. At the same time, Lady Ada Lovelance (1815-1852) thought about the computing power of such a machine. She argued that such a machine could only perform what it was told to do; such a machine could not generate new knowledge.

The term "artificial intelligence" itself was invented by the American computer scientist John McCarthy. It was used in the title of a conference that took place in the year 1956 at Dartmonth College in the USA. During this meeting, programs were presented that played chess and checkers, proved theorems and interpreted texts. The programs were thought to simulate human intelligent behavior. However, the terms "intelligence"

1

and "intelligent human behavior" are not very well defined and understood. The definition of artificial intelligence leads to the paradox of a discipline whose principal purpose is its own definition.

A.M. Turing (1912-1954), in 1950, wrote the essay "Computing Machinery and Intelligence", in which he poses the question of how to determine whether a program is intelligent or not [Turing (1950)]. He defines intelligence as the reaction of an intelligent being to certain questions. This behavior can be tested by the so-called Turing test. A subject communicates over a computer terminal with two non-visible partners, a program and a human. If the subject cannot differentiate between the human and the program, the program is called intelligent. The questions posed can originate from any domain. However, if the domain is restricted, then the test is called a restricted Turing test. A restricted domain could be, for example, a medical diagnosis or the game of chess.

Human problem-solving algorithms are studied in Artificial Intelligence. The key idea behind these algorithms is the symbolic representation of the domain in which the problems are solved. Symbols are used to denote or refer to something other than themselves, namely other things in the world (according to the, pioneering work of Tarski [Tarski (1944, 1956, 1995)]). They are defined by their occurrence in a structure and by a formal language which manipulates these structures [Simon (1991); Newell (1990)] (see Figure 1.1). In this context, symbols do not, by themselves, represent any utilizable knowledge. For example, they cannot be used for a definition of similarity criteria between themselves. The use of symbols in algorithms which imitate human intelligent behavior led to the famous physical symbol system hypothesis by Newell and Simon (1976) [Newell and Simon (1976)]: "The necessary and sufficient condition for a physical system to exhibit intelligence is that it be a physical symbol system." Symbols are not present in the world; they are the constructs of a human mind and simplify the process of representation used in communication and problem solving.

1.2   Motivation and Goals

Traditional AI is built around abstract algorithms and data structures that manipulate symbols. One of the important algorithms is the tree or graph search. Common forms of knowledge representation are symbolic rules and semantic nets. Traditional AI attempts to imitate human behavior without

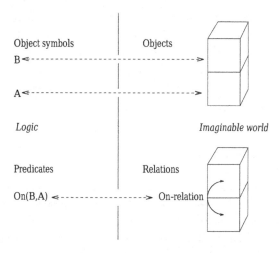

Fig. 1.1 Object represented by symbols and relation represented by predicate.

any relationship to physical reality, for example, in biological hardware. Sub-Symbolical processing, on the other hand, belongs to biology-inspired AI, which involves methods such as neural networks or behavioral systems. Could the physical nature, as described by quantum physics, also lead to algorithms that imitate human behavior? What are the possibilities for the realization of artificial intelligence by means of quantum computation? Computational algorithms that are inspired by this physical reality are described by quantum computation. We will answer questions such as why and how to use quantum algorithms in artificial intelligence.

Questions that appear to be quite simple, such as: what are random numbers and how can we generate them, cannot be answered by traditional computer science. The widely used pseudo random generators are based on deterministic procedures and do not generate randomness; instead, they generate pseudo-randomness. Pseudo random generators are related to deterministic chaos sequences, which are described by mathematical chaos theory. Chaotic patterns can arise from very simple mathematics. While the results can be similar to true randomness, the output patterns are generated by deterministic rules. Chaotic patterns differ from most deterministic systems because any small change made to their variables can result in unpredictable changes to the system behavior.

Recently, quantum algorithms for AI were proposed, including a quantum tree search algorithm and a quantum production system [Tarrataca and Wichert (2011b,a, 2012b, 2013b)]. In this book, we introduce quantum computation and its application to AI. Based on information science, we will illustrate the general principles that govern information processing and information structures.

1.3 Guide to the Reader

This book is about some core ideas of artificial intelligence and quantum computation and is composed of two sections: the first is on classical computation and the second section is on quantum computation. In the first section, we introduce the basic principles of computation, representation and problem solving. Quantum physics is based on information theory and probability theory. We present both theories and indicate their relationships to artificial intelligence by associative memory and Bayesian networks. In the second section, we introduce the principles of quantum computation and its mathematical framework. We present two principles on which quantum computation is based, the discrete Fourier transform and Grover's algorithm. Based on these principles, we introduce the iterative quantum tree search algorithm that speeds up the search. In the next step we introduce a quantum production system on which a universal quantum computer model is based. Finally, related topics such as quantum cognition and quantum random walk are presented. Readers who want to develop a general understanding of the quantum computation mathematical framework should read the second section, beginning with the chapter "Introduction to Quantum Physics". Sections that go more into detail are marked by a star "∗" and can be skipped on the first reading.

1.4 Content

1.4.1 *Classical computation*

Computation - Chapter 2 The Entscheidungsproblem is presented, and the Turing machine is introduced. The proof of the Entscheidungsproblem is based on Cantor's diagonal argument and Gödelization. The Universal Turing machine is an abstract model of a computer. Computational complexity theory addresses questions regarding which problems can be solved in a finite amount of time on a computer. The Church–Turing thesis states that any algorithmic process can be simulated on a Turing machine. Two classes of practical computers are presented: analog and digital computers.

Problem Solving - Chapter 3 In the first step, the knowledge representation framework is introduced: rules, logic-based operators, frames and categorical representations. In the next step, production systems are introduced. A production system is a model of human problem solving. It is composed of long-term memory and working memory, which is also called short-term memory. We distinguish between deduction systems and reaction systems. Planning can be performed more easily by reaction systems in which the premise specifies the conditions that must be satisfied; in this way, the condition that specifies an action can be undertaken. An 8-puzzle example is presented. There is an assumption that the distance between states in the problem space is related to the distance between the sub-symbols that represent the states in sub-symbolical problem-solving. Sub-symbolical problem-solving takes advantage of the geometric nature of the world.

Information - Chapter 4 Information theory is highly related to mathematical probability theory and thermodynamics. Entropy is a measure of the disorder of the configuration of states and can be described by a dice model. The Maxwell paradox identifies information with a negative measure of entropy. The ideal entropy represents the minimal number of optimal questions that must be addressed to know the result of an experiment. We will indicate the relationships between information and hierarchical structures and measurement. In the section on information and memory, we will introduce a biologically inspired model of associative memory. The Information and storage capacity of the model is high, given that the binary representation is sparse. Finally, a deduction system based on associative memory is presented.

Reversible Algorithms - Chapter 5 Bennett (1973) showed that irreversible overwriting of one bit causes at least $k \cdot T \cdot log2$ joules of energy dissipation, where k is Boltzmann's constant and T is the absolute temperature. Bennett also indicated that this lower bound can be ignored when using reversible computation. Reversible computing is a model of computing in which the computational process is reversible. Reversible Boolean gates and circuits are described.

Probability - Chapter 6 Probability theory is built around Kolmogorov's axioms. For a joint distribution of n possible variables, the exponential growth of combinations being true or false becomes an intractable problem for large n. There are two possible solutions to this problem, Naïve Bayes and Bayesian networks. Naïve Bayes is related to counting and categorization. For the unobservable variables, the Bayesian networks are based on the law of total probability. A Markov chain is a mathematical system that undergoes transitions described by a stochastic matrix. A stochastic matrix evolution that occurs when describing the evolution of a physical system is usually non-reversible.

1.4.2   Quantum computation

Introduction to Quantum Physics - Chapter 7 The unitary deterministic evolution represented by the Schrödinger equation and two interpretations of quantum mechanics are presented. We indicate the difference between stochastic Markov evolution and unitary evolution. The mathematical framework of quantum theory is based on linear algebra in Hilbert space. The relationships between the unitary operators represented by unitary matrices and the Schrödinger equation and the Hamiltonian are described by a spectral representation. A 2-state quantum system is described by a two-dimensional Hilbert space. Such a 2-state quantum system corresponds to a qubit. A register is composed of several qubits and is defined by the tensor product. The von Neumann entropy of a superposition of qubits measures the distribution of the probabilities. It describes the departure of the state from a pure state. For a pure state, there is no uncertainty during the measurement. The higher the entropy is, the higher the uncertainty during the measurement.

Computation with Qubits - Chapter 8 A unitary operator on a qubit is called a unary quantum gate. An operation on several qubits can be represented by unitary matrices. The matrix representation of serial and parallel operations is composed of either a product or a tensor operation between the matrices. A reversible circuit of m bits corresponds to a unitary mapping. A reversible circuit can be represented by a unitary permutation matrix or by quantum Boolean gates. The Deutsch algorithm exploits the superposition of qubits that are generated by Hadamard gates; the Deutsch algorithm is more powerful than any other classical algorithm and determines whether an unknown function of one bit is constant or not by calling the function one time. A classical algorithm requires two calls. The Deutsch Jozsa algorithm generalizes the working principle even to a more powerful algorithm for a function of m bits.

Periodicity - Chapter 9 The Fourier transform changes a signal from the time domain to the frequency domain. The discrete Fourier transform changes discrete time-based or space-based data into frequency-based data. The discrete Fourier transform (DFT) can be seen as a linear transform represented by a unitary matrix F. This unitary matrix F also defines the quantum Fourier transform (QFT). The decomposition of the matrix is described by the fast Fourier transform (FFT). The QFT decomposition is equivalent to the FFT. The QFT period algorithm determines the period of a periodic function in polynomial time and is the basis of Shor's Algorithm for the factorization of numbers in polynomial time. An alternative approach is described in Kitaev's phase estimation algorithm, which determines the eigenvalue for a unitary operator and an eigenvector.

Search - Chapter 10 We want to find x for which $f(x) = 1$, $x = \xi$. This task is equivalent to a decision problem with a binary answer $1 = yes$ and $0 = no$ and the instance x. There is a lower bound for a quantum search on a quantum computer using a quantum oracle. The possible speedup is quadratic; $NP - complete$ problems remain $NP - complete$. The search is described by Grover's algorithm and is based on the Householder reflection. In the case, the number of the solutions is unknown, we can apply a quantum counting algorithm. The generate-and-test method is a simple AI paradigm that can directly benefit from Grover's algorithm.

Quantum Problem-Solving - Chapter 11 Problem-solving can be modeled by a production system that implements a search algorithm. The search defines a problem space and can be represented as a tree. In an uninformed search, no additional information about the states is given. A heuristic search is based on a heuristic function $h(\nu)$ that estimates the cheapest cost from the node ν to the goal. However, inventing heuristic functions is difficult. An alternative approach is that of the quantum tree search algorithm. Using Grover's algorithm, we search through all possible paths and verify, for each path, whether it leads to the goal state. We present the iterative quantum tree search, which is the basis of the quantum production system. We explain the principles of Tarrataca's quantum production system on a trivial example, the 3-puzzle. Finally, we present a universal quantum computer model that is capable of more quickly executing programs. The corresponding principles can be integrated into the unified theories of human cognition.

Quantum cognition - Chapter 12   Quantum cognition uses mathematical quantum theory to model cognitive phenomena. It is assumed that the computation itself is performed on a classical computer and not on a quantum computer. The brain is considered a classical computer in a quantum world. The quantum probabilities, when observed, correspond to classical probability theory. If not observed, the state of a system is described by a complex vector with a length of one. Two equivalent states represent the same state when a measurement is performed, but they can behave differently during the unitary evolution. Humans, when making decisions, violate the law of total probability. The violation can be explained as a quantum interference.

Related approaches - Chapter 13   Quantum random walks correspond to Grover's algorithm and the quantum tree search algorithm. A quantum random walk corresponds to the random walk. We will introduce a quantum insect and demonstrate the principles of quantum walk by a discrete walk on a line. Adiabatic quantum computation is an alternative approach to quantum computation and is based on the evolution time of a quantum system. The energy of a system can be described by a function. In quantum annealing, the quantum fluctuation parameter replaces a local minimum state by a randomly selected neighboring state in a fixed radius. Quantum annealing can speed up some machine learning tasks that are based on the gradient descent method.

Chapter 2

Computation

2.1 Entscheidungsproblem

David Hilbert, one of the most famous German mathematicians, attended a banquet in 1934, and he was seated next to the new minister of education, Bernhard Rust [Reid (1996)]. Rust asked, "How is mathematics in Göttingen now that it has been freed of the Jewish influence?" Hilbert replied, "Mathematics in Göttingen? There is really none any more." David Hilbert died in 1943. On his tombstone, at Göttingen, one can read his epitaph:

- Wir müssen wissen (We have to know)
- Wir werden wissen (We shall know!)

At the International Congress of Mathematicians in Paris in 1900, he put forth an influential list of 23 unsolved problems in mathematics. Hilbert's 23rd problem became known as the Entscheidungsproblem. Hilbert's Entscheidungsproblem is formulated as the following question:

- Is there a general algorithm to determine whether a mathematical conjecture is true or false?

It was commonly believed that there was no such thing as an unsolvable problem. However, Alonzo Church and Alan Turing discovered independently, around 1936, that a general solution to the Entscheidungsproblem is impossible. They showed that it is impossible to decide algorithmically whether statements in arithmetic are true or false. This result is now known as Church's Theorem or the Theorem Church-Turing Theorem.

Alonzo Church created the method for defining recursive functions λ-calculus [Church (1936a)], [Church (1936b)], [Church (1941)] and Alan Turing created a simple model called the Turing machine [Turing (1936)] (see Figure 2.1). The Turing machine constitutes an infinitely long tape that is divided into a sequence of cells. In each cell, a certain symbol can be written and later read by a head. The head can move along the tape and exist in one state of a finite set of internal states. A set of rules specifies a new state given the current state and the symbol being read. The new state determines in which direction the head must move and if it must write or read a symbol. For each state, only one rule describes one action. Turing

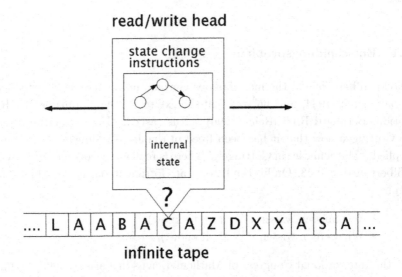

read/write head

infinite tape

Fig. 2.1 The Turing machine constitutes an infinitely long tape that is divided into a sequence of cells. In each cell, a certain symbol can be written and later read by a head. The head can move along the tape and exist in one state of a finite set of internal states. A set of rules specifies a new state given the current state and the symbol being read. The new state determines in which direction the head must move and if it must write or read a symbol. For each state, only one rule describes one action.

realized that one could encode the transformation rules of any specific Turing machine T as some pattern of symbols on the tape that fed into a special Turing machine U. U had the effect of reading in the pattern, specifying the transformation rules for T and then simulating T. Any algorithmic process can be simulated on a Turing machine U. Entscheidungsproblem corresponds to the halting problem. Whether a program will halt or run forever can be determined and is based on the given program with a finite input. We will sketch the proof, assuming a common computer model and not the Turing machine, to make the explanation easier.

The proof uses a technique called reduction ad absurdum, in which we assume the truth of the opposite of what we want to prove and then derive a logical contradiction. The proof is based on Cantor's diagonal argument and a form of coding in which a function or a program can be represented by a number. This form of coding is called Gödelization. It allows self-reference, which means that the code of the program that is represented by a number can form an input to the program. The program can make statements about itself.

2.1.1 Cantor's diagonal argument

Cantor's diagonal argument indicates that there is no bijection between infinite sets and natural numbers [Lewis and Papadimitriou (1981)]. Natural numbers are countably infinite, and infinite sets are uncountably infinite. Suppose that infinite sets are represented by binary infinite strings, and we list all of the sets in a table. This list is infinitely long, and we can write each entry as an infinitely long binary string. It is possible to build a new infinite binary string in such a way that its first element is different from the first element of the first infinite binary string in the list, its second element is different from the second element of the second infinite binary sting in the list, and so on. In general, its nth element is different from the nth element of the nth infinite binary string in the list. The new infinite binary string corresponds to the diagonal elements of the list in which its element is zero if the diagonal element is one and is zero if the diagonal element is one. The procedure can be repeated many times; the infinite list of infinite sets is never complete, and the set of all infinite sets is uncountable. It should be noted that to deny the Cantor's diagonal argument implicates the rejection of infinity. Because the size of the power set is 2^n, it follows from Cantor's diagonal argument

$$\lim_{n \to \infty} n < \lim_{n \to \infty} 2^n.$$

2.1.2 Reductio ad absurdum

Using Gödelization, we can represent a program with binary numbers. A binary number can be easily mapped to a binary string. A program can be infinite because the Turing machine has an infinite tape [Lewis and Papadimitriou (1981)]. As previously observed, we cannot list all of the infinite programs. Suppose that the program is finite. The program and the finite input are encoded as a pair of positive binary numbers. Is there a program that solves the halting problem? Let us suppose that such a program exists and that it is using a self-referent function $halt(x)$. The binary number x is its representation using the Gödelization principle. The function $halt(x)$ returns a one if the corresponding program represented by the binary number x with the input x halts and otherwise returns a zero.

$$halt(x) = \begin{cases} 1 \; program \; x \; halts \; on \; input \; x \\ 0 \; otherwise \end{cases}$$

Using the modified diagonal argument we define the program with the name "Diagonal"

```
Diagonal(x)
{
  if halt(x)=0 then halt;
  else loop forever;
}
```

The program "Diagonal" is represented by the binary number u. Does the program Diagonal(u) halt? If yes, then we have a contradiction to the definition of $halt(x)$. If it does not halt, then there is also a contradiction to the definition of $halt(x)$. From the contradiction, it would follow that there is no program that solves the halting problem.

2.2 Complexity Theory

The elegant way of modeling a computer by a Turing machine leads us to computational complexity theory. Computational complexity theory addresses the questions of which problems can be solved in a finite amount of time on a computer. Time is the most important resource during computation besides space and energy. Space and energy are negligible when using the Turing machine because the Turing machine itself is composed of infinitely long tape and does not require any energy resources [Lewis and Papadimitriou (1981)]. To simplify the analysis of the correspondence to time, special computational problems are investigated, namely decision problems.

2.2.1 Decision problems

A decision problem is a computational problem with instances formulated as a question with a binary "yes" or "no" answer. An example is the question of whether a certain number n is a prime number. Most problems can be converted into a decision problem. A problem is easy if a certain Turing machine can determine the instances related to the input for the answer "yes" in polynomial time. Otherwise, we state that the problem is hard. The relationship to the size of the input accounts for the reading time of the input. It should not influence the time complexity. A number is usually represented by the base $B > 1$, which means that k digits can represent B^k different numbers. In other words, the hierarchical organized structure of the numbers exponentially speeds up the reading time of a deterministic Turing machine. This relationship is not valid for a unary representation in which the input size is equivalent to the numbers that can be represented.

2.2.2 P and NP

The formal definition for easy problems represented by P is as follows: The set of all decision problems that have instances that are solvable in polynomial time using a deterministic Turing machine. In a deterministic Turing machine, all of the transitions are described by some fixed rules [Lewis and Papadimitriou (1981)]. An example for an easy problem is multiplication $x \times b = c$, where x is the instance and the values b and c are given; determine x so that the answer to the question is $x \times 7 = 28$ is yes. On the other hand, it is thought that the factoring determines the integers for which the product is equal to for a given number d; for example, integers a, b with $a \times b = d$ is not in P, which indicates that it is hard. The class NP is the set of all decision problems that have instances that are solvable in polynomial time using a non-deterministic Turing machine. In a non-deterministic Turing machine, in contrast to a deterministic Turing machine, for each state, several rules with different actions can be applied.

Non-deterministic Turing machine branches into many copies that are represented by a computational tree in which there are different computational paths. The class NP corresponds to a non-deterministic Turing machine that guesses the computational path that represents the solution. By doing so, it guesses the instances of the decision problem. In the second step, a deterministic Turing machine verifies whether the guessed instance leads to a "yes" answer. It is easy to verify whether a solution is valid or not. This statement does not mean that finding a solution is easy. Clearly, the class $P \subseteq NP$ is known, and it follows that $NP \neq P$ or $NP = P$; however, other relationships are not known. The class $NP - complete$ is present if the problem is in NP and every other problem in NP can be reduced to the class $NP - complete$.

It was not obvious that an $NP - complete$ problem exists. Cook-Levin described the first example of an $NP - complete$ problem, the satisfiability problem. Until recently, thousands of other problems are known to be $NP - complete$, including the well-known traveling salesman and Hamiltonian cycle problem [Cormen *et al.* (2001)].

The structure of $NP - complete$ problems is equivalent to a computational tree of a non-deterministic Turing machine in which all different computational paths must be searched by a deterministic Turing machine. A simple algorithm for solving $NP - complete$ problems by a deterministic Turing machine is to perform an iterative search for all possible instances.

- The formal definition for NP is as follows: a deterministic Turing machine verifies whether an instance (ticket) leads to a "yes" answer in polynomial time.
- The formal definition of an $NP - complete$ problem is as follows: The problem is NP and the problem is $NP - hard$. $NP - hard$ means that every other problem in NP can be reduced to it in polynomial time.

2.3   Church–Turing Thesis

The definition of P and NP should not depend upon the currently used computational model. The following is stated in the Church–Turing thesis: Any algorithmic process can be simulated on a Turing machine. The extended Church–Turing thesis, which is also called the strong Church–Turing thesis, states that everything that can be computed in a certain amount of time on any physical computer can be also be computed on a Turing machine with a polynomial slowdown. In other words, any reasonable algorithmic process can be simulated on a Turing machine, with the possibility of a polynomial slowdown, in the number of steps required to run the simulation. The problems in P are precisely those for which a polynomial-time solution is the best possible, in any physically reasonable model of computation.

The hypothesis that the universe is equivalent to a Turing machine, which is related to the Church–Turing thesis, is similar to that stated in digital physics. However, Richard Feynman observed in the early eighties that it did not appear possible for a Turing machine to simulate certain quantum physical processes without incurring an exponential slowdown. This fact would contradict the strong Church–Turing thesis, which led Feynman to ask whether a quantum system can be simulated on an imaginary quantum computer.

2.3.1 *Church–Turing–Deutsch principle*

In 1985, David Deutsch [Deutsch (1985)] reformulated the Church–Turing thesis based on the observation of Richard Feynman in physical terms: "Every finitely realizable physical system can be perfectly simulated by universal computing machine operating by finite means." The Turing machine was replaced by the universal computing machine which operates by finite means.

2.4 Computers

The Turing machine is a theoretical mathematical model, not a practical engineering model of a computer. There are two distinct classes of practical computers, analog and digital computers.

2.4.1 *Analog computers*

An analog computer represents information by analog means, such as voltage. In such a computer, information is represented by a voltage wave and the algorithm is represented by an electrical circuit. Such a circuit is composed of resistors and capacitors that are connected together. An algorithm represents a mathematical model of a physical system, which can be described, for example, by specific differential equations. In the first step, the mathematical model is determined. Then, a block diagram that models the analogous system is developed. This model defines the electrical components that specify the computation. The input and output of the computation are voltage waves that can be observed by an oscilloscope. The represented values are usually less accurate than digitally represented values. The results of each computation can vary due to external influences.

For this reason, each result of the computation is unique. The exact value cannot be reproduced without an error. This type of noise, which results from an external influence, makes it impossible to recompute the output of chaotic deterministic functions. Even making the smallest change to the initial condition can cause the results to greatly diverge. It is important to note that analog computers are not covered by the Church–Turing thesis because they cannot be simulated by a Turing machine; however, analog computers are covered by the Church–Turing–Deutsch principle because they correspond to a computing machine that operates by finite means. Analog computers were popular in the 1950s. However, analog computers fell into decline with the advent of the development of the microprocessor, which led to the development of digital computers.

2.4.2 Digital computers

A digital computer is a device that processes information that is represented in discrete means such as symbols. Usually, the symbols are represented in binary form. Modern digital computers are based on digital circuits. In a digital circuit, the information is represented by binary digits. Due to a digital representation, the exact values of each computation can be reproduced without any error. The computation can be repeated, and the result remains the same (this scenario is not the case with analog computers). Binary digits are represented by the minimal unit of information, the bit. The binary information is manipulated by Boolean digital circuits. Emil Post has proven the complete sets of truth functions. It follows that they can be computed using Boolean circuits, which are composed of Boolean gates and represent Boolean logic, which operates on bits [Cormen *et al.* (2001)]. An algorithm can be described by a circuit. The construction of a circuit requires the exact knowledge of the values that must be computed. For this reason, a circuit is not an algorithmic device; by itself, it does not correspond to a universal Turing machine. The Halting problem cannot by represented by a circuit.

2.4.3 Von Neumann architecture

The ENIAC (Electronic Numerical Integrator And Computer) was one of the first Turing-complete universal digital computers that was capable of being programmed. John von Neumann learned in 1945 of the ENIAC Project and described this model in a technical report called "First Draft of a Report on the EDVAC" [von Neumann (1945)]. The model become known as the Van Neumann architecture [Aspray (1990)]. This technology is composed of five main concepts:

- An arithmetic logic unit (ALU) unit that is capable of performing both arithmetic and logic operations on the data.
- A control unit (CU) that interprets an instruction retrieved from the memory and that selects alternative courses of action based on the results of the previous operations.
- Main memory stores both data and instructions and read-write random-access memory (RAM).
- Secondary memory represents the external mass storage.
- Input and output mechanisms.

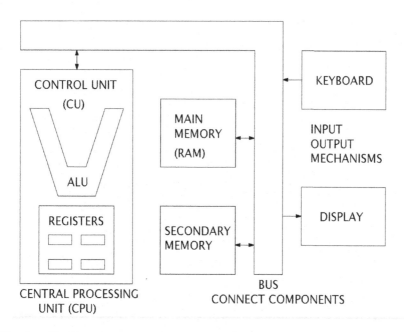

Fig. 2.2   The Van Neumann architecture. In modern computers, the ALU and the CU are parts of the central processing unit (CPU) that are represented by a single silicon chip called a microprocessor. The subsystem called a bus transfers the data between the random-access memory, the CPU, and the input and output.

In modern computers, the ALU and the CU are parts of the central processing unit (CPU) that are represented by a single silicon chip called a microprocessor. The subsystem called a bus transfers the data between the random-access memory, the CPU, and the input and output (see Figure 2.2). Most modern computers are based on the von Neumann architecture.

Chapter 3

Problem Solving

It is quite certain for the cognitive psychologist that the human computational model is not at all based on the Van Neumann architecture. Instead, they propose that the human computational model is based on production systems. A production system is a mathematical as well as a practical model that can be realized as a computing machine. Production systems are closely related to the approach taken by Markov algorithms [Markov (1954)], and similar to these approaches, production systems are equivalent in power to a Turing machine [Turing (1936)]. A Turing machine can also be easily simulated by a production system. The production system is a model of actual human problem-solving behavior [Newell and Simon (1972); Anderson (1983); Klahr and Waterman (1986); Newell (1990)].

3.1 Knowledge Representation

Production systems are composed of if-then rules that are also called productions. A rule contains several "if" patterns and one or more "then" patterns. A pattern in the context of rules is an individual predicate, which can be negated together with arguments. A rule can establish a new assertion by the "then" part (its conclusion) whenever the "if" part (its premise) is true. Productions can be represented by rules or logic-based operators. Alternative sub-symbolical representation is based on categorial representation. Binary vector representation is the basis of the quantum production systems.

3.1.1 *Rules*

A rule [Winston (1992); Russell and Norvig (1995); Luger and Stubblefield (1998)] contains several "if" patterns and one or more "then" patterns.

A pattern in the context of rules is an individual predicate which can be negated together with arguments. The rule can establish a new assertion by the "then" part, the conclusion whenever the "if" part, the premise, is true. When variables become identified with values they are bound to these values. Whenever the variables in a pattern are replaced by values, the pattern is said to be instantiationed. Here is an example of rules with a variable x:

- If $\underbrace{\text{(flies}(x) \vee \text{feathes}(x)) \wedge \text{lays eggs}(x)}_{premise}$ then $\underbrace{\text{bird}(x)}_{conclusion}$
- If $\text{bird}(x) \wedge \text{swims}(x)$ then $\text{penguin}(x)$
- If $\text{bird}(x) \wedge \text{sings}(x)$ then $\text{nightinagle}(x)$

The following assertions are present:

- feathers(Pit)
- lays eggs(Pit)
- swims(Pit)
- flies(Airbus)

Pit is a bird because the premise of the first rule is true when x is bound to Pit. Because bird(Pit), the premise of the second rule is true and Pit is a penguin.

3.1.2 *Logic-based operators*

Logical representation is motivated by philosophy and mathematics [Kurzweil (1990); Tarski (1995); Luger and Stubblefield (1998)]. Predicates are functions that map objects' arguments into true or false values. They describe the relation between objects in a world which is represented by symbols. Whenever a relation holds with respect to some objects, the corresponding predicate is true when applied to the corresponding object symbols.

Predicates can be negated by the function $\neg$ (not) and combined by the logical connectives $\vee$ (disjunction), $\wedge$ (conjunction) and the implies ($\rightarrow$) operator. $\neg$, $\vee$, $\wedge$, and $\rightarrow$ determine the predicate's value. To signal that an expression is universally true, the universal quantifier and a variable standing for possible objects is used.

$$\forall\, x[\text{Feathers}(x) \rightarrow \text{Bird}(x)].$$
An Object having feathers is a bird.

Some expressions are true only for some objects. This is represented by an existential quantifier and a variable.

$$\exists\, x[\text{Bird}(x)].$$
There is at least one object which is a bird.

An interpretation is an accounting of the correspondence between objects and object symbols and between relations and predicates. An interpretation can be only either true or false. These are some basic ideas about representation in predicate calculus, which is a subset of formal logic. A world state can be described including properties and relations using predicate calculus. This kind of description can be used to define operators like those used in the STRIPS computer science approach (see Figure 3.1) [Fikes and Nilsson (1971); Nilsson (1982); Givan and Dean (1997)].

ontable(A).
ontable(C).
on(B,A).
clear(B).
clear(C).
gripping().

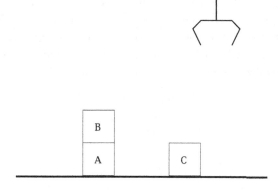

Fig. 3.1   ABC block world.

Using the block examples, four operations "pickup", "putdown", "stack" and "unstack" can be defined [Nilsson (1982)]: [1]

$$pickup(x) \begin{cases} P : gripping() \land clear(x) \land ontable(x) \\ A : gripping(x) \\ D : ontable(x) \land gripping() \end{cases}$$

$$putdown(x) \begin{cases} P : gripping(x) \\ A : ontable(x) \land gripping() \land clear(x) \\ D : gripping(x) \end{cases}$$

$$stack(x,y) \begin{cases} P : gripping(x) \land clear(x) \\ A : on(x,y) \land gripping() \land clear(x) \\ D : clear(y) \land gripping(x) \end{cases}$$

$$unstack(x,y) \begin{cases} P : gripping() \land clear(x) \land on(x,y) \\ A : gripping(x) \land clear(y) \\ D : on(x,y) \land gripping() \end{cases}$$

Each of the operators is represented as triples of description. The first element is the precondition, the world state that must be met for an operator to be applied. It can be true or false when variables become identified with the values, which describe the state. The second element is the additions to the state description that are a result of applying the operator. The last element is the items that are removed from the state description to create a new state when the operator is applied. These operators obey the frame axiom since they specify what is true in one state of the world and what exactly has changed by performing some action by an operator. The problem of specifying which part of the description should change and which should not is called the frame problem [Winston (1992)].

$$ontable(A).$$
$$clear(A)$$
$$ontable(C).$$
$$clear(C).$$
$$gripping(B).$$

---

[1] The expressions are always universally true, and therefore the universal quantifier is omitted.

The state after the operator *pickup(B)* was applied to the state of Figure 3.1 (see Figure 3.2).

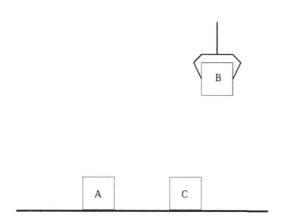

Fig. 3.2   The state after the operator *pickup(B)* was applied to the state of Figure 3.1.

3.1.3   *Frames*

Frames describe individual objects and entire classes [Minsky (1975, 1986); Winston (1992)] and can be used to represent states of the world. They are composed of slots which can be either attributes, which describe the classes or object, or links to other frames. With the aid of links, a hierarchy can be represented in which classes or objects are parts of more general classes. In this taxonomic representation, frames inherit attributes of the more general classes (see Figure 3.3). Frames can be viewed as generalization of semantic nets. They are psychologically motivated and were popularized in computer science by Marvin Minsky. One important result of the frame theory is the object-oriented approach in programming.

3.1.4   *Categorial representation*

Humans divide the world into categories so that they can make sense of it [Smith (1995)]. The categorization task consists of the determination if an object belongs to a category [Osherson (1995); Lakeoff (1987)]. Objects can be described by a set of discrete features, such as red, round and

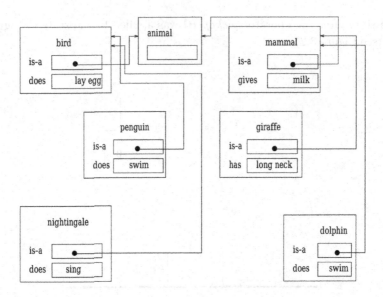

Fig. 3.3   Taxonomic frame representation of some animals.

sweet [Tversky (1977); McClelland and Rumelhart (1985)]. The similarity between them can be defined as a function of the features they have in common [Osherson (1995); Sun (1995); Goldstone (1999); Gilovich (1999)]. The contrast model of Tversky [Tversky (1977)] is one well known model in cognitive psychology [Smith (1995); Opwis and Plötzner (1996)] which describes the similarity between two objects which are described by their features. Rather than relying on prototypical features, picture categorization often relies on detailed shape representation [Smith *et al.* (1978); Murphy and Brownell (1985); Smith (1995)]. Objects and scenes can be represented by binary pictures which are normalized for size and orientation [Feldman (1985)]. Similarity between the objects or scenes is measured by the amount of shared area between the overlaid patterns [Biederman and Ju (1988); Kurbat *et al.* (1994); Smith and Sloman (1994)]. Categorial representation represents the basis of sub-symbolical representation.

3.1.5   *Binary vector representation*

Binary vectors can represent discrete features. A one represents a discrete feature at the corresponding position of a binary vector, its absence is denoted by a zero. The feature set A, B, C, D, E, F, G, H, I, J, K is represented by a binary vector of dimension 11. The presence of features C and E is represented by the binary vector [0 0 1 0 1 0 0 0 0 0 0]. Binary vectors can represent transitions between states. The first binary vector describes the state which should be present before the transition (the premise). The second binary vector describes the world state after the transition (the conclusion).

3.2 Production System

Human problem solving can be described by a problem-behavior graph constructed from a protocol of the person talking aloud, mentioning considered moves and aspects of the situation. According to the resulting theory, searching whose state includes the initial situation and the desired situation (goal) in a problem space [Newell (1990); Anderson (1995b)]. This process can be described by the production system theory. The production system in the context of classical Artificial Intelligence and Cognitive Psychology is one of the most successful computer models of human problem solving. The production system theory describes how to form a sequence of actions, which lead to a goal, and offers a computational theory of how humans solve problems [Anderson (1995b)]. A production system is composed of [Brownston *et al.* (1985); Luger and Stubblefield (1998)] (see Figure 3.4):

- Set of rules. These rule are also called productions. The set of rules models the human long-term memory.
- Working memory. This memory contains a description of the state in a problem solving process. The state is described using predicate calculus and is simply called a pattern. Whenever a premise is true, the conclusions of the rules change the contents of the working memory. The working memory models the human short-term memory.
- Recognize-act cycle. The current state of the problem-solving process is maintained as a set of patterns in the working memory. Working memory is initialized with the initial state description. The patterns in working memory are matched against the premise of the rules. The premise of the rules that match the patterns in working memory produces a set, which is called the conflict set. One of the rules of this set is chosen and the conclusion of the rule changes the content of the working memory. This process is denoted as firing of the rule. This recognize-cycle is repeated on

the modified working memory until a desired state is reached or no rules can be fired. The recognize-act cycle models the current focus of attention triggering one of the set of permanent skills. This, in turn, changes the focus of attention.

Conflict resolution chooses a rule from the conflict set for firing. There are different conflict resolution strategies, such as choosing a random rule from the set, or selecting a rule by some certain function. In a pure production system which was proposed as a formal theory of computation [Post (1943)] the system halts if no production can fire in a state.

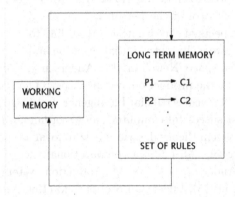

Fig. 3.4 A production system is composed of the long term memory and the working memory also called short term memory. This recognize-cycle is repeated on the modified working memory until a desired state is reached or no rules can be fired.

3.2.1 *Deduction systems*

Problems without side effects of actions can be described by deduction systems which are a subgroup of production systems [Winston (1992)]. In deduction systems the premise specifies combinations of assertions, by which a new assertion of the conclusion is directly deduced. This new assertion is added to the working memory. Deduction systems do not need strategies for conflict resolution because every rule presumably produces reasonable assertions and there is no harm in firing all triggered rules. Deduction systems may chain together rules in a forward direction, from assertions to conclusions, or backward from hypotheses to premises. During backward chaining it is ensured that all features are properly focused. Backward chaining is used if no features are present. If all features are given, forward chaining is used to prevent wasting of time pursuing hypotheses, which are not specified by the features. The chained rules describe the complete problem space which can be represented by a graph [Quillian (1968); Shastri (1988)]. Examples of deduction systems are semantic nets, diagnostic systems and expert systems. Simple if then rules can be represented by a knowledge base. We present a compendium of six rules concerning problems with the oil of a car expert system:

(1) oil lamp lights during driving round a bend **or** oil lamp lights during braking **then** cable of the oil pressure lamp is loose
(2) driving round a bend **and** problems with oil **then** oil lamp lights during driving round a bend
(3) braking **and** problems with oil **then** oil lamp lights during braking
(4) oil lamp goes out after some time **and** problems with oil **and** during idling **then** oil pressure too low
(5) problems with oil **and** during idling **then** oil level too low
(6) oil lamp lights up **then** problems with oil

For clarity we can replace the names of features and categories by symbols, each symbol representing a name, for example B representing "oil lamp lights during driving round a bend":

(1) B ∨ C then A
(2) D ∧ F then B
(3) E ∧ F then C
(4) H ∧ F ∧ I then G
(5) F ∧ I then J
(6) K then F

The representation of the logical relationship defined by these rules requires an extension to the basic graph model known as AND/OR graph [Luger and Stubblefield (1998)]. We can represent the set of rules (for example describing an ontology) by a directed AND/OR graph. In Figure 3.5 we see the representation of the six rules. During the deduction a subgraph is constructed. The deduction system is a simple model. It is not practical therefore to use it for planning, as planning is mostly described by fewer rules, but it characterizes a much bigger problem space. Dynamical representation of the problem space is suitable instead of static for reaction systems.

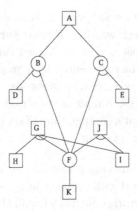

Fig. 3.5　Representation of six rules by a directed AND/OR graph. The 'and' rules are indicated by an arc between the links connecting the nodes indicating the manifestations.

3.2.2　Reaction systems

Problems with side effects of actions like planning can be resolved by reaction systems [Winston (1992)]. Reaction systems are a subgroup of production systems. The premise specifies the conditions that must be true before the action described in the conclusion can be taken. Reaction systems need strategies for conflict resolution. We will call the reaction systems simply "production system" if no confusion with a deduction system is possible.

3.2.3　Conflict resolution

Conflict resolution strategies are often specified by general provisions [Jackson (1999)]:

- chose randomly a rule;
- a rule should be not allowed to fire more than once on the same data;
- rules that have used more recent data are preferred;
- rules that have a greater number of patterns in the premise are preferred.

Rules also can be evaluated by a heuristic function. There are two different kinds of heuristic functions:

- the probability that the function is on the best path;
- the distance or difference between a given state and the desired state.

It is difficult to define heuristic functions, though frequently features can be picked out which describe the distance to the goal [Russell and Norvig (1995)]. The other possibility is the reuse of solutions to solved problems to indicate which rule to use.

3.2.4 *Human problem-solving*

In systems which model human behavior and in practical applications, backtracking to a previous state of working memory is allowed. By allowing backtracking and the exclusion of loops, a search from the initial state to the desired state is executed. The search defines a problem space and can be represented as a tree. However, it may not reach the desired goal either because the branches are infinite, or because after backtracking to the initial state no rule can fire. A problem is described by the productions in the long term memory, by the initial state, and by the desired state. The solution to the problem is represented by a set of the productions which successively change the state from the initial state to the desired state. One of the best-known cognitive models, based on the production system, is SOAR. The SOAR state, operator and result model was developed to explain human problem-solving behavior [Newell (1990)]. It is a hierarchical production system in which the conflict-resolution strategy is treated as another problem to be solved. All satisfied instances of rules are executed in parallel in a "temporary" mode. After the temporary execution, the best rule is chosen to take action. The decision takes place in the context of a stack of earlier decisions. Those decisions are rated utilizing preferences and added to the stack by chosen rules. Preferences are determined together with the rules by an observer using knowledge about a problem.

3.2.5 *Example*

The 8-puzzle is composed of eight numbered movable tiles in a 3×3 frame. One cell of the frame is empty; as a result, tiles can be moved around to form different patterns. The goal is to find a series of moves of tiles into the blank space that changes the board from the initial configuration to a desired configuration (see Figure 3.6). The production of long-term memory can be specified by four productions [Luger and Stubblefield (1998)]:

- *If* the empty cell is not on the top edge, *then* move the empty cell up;
- *If* the empty cell is not on the left edge, *then* move the empty cell left;
- *If* the empty cell is not on the right edge, *then* move the empty cell

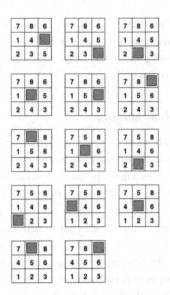

Fig. 3.6   The first pattern (upper left) represents the initial configuration and the last (low right) the desired configuration. The series of moves describe the solution to the problem.

right;
- *If* the empty cell is not on the bottom edge, *then* move the empty cell down.

The control strategy for the search would be

- halt when goal is in the working memory;
- chose a random production;
- do not allow loops.

3.3   Sub-Symbolic Models of Problem-Solving

Perception-oriented representation is an example of sub-symbolical representation, such as the representation of numbers by the Oksapmin tribe of Papua New Guinea. The Oksapmin tribe of Papua New Guinea counts by associating a number with the position of the body [Lancy (1983)]. The sub-symbolical representation often corresponds to a pattern that mirrors the way the biological sense organs describe the world. Vectors represent patterns. A vector is only a sub-symbol if there is a relationship between the vector and the corresponding similarity of the represented object or state in the real world through sensors or biological senses. Feature-based representation is an example of sub-symbolical representation.

Living organisms experience the world as a simple Euclidian geometrical world. The actual perception of the world and manipulation in the world by living organisms lead to the invention or recreation of an experience that, at least in some respects, resembles the experience of actually perceiving and manipulating objects in the absence of direct sensory stimulation [Wichert (2009)].

This kind of representation is called sub-symbolic. Sub-symbolic representation implies heuristic functions. The assumption that the distance between states in the problem space is related to the similarity between the sub-symbols representing the states is only valid in simple cases. However, simple cases represent the majority of exiting problems in domain. Sense organs sense the world by receptors which a part of the sensory system and the nervous system.

According to the production system theory (reaction systems), we can define a geometrically-based problem-solving model as a production system operating on vectors of fixed dimensions. Instead of rules, we use associations and vectors represent the states. Our goal is to form a sequence of associations, which lead to a desired state represented by a vector, from an initial state represented by a vector. Each association changes some parts of the vector. In each state, several possible associations can be executed, but only one has to be chosen. Otherwise, conflicts in the representation of the state would occur. To perform these operations, we divided a vector representing a state into sub-vectors. An association recognizes some sub-vectors in the vector and exchanges them for different sub-vectors. It is composed of a precondition of fixed arranged α sub-vectors and a conclusion [Wichert (2009)], [Wichert (2013)].

3.3.1 *Proto logic*

The manipulation of the states is described by simple proto logic, which verifies if a subset of symbols is present in a certain set of symbols. Suppose a vector is divided into α sub-vectors with $\alpha > \beta$. A production recognizes β different sub-vectors and exchanges them for β different sub-vectors. Let $\alpha = 7$ objects that were recognized in the visual scene. The seven visual objects are indicated at a certain position of the scene by symbols A, B, C, D, E, F and G. The task of proto logic is to identify a precondition formed by visual objects represented by the set B, C, G, $\beta = 3$. Each of the symbols B, C, G is checked for presence in the set that represents the scene. It is verified if a set representing a precondition is a subset of the set representing a scene. *Proto logic operates on sets. It verifies whether a subset is present in a certain set* [Wichert (2013)]. The task of proto logic is trivial when working with sets. For an associative memory the direct access to the stored information is not present, a solution to this problem is described in [Wichert (2011)].

3.3.2   Binding problem

The "binding problem" determines how to connect together all physically separated fragments of a complex object so that they can be processed as a whole in sub-symbolical representation [Miikkulainen (1993); Kurfess (1997); Wennekers (1999); Hummel (1999)]. For example, a red block is obviously a different object then a blue block. The fragments in this example are the form and the color. Sub-vectors representing different fragments can be concatenated to a sub-vector representing the object [Wichert (2011)].

3.3.3   Icons

Out of several possible associations, we chose the one, which modifies the state in such a way that it becomes more similar to the desired state according to the Euclidean distance [Wichert (2009)] (see Figure 3.7).

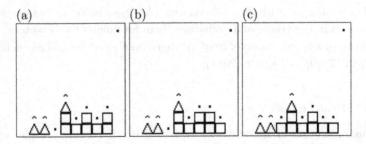

Fig. 3.7   The Euclidean distance between the corresponding vectors can compute the distance between the icons. The distance between the states in the problem space is actually related to the distance between the icons representing the states. Euclidian distance of state (a) and state (c) is smaller than the distance between state (b) and (c). The distance in the problem space as well between state (a) and state (c) is smaller than the distance between state (b) and (c).

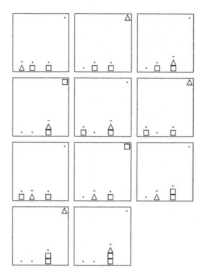

Fig. 3.8   The simplest method corresponds to a random choice, and does not offer any advantage over simple symbolical representation. An example of visual planning of the tower building task of three blocks using the random choice is shown. The upper left pattern represents the initial state; the bottom right pattern, the desired state.

With the aid of this heuristic hill climbing is performed. Each element represents an object. Objects are represented by some dimensions of the space and form a sub-space by themselves.

The example of Figure 3.8 and Figure 3.9 consists of the task of building a tower from a collection of blocks [Nilsson (1982)]. A robot arm can stack, unstack, and move the blocks within a plane on three different positions at a table. There are two different classes of blocks: cubes and pyramids. While additional blocks may be stacked on top of a cube, no other blocks may be placed on top of a pyramid. The robot arm, which is represented in the upper right corner, has a gripper that can grasp any available block. It can move the block to eight different positions on the tabletop or place it on top of another cube [Wichert (2001, 2005a)].

The computation can be improved by a simple and universal heuristics function, which takes into account the relationship between the vector and the corresponding similarity of the represented states (see Figure 3.8 and Figure 3.9). The heuristics function makes a simple assumption that the distance between the states in the problem space is related to the similarity

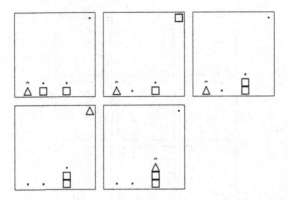

Fig. 3.9 An example of visual planning of the tower building task of three blocks using hill climbing shown. The upper left pattern represents the initial state; the bottom right pattern, the desired state..

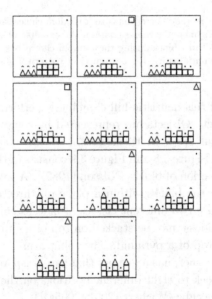

Fig. 3.10 An example of visual planning of the tower building task of eleven blocks using hill climbing shown. The upper left pattern represents the initial state; the bottom right pattern, the desired state.

of the vectors representing the states. This becomes more obvious with the growth of objects that can be manipulated (see Figure 3.10).

3.3.4   *Euclidian geometry of the world*

The similarity between the corresponding vectors can indicate the distance between the sub-symbols representing the state. Empirical experiments in popular problem-solving domains of Artificial Intelligence, like robot in a maze, block world or 8-puzzle indicated that the distance between the states in the problem space is actually related to the similarity between the images representing the states [Wichert (2001); Wichert *et al.* (2008); Wichert (2009)].

Sub-symbolical problem solving takes advantage of the geometric nature of the world. The assumption that the distance between states in the problem space is related to the distance between the sub-symbols representing the states is only valid in simple cases. For example, our simple heuristics and the resulting hill climbing cannot overcome problems in which one cannot perform either of the necessary first actions without undoing them at a later stage. These kinds of problems are very often called anomalies, such as the "Sussman anomaly" [Sussman (1975)].

Chapter 4

Information

4.1 Information and Thermodynamics

Information can be presented in a variety of forms that differ from one another: natural language, symbols, acoustic speech and pictures [Resnikoff (1989)] (see Figure 4.1).

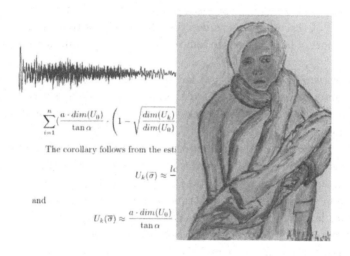

Fig. 4.1 Information can be presented in a variety of forms which differ from one another: natural language, symbols, acoustic speech, pictures.

Information appeared as a unifying scientific concept before the invention of the first computers. Information does not concern the substance and the forces of the physical world [Stonier (1990)]. Information is what remains after one abstracts from the material aspects of physical reality. Information theory is highly related to mathematical probability theory and thermodynamics. A thermodynamic description similar to information is not a description of a physical property and relationships, but rather, this description is a fundamental property. Thermodynamic relations might remain valid for all physical theories that can describe an aspect of reality. They link physical entities to their organization and to their informational structure. Thermodynamics is the study of the collective behavior of entities on a macroscopic scale and uses statistics to describe microscopic states of entities. The microscopic behavior corresponds to the motion of the entities; on a macroscopic scale, this behavior is represented by the temperature, pressure, and volume of physical systems such as a gas or a fluid. The statistical description gives us freedom of abstraction [Maxwell (2001)]. It was James Clerk Maxwell, (1831 – 1879), a Scottish mathematician, who was one of the first to recognize the connection between thermodynamic quantities that are associated with gas, such as temperature, and the statistical descriptions of the molecules. We do not need to specify each entity as a molecule or specify its exact speed or position. It is sufficient to describe the statistical behavior of specific molecules. The three laws of thermodynamics describe the processes that are involved in the transport of heat. They are some of the most important laws of physics.

- Conservation of energy (first law of thermodynamics): The change in the internal energy of a closed thermodynamic system is equal to the sum of the amount of heat energy supplied to the system and the work performed on the system.
- The second law deals with entropy. Entropy is a measure of disorder of the configuration of the states of the atoms or other particles, which make up the system. The total entropy of any isolated thermodynamic system tends to increase over time, approaching a maximum value.
- Third law of thermodynamics: absolute zero temperature As a system asymptotically approaches the absolute zero of the temperature, all processes virtually cease and the entropy of the system asymptotically approaches a minimum value. The entropy of all systems and of all states of a system is zero at absolute zero.

"A physical system that is made up of many, many tiny parts will have microscopic details to its physical behavior that are not easy to observe. There are various microscopic states the system can have, each of which is defined by the state of motion of every one of its atoms, for instance." a

Table 4.1 Each of the two die can have one out of six microstates.

macrostate	(die1, die2)	number of microstates
2	1,1	1
3	1,2;2,1	2
4	1,3; 2,2; 3,1	3
5	1,4; 2,3; 3,2; 4,1	4
6	1,5; 2,4; 3,3; 4,2; 5,1	5
7	1,6; 2,5; 3,4; 4,3; 5;2, 5,1	6
8	2,6; 3,5; 4,4; 5,3; 6,2	5
9	3,6; 4,5; 5,4; 6,3	4
10	4,6; 5,5; 6,4	3
11	5,6; 6,5	2
12	6,6	1

quote from Matt McIrvin.[1] We can choose to measure a physical system at the macroscopic level. Macroscopic properties such as density or pressure are the result of microscopic properties. A macroscopic property can be realized by different microscopic states. Macroscopic states are not static, but they continuously change corresponding to the motion of atoms or molecules. Statistical mechanics describes this motion by some random parameters, whereby each atom is moving randomly from a macroscopic viewpoint. A set of atoms is described by a distribution of random variables that express the random movements.

4.1.1 *Dice model*

Suppose that we have two dice; the macrostate is the total of the two dice, and the microstate corresponds to the number on each of the die. There are six ways to get a total of 7 from the microstates of the two dice but only one way to get a total of 2 or 12. For this reason, throwing two dice to sum a total of seven is more likely to occur; a sum of seven is six times more likely to occur than two or twelve. Each die can have one out of six microstates. The number of microstates of the whole system of two dice is $6 \times 6 = 36$, the number of possible microstates is multiplied together. The number of different macrostates adds, for example, $(6 + 6) - 1 = 11$. We must subtract a one because the smallest macrostate is two and not one (see Table 4.1). For four dice the number of microstates is already $6 \times 6 \times 6 \times 6 = 1296$. In general, when several systems are combined into a larger system, the number of possible microstates of each system is multiplied, and the number of macrostates is added. For n fair dice,

---

[1]Matt McIrvin physics- group posting.

the total number of possible microstates is at a maximum at a macrostate value of $3.5 \times n$. The value corresponds to the median of the Gaussian distribution. The median of a finite list of microstates can be found by arranging all of the microstates from the lowest value that represents a macrostate to the highest value of a macrostate and picking the middle value (see Table 4.1). The value of $3.5 \times n$ can be derived for n dice, as follows; the median is also represented as follows,

$$\frac{min + max}{2} \tag{4.1}$$

for n dice it follows:

$$\frac{n + n \cdot 6}{2} = n \cdot 3.5. \tag{4.2}$$

If we shake n dice in a bag and measure the uppermost faces, and we repeat the experiment, the dice will converge rapidly on the value (the "macrostate") for which the number of ways to make the value from individual dice ("microstates") is at a maximum. By performing this action, we model an isolated system, the second law of thermodynamics. We model the thermal fluctuations by "shaking" the bag. The macroscopically measurable quantities converge to the values that have the largest number of microstates. It appears that the basis of the time direction, as expressed by the second law of thermodynamics, is a type of Gaussian randomness.

4.1.2 *Entropy*

When several systems are combined into a larger system, the number of possible microstates of each system are multiplied. This operation leads to a very large number, which becomes intractable very quickly. A solution to this problem is to use the logarithms of numbers; in this case, the log of the product is the sum of the logs. In statistical thermodynamics, Boltzmann's equation relates the entropy S of an ideal gas to the *number of microstates*, where W corresponds to a given macrostate [Boltzman (1995)]. We add the number of microstates when we put systems together by taking the logarithm. The result indicates the relationship between entropy and the number of ways that the atoms or molecules of a thermodynamic system can be arranged. Entropy corresponds to the number of ways that the microstate can rearrange itself without affecting the macrostate. In the equation, k is Boltzmann's constant, which is equal to 1.38062×10^{-23} joule/kelvin.

$$S = k \cdot \log \cdot W \tag{4.3}$$

The Second Law states that isolated systems tend toward an equilibrium macrostate with as large total entropy as possible corresponding to the largest number of microstates. For example, atoms moving around in a gas possess a large number of possible microstates. This number is less for a crystalline structure and, finally, it is one at $0K$, where all microstates become identical.

4.1.3 Maxwell paradox and information

In 1929, Leó Szilárd explained the thermodynamic Maxwell paradox by identifying information with the negative measure of entropy [Szilárd (1929)]. Suppose that we have two chambers that are separated by a common partition, which could be removed to permit the objects in one to move freely to the other. One chamber contains gas and the other chamber contains nothing; on the removal of the partition, the gas will rapidly diffuse and fill the empty chamber (see Figure 4.2). Reverse evidence of this

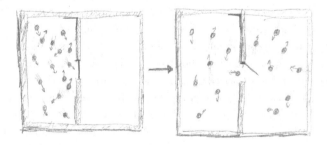

Fig. 4.2 Suppose that we have two chambers that are separated by a common partition, which could be removed to permit the objects in one to move freely to the other. One chamber contains gas and the other chamber contains nothing; on the removal of the partition, the gas will rapidly diffuse and fill the empty chamber.

sequence mostly does not occur because an isolated systems tends toward an equilibrium macrostate that corresponds to the largest number of microstates that are present when the gas is diffused over the two chambers. Thinking in terms of the dice model, the probability of reverse evidence approaches zero but is never equal to zero. In the paradox, there is a demon that observes the gas molecules. Between the chambers, there is a small door. The demon can open and close the small door, passing only one molecule into a chamber. When a molecule in its random motion heads toward the door of the chamber, it opens the door, briefly permitting the molecule to pass into the other chamber. Soon there will be more molecules in one chamber than the other. Because the demon requires almost no energy to operate the door, the process decreases the entropy, which is a contradiction to the second law of thermodynamics. Szilard's explanation is the following: to perform this task, the demon must be very well informed about the position and velocity of the molecules that approached the door. Only with this information can he judge when and for how long the door should be opened to pass a molecule through and into the chamber without allowing any molecules to pass in the opposite direction. As the demon's information about the distribution of the gas increases, the entropy of the gas decreases.

4.1.4   *Information theory*

Instead of a demon that operates a door between two chambers, let us imagine a simple experiment, for example, throwing a fair coin [Topsoe (1974)]. Before we perform the experiment, we do not know what will be the result; we are uncertain about the outcome. We measure the uncertainty by the entropy of the experiment. The experiment starts at t_0 and ends at t_1. At t_0, we have no information about the results of the experiment, and at t_1, we have all of the information, so that the entropy of the experiment is 0. We can describe an experiment by probabilities. For the outcome of the flip of an honest coin, the probability for a head or tail is 0.5, $p = (0.5, 0.5)$. How can we define entropy? A person A knows the outcome, but person B does not. Person B could ask A about the outcome of the experiment. If the question is of the most basic nature, then we could measure the minimal number of optimally required questions B must pose to know the result of the experiment. A most basic question corresponds to the smallest information unit that could correspond to a yes or no answer. The smallest information unit is called a binary digit, or bit. For a fair coin, we pose just one question, for example, is it a tail?

For a card game, to determine if a card is either red, clubs or spades, we have a different number of possible questions. If the card is red, then we need only one question. However, in the case in which the card is not red, we need another question to determine whether it is a spade or a club. The probability of being red is 0.5, of clubs 0.25 and spades 0.25, $p = (0.5, 0.25, 0.25)$. If the card is red, then we need only one question (with probability 0.5). For clubs and spades, we need two questions. In the meantime, we must ask $1 \cdot 0.5 + 2 \cdot 0.25 + 2 \cdot 0.25$ questions, which would result in 1.5 questions. Thus, we must measure the mean number of optimal questions. For four cards, of which one is the joker, the probability of a joker is 0.25 and of the other cards $1 - 0.25 = 0.75$, $p = (0.25, 0.75)$. In the meantime, we must ask $1 \cdot 0.25 + 1 \cdot 0.75$ questions to determine if the card is a joker or not. This approach results in one question. Given n cards, of which one is the joker, the probability of a joker is $1/n$ and of the other cards is $1 - 1/n$. In the meantime, we must ask $1 \cdot 1/n + 1 \cdot (1 - 1/n)$ questions to determine if the card is a joker or not. This approach results in one question that is independent of the size of n. How could it be that the result is independent of the size of n? It appears that something is missing in our definition. Our result is correct for one independent experiment; however, for several experiments, the mean number of questions is lower. We define the real entropy for one experiment as $H_0(F^1)$, for two experiments as $H_0(F^2)$, and for k experiments as $H_0(F^k)$. Here, we have the mean number of questions for the first experiment, the second, and the third to the kth experiment. The mean number of questions for one experiment in the sequence of k experiments is $1/k \cdot H_0(F^k)$.

For four cards of which one is the joker the probability of a joker is 0.25 and of other cards $1 - 0.25 = 0.75$ The real entropy for one experiment is $H_0(F^1)$:

$$H_0(F^1) = 1 \cdot 0.75 + 1 \cdot 0.25 = 1$$

$$\frac{H_0(F^1)}{1} = 1$$

The binary search tree corresponding to one experiment is represented in the Figure 4.3.

The hierarchy of the probabilities for two experiments is shown in Table 4.2 and the resulting binary search tree is represented in the Figure 4.4. The real entropy for two experiments is $H_0(F^2)$:

$$H_0(F^2) = 1 \cdot 0.75 \cdot 0.75 + 2 \cdot 0.75 \cdot 0.25 + 3 \cdot 0.25 \cdot 0.75 + 3 \cdot 0.25 \cdot 0.25$$

$$H_0(F^2) = 1.6875$$

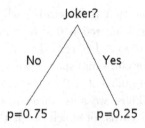

Fig. 4.3 For four cards of which one is the joker the probability of a joker is 0.25 and of other cards $1 - 0.25 = 0.75$, $p = (0.25, 0.75)$. In the mean we have to ask $1 \cdot 0.25 + 1 \cdot 0.75$ questions to determine to determine if the card is a joker or not. The real entropy for one experiment as $H_0(F^1)$

Table 4.2   Hierarchy of the probabilities for two experiments.

results	probability
card, card	$0.75 \cdot 0.75$
joker, card	$0.25 \cdot 0.75$
card, joker	$0.75 \cdot 0.25$
joker, joker	$0.25 \cdot 0.25$

$$\frac{H_0(F^2)}{2} = 0.84375$$

The hierarchy of the probabilities for three experiments is shown in Table 4.3 and the resulting binary search tree is represented in the Figure 4.5. The real entropy for two experiments is $H_0(F^3)$:

$$H_0(F^3) = 1 \cdot 0.42188 + 3 \cdot 0.14062 + 3 \cdot 0.14062 + 3 \cdot 0.14062+$$

$$+5 \cdot 0.046875 + 5 \cdot 0.046875 + 5 \cdot 0.046875 + 5 \cdot 0.015625$$

$$H_0(F^3) = 2.4688$$

$$\frac{H_0(F^3)}{3} = 0.82292$$

Does the sequence $h_k := \frac{H_0(F^k)}{k}$, with the values $\{1, 0.84375, 0.82292, ...\}$ for $k = 1, 2, 3, ..$ have a limit for $\lim_{k \to \infty} h_k$?
It has. The limit is defined as

$$H(F) := \lim_{k \to \infty} \frac{H_0(F^k)}{k} \leq H_0(F) \tag{4.4}$$

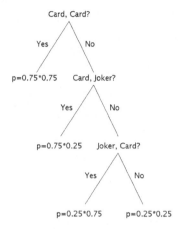

Fig. 4.4   The real entropy for two experiments as $H_0(F^2)$

Table 4.3   Hierarchy of the probabilities
for three experiments.

results	probability
card, card, card	$0.75 \cdot 0.75 \cdot 0.75$
card, card, joker	$0.75 \cdot 0.75 \cdot 0.25$
card, joker, card	$0.75 \cdot 0.25 \cdot 0.75$
joker. card card	$0.25 \cdot 0.75 \cdot 0.75$
joker, joker, card	$0.25 \cdot 0.25 \cdot 0.75$
joker, card, joker	$0.25 \cdot 0.75 \cdot 0.25$
card, joker, joker	$0.75 \cdot 0.25 \cdot 0.25$
joker, joker, joker	$0.25 \cdot 0.25 \cdot 0.25$

it is called the ideal entropy, it converges to [Shannon (1948)]

$$H(F) = -\sum_i p_i \log_2 p_i. \tag{4.5}$$

In our case it is simply

$$H(F) = -0.25 \cdot \log_2 0.25 - 0.75 \cdot \log_2 0.75 = 0.81128.$$

The ideal entropy indicates the minimal number of optimal questions that B must pose to know the result of the experiment on A [Shannon (1948)], [Topsoe (1974)]. Suppose that A repeated the experiment an infinite number of times. The ideal entropy is the essential information obtained by taking out the redundant information that corresponds to the ideal distribution to which the results converge. An experiment is described by the

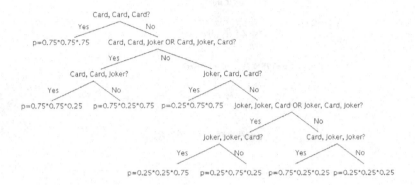

Fig. 4.5   The real entropy for two experiments as $H_0(F^3)$

probabilities $p = (p_1, p_2, ..., p_n)$. Does the distribution of these probabilities have an effect on the ideal entropy? It turns out that the ideal entropy is maximal in the case in which all probabilities are equal, which means that $p = (1/n, 1/n..., 1/n)$. In this case, the maximal ideal entropy is

$$H(F) = - \sum_i p_i \log_2 p_i = - \log_2 1/n = \log_2 n \qquad (4.6)$$

in which n describes the number of states. For $2^{16} = 65536$ states that present with the equal probability $1/65536$, the optimal number of questions is 16, which corresponds to 16 bits. If we suppose the letters of the alphabet (26 of them) occur with equal probability in a message, then the average information content per letter in a message is

$$H(F) - \sum_i^{26} 1/26 \cdot \log_2 1/26 = \log_2 26 = 4.7004 \; bit.$$

A word of five letters has an average information content of $5 \cdot \log_2 6 = 23.502$ bits. However, in a real human language, the average information content per letter is much lower because the distribution is not equal [Topsoe (1974)]. Some letters are more frequent than others; an e is more frequent than an x. We say that events that seldom happen, for example, the letter x in a message, have a higher surprise. Surprise is inversely related to probability. The larger the probability that we receive a character, the less surprised we are. A message over events that are not equally distributed has less information than a message over events that are equally distributed, but that message allows a higher surprise.

The equation $H(F) = \log_2 n$ is very similar to Boltzmann's equation, in which W *number of microstates* corresponds to a given macrostate. It follows, then, that the *number of microstates* is evenly distributed, and each microstate has the same probability of appearance. There are, however, two differences between the two equations. Boltzmann's equation includes Boltzmann's constant, and it uses log instead of $\log_2$. Instead of measuring the information in bits (yes/no questions) it measures the information in nepit (nat), which is based on Euler's number $e = 2.7182818...$ (sometimes also called Napier's constant). Euler's number is irrational and cannot be attributed to any questions. However, in the next section, we indicate that Euler's number is the ideal number that minimizes the depth of an idealistic search tree.

4.2 Hierarchical Structures

The principles of hierarchical organization appear in nature, for example, the structure of matter itself is hierarchically organized, including elementary particles, atomic nuclei, atoms, and molecules [Resnikoff (1989)]. The idea of hierarchical structures is based on the decomposition of a hierarchy into simpler parts. One of the greatest inventions of human civilization is the possibility of representing numbers by a hierarchically organized structure, which was begun approximately 5000 years ago by the Sumerian and Akkadian civilizations and later popularized by the Babylonians. An ancient way to denote a positive whole number is a sequence of marks used for counting. A requirement for the sequence is to provide a way to write down the next mark. An example is the arrangement of a number as a set of similar strokes; however, this representation takes up a large amount of space. This type of representation is called the unary numeral system. Positional notation is itself a hierarchical organized structure in which the whole number is mapped to positional notation to a certain base. For a unary numeral system, the base is one, and no hierarchy is present. For base $B > 1$ (a whole number), the hierarchy for a number N corresponds to determining the largest integer k such that $B^k \leq N$, where k indicates the number of digits that correspond to the depth of the hierarchy for the basis B. B^k represents the number of possible numbers that can be represented by the corresponding hierarchy. In the next step, k questions for each layer of the hierarchy must be answered to indicate which combination out of the B^k possible numbers is present. Each question has B possible answers, which correspond to the digits $B - 1, B - 2, .., 0$. The first question is: what is the leading digit n_k of the base B representing N, $n_k \cdot B^k \leq N$. The next question asks about the digit,

$$n_{k-1} \cdot B^{k-1} \leq N - n_k \cdot B^k. \tag{4.7}$$

The following questions ask about the digit

$$n_{k-2} \cdot B^{k-2} \leq N - n_k \cdot B^k - n_{k-1} \cdot B^{k-1} \tag{4.8}$$

and so forth.

For a binary base, the hierarchical structure corresponds to the ideal Entropy in which all of the probabilities of occurrences of the numbers are equal. Each question receives a reply of either yes or no. For each base, each question has B possible answers. This representation is related to a tree in computer science that has a constant branching factor of B. However, there are some differences; the nodes are organized in levels, the root of the tree corresponds to the level 0, and each node at each level has B children, which means that, at each level k, there are B^k nodes. A has the highest level L, and there are $B^L = N$ leaves that correspond to the N represented objects. For N objects and the number of levels L, the branching factor B is equal to

$$B = N^{\frac{1}{L}}. \tag{4.9}$$

For each level k there are

$$N(K) = B^k = N^{\frac{1}{L}} \tag{4.10}$$

nodes with $N(L) = L$. For a search of an object out of N at each level, B questions must be answered. The costs are $B \cdot log(N)/(log(B)$. Is there a B for which the cost becomes minimal? If we suppose that the tree is an ideal tree in which the branching factor can be an irrational number, then the solution is easy

$$cost = B \cdot \frac{\log(N)}{\log(B)} \tag{4.11}$$

$$0 = \frac{\partial cost}{\partial B} = \frac{\log(N)}{\log(B)} - \frac{\log(N)}{\log(B)^2}$$

with the solution

$$B = e = 2.7182818...$$

which corresponds to Euler's number. The closest whole number is three, followed by two. Euler's number minimizes the cost of an idealistic search tree; it is the minimal mean number of questions that must be answered. The minimal value of the number of questions corresponds to the essential information represented by nepit (nat) in the Boltzmann's equation. We assumed that we can answer all of the questions. Suppose that we cannot. In this case, we do not know which path to follow, and we must perform a search. Either we chose the path (answer to a question) randomly, or we perform a blind search, or we get a hint of which path (which answer) is right. In computer science, the hint is expressed by a heuristic function that rates the value's different paths according to how far the paths are from the goal object.

4.2.1 Example of a taxonomy

One of the most effective ways to structure knowledge is the taxonomic arrangement of the information that represents it [Resnikoff (1989)]. In 1887 Professor Harry Govier Seeley grouped all dinosaurs into the Saurischia and Ornithischia groups according to their hip design [Haines (1999)]. In Figure 4.6 and we 4.7 can see some examples of the two categories [Wichert (2000)].

Fig. 4.6 Stenonychosaurus is an example of the category Saurischia.

Fig. 4.7 Stegosaurus is an example of the category Ornithischia.

The saurischian were divided later into two subgroups: the carnivorous, bipedal theropods and the plant-eating, mostly quadruped sauropodomorphs. The ornithischians were divided into the subgroups birdlike ornithopods, armored thyreophorans, and margginoncephalia. The subgroups can be divided into suborders and then into families and finally into genus. The genus includes the species. It must be noted that in this taxonomy many relations are only guesswork, and many paleontologists have different ideas about how the taxonomy should look [Lambert (1983, 1993)] (see Figure 4.8).

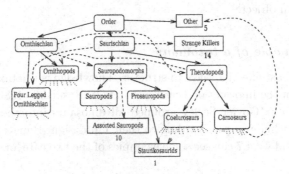

Fig. 4.8 Taxonomy of dinosauria. The number written below the rectangular boxes represents the categories which are not divided, the species. Uncertain categories are represented by dotted arrows.

4.3 Information and Measurement

Numbers are used in two fundamentally different ways. Either they can describe measurements of observed phenomena or they are used for mathematical calculations. Numbers that are attached to an observed magnitude represent the gained information. A real number a will be represented as decimal expansions of the form

$$a = a_{-N} \cdots a_{-1} a_0 . a_1 a_2 \cdots \tag{4.12}$$

it is a shorthand of notation of

$$a = a_{-N} 10^N + \cdots + a_{-1} 10 + a_0 10^0 + a_1 10^{-1} + a_2 10^{-2} + \cdots . \tag{4.13}$$

Increasingly precise variants of the measurement yield to least significant digit (right one) in the decimal expansion. How much additional information is provided by increasing the process of measurement? The measurement of a quantity Ξ is made. Its numerical value is h with infinitely many digits. The measurement provides a range of values in which h will be contained. Suppose the measurement provides numbers x_1 and y_1 with [Resnikoff (1989)]

$$x_1 < h < y_1, \tag{4.14}$$

(see Figure 4.9). In terms of decimal expansion, the measurement has

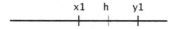

Fig. 4.9 The measurement provides numbers x_1 and y_1 with $x_1 < h < y_1$.

determined a certain fixed numbers of the expansion of h. The second measurement is done with a greater precision x_2 and y_2 with

$$x_1 < x_2 < h < y_2 < y_1, \tag{4.15}$$

(see Figure 4.10). The gain of information after the second measurement

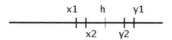

Fig. 4.10 The second measurement is done with a greater precision x_2 and y_2 with $x_1 < x_2 < h < y_2 < y_1$.

can be expressed by

$$I_{10} = \log_{10}\left(\frac{y_1 - x_1}{y_2 - x_2}\right) = \log_{10}(y_1 - x_1) - \log_{10}(y_2 - x_2) \tag{4.16}$$

with $\log_{10}(y_2 - x_2)$ being approximately number of digits in decimal expansion. The information can be measured in different units, for example binary digit expansion is

$$I_2 = \log_2\left(\frac{y_1 - x_1}{y_2 - x_2}\right) = \log_2(y_1 - x_1) - \log_2(y_2 - x_2). \tag{4.17}$$

The Equation 4.16 represents the information, which depends only on the endpoints x and y of the measurement of the interval. It does not depend on

- the choice of the zero point

$$I(x + b, y + b) = I(x, y)$$

- nor the scale

$$I(x \cdot a, y \cdot a) = I(x, y).$$

4.3.1 *Information measure I*

We determine the function I which satisfies both conditions [Resnikoff (1989)]. With $b = -x$ we get

$$I(x, y) = I(x + b, y + b) = I(0, y - x) \tag{4.18}$$

and with $a = \frac{1}{x}$ we get

$$I(x, y) = I(a \cdot x, a \cdot y) = I\left(1, \frac{y}{x}\right). \tag{4.19}$$

If we apply $a = \frac{1}{y-x}$ to Equation 4.18 we get

$$I(x, y) = I(0, y - x) = I(a \cdot 0, a \cdot (y - x)) = I(0, 1) = constant \tag{4.20}$$

One measurement results always in a constant gain. Information gain does not depend on the results of one measurement described by x and y. Suppose that I is a function of 3 variables x, y, z which were the results of a measurement (see Figure 4.11). The function does not depend on

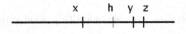

Fig. 4.11 I is a function of 3 variables x, y, z which were the results of a measurement.

- the choice of the zero point

$$I(x + b, y + b, z + b) = I(x, y, z)$$

- nor the scale

$$I(x \cdot a, y \cdot a, z \cdot a) = I(x, y, z).$$

Setting $b = -x$ and $a = \frac{1}{y}$ we get

$$I(x, y, z) = I(x + b, y + b, z + b) = I(0, y - x, z - x) \tag{4.21}$$

$$I(x, y, z) = I(a \cdot x, a \cdot y, a \cdot z) = I\left(\frac{x}{y}, 1, \frac{z}{y}\right) \tag{4.22}$$

Combining this two results together we get

$$I(x, y, z) = I\left(0, 1, \frac{z-x}{y-x}\right). \tag{4.23}$$

Information measurement which yields the numbers x, y, z can be expressed as a function of the ratio of the difference $z - x$ to the difference $y - x$. This ratio corresponds to two measurements for h with $x < y < z$ (see Figure 4.11):

- first with the bounds $x < h < z$,
- second with the bounds $x < h < y$.

We can preform a third measurement h with $x < w < y < z$, see Figure 4.12. The information content of the second measurement relative to the

Fig. 4.12 x, y, z, w describe two measurements for h with $x < w < y < z$.

first one is

$$I(x, y, z) = I\left(0, 1, \frac{z-x}{y-x}\right) \tag{4.24}$$

and the information content of the third measurement relative to the second one is

$$I(x, y, z) = I\left(0, 1, \frac{y-x}{w-x}\right). \tag{4.25}$$

The information content of the third measurement relative to the first should remain unchanged

$$I\left(0, 1, \frac{z-x}{w-x}\right) = I\left(0, 1, \frac{z-x}{y-x}\right) + I\left(0, 1, \frac{y-x}{w-x}\right). \tag{4.26}$$

We simplify

$$I\left(\frac{z-x}{w-x}\right) = I\left(\frac{z-x}{y-x}\right) + I\left(\frac{y-x}{w-x}\right) \tag{4.27}$$

with

$$t := z - x, \quad u := y - x, \quad v := w - x$$

$$I\left(\frac{t}{v}\right) = I\left(\frac{t}{u}\right) + I\left(\frac{u}{v}\right) \tag{4.28}$$

and with

$$s := \frac{1}{v}, \quad u := 1$$

$$I(s \cdot t) = I(t) + I(s). \tag{4.29}$$

I must be a Logarithm with respect to chosen base, for $\log_2$

$$I(s) = \log_2 s \tag{4.30}$$

and

$$I\left(\frac{z-x}{w-x}\right) = \log_2\left(\frac{z-x}{w-x}\right) \tag{4.31}$$

represent the gain of information in bits. The general case is the one of the two measurements, with the first measurement $x < h < z$ and second one is a more precise measurement $u < h < v$ with $x < u < v$ (see Figure 4.13). Additivity of the information function I provides

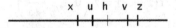

Fig. 4.13   The general case is the one of the two measurements, with the first measurement $x < h < z$ and second one is a more precise measurement $u < h < v$ with $x < u < v$.

$$I\left(\frac{z-x}{z-u}\right) + I\left(\frac{z-u}{v-u}\right) = I\left(\frac{z-x}{v-u}\right) \tag{4.32}$$

- First term is the information increment obtained by narrowing the estimate $x < h < z$ to $u < h < z$ where $x < u$.
- Second term is the information increment gained by narrowing the estimate $u < h < z$ to $u < h < v$ where $v < z$.
- Sum as in formation gained by passing from the estimate $x < h < z$ to the more precise estimate $u < h < v$.

4.3.2 *Nature of information measure*

Information measure is relative [Resnikoff (1989)]:

- The information remains unchanged when each of the variables is increased by a value or multiplied by a constant.
- A single measurement does not provide information.

Information gained from the measurement of an interval must always be considered relative to some prior measurement. This prior measurement can be represented by a pre defined scale representing the first measurement, like defined by the metric system.

4.3.3 *Measurement of angle*

In a circle a measurement is represented by an angle α and a more exact one by the angle β with $\alpha > \beta$ (see Figure 4.14). The information gain is

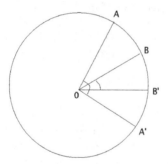

Fig. 4.14   In a circle a measurement is represented by two angles.

$$I\left(\frac{\alpha}{\beta}\right) = \log_2\left(\frac{\alpha}{\beta}\right)$$
(4.33)

bits. The angle measure of a direction must lie between 0 and $2 \cdot \pi$ With a priori knowledge $\alpha = 2 \cdot \pi$ only one measurement β is required [Resnikoff (1989)]

$$I\left(\frac{2 \cdot \pi}{\beta}\right) = \log_2\left(\frac{2 \cdot \pi}{\beta}\right).$$
(4.34)

For a straight line $\beta = \pi$ and the information content is

$$I(\pi) = \log_2\left(\frac{2 \cdot \pi}{\pi}\right) = 1 \; bit.$$
(4.35)

The observed direction lies in one half-of the planes. Smaller angles correspond to greater information, $I(\pi/2) = 2\ bits$, $I(\pi/4) = 3\ bits$.

4.3.4   *Information and contour*

A contour is subdivided into short segments of equal length. Each segmenting point can be thought as the vertex of an angle formed with two neighboring points [Resnikoff (1989)]. Associated with that angle is its measure of information gain. In a simple example there are three points P, Q, R (see Figure 4.15). We move on a line from P to Q. The corresponding information is 1 bit. The information gain passing from one straight line to the next is

$$I\left(\frac{\pi}{\pi}\right) = 0\ bits$$

since the angle remains unchanged. When the right angle at vertex Q is reached, there is a positive gain of information

$$I\left(\frac{\pi}{\pi/2}\right) = 1\ bits.$$

At the next step, passing from right angle to the straight angle there is an information loss

$$I\left(\frac{\pi/2}{\pi}\right) = -1\ bits.$$

In the example the right angle is where the contour changes its direction.

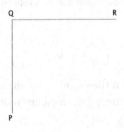

Fig. 4.15   There are three points P, Q, R.

Corners yield the greatest information, more strongly curved points yield more information.

4.4   Information and Memory

"Human memory is based on associations with the memories it contains. Just a snatch of well-known tune is enough to bring the whole thing back to mind. A forgotten joke is suddenly completely remembered when the next-door neighbor starts to tell it again. This type of memory has previously been termed content-addressable, which means that one small part of the particular memory is linked - associated -with the rest." Cited from [Brunak and Lautrup (1990)], page 104.

Associative memory models human memory [Palm (1990); Churchland and Sejnowski (1994); Fuster (1995); Squire and Kandel (1999)]. The associative memory and sub-symbolic distributed representation incorporate the following abilities in a natural way [Palm (1982); Hertz *et al.* (1991); Anderson (1995b); Kohonen (1989)]:

- The ability to correct faults if false information is given.
- The ability to complete information if some parts are missing.
- The ability to interpolate information. In other words, if a sub-symbol is not currently stored the most similar stored sub-symbol is determined.

The Lernmatrix, also simply called "associative memory", was developed by Steinbuch in 1958 as a biologically inspired model from the effort to explain the psychological phenomenon of conditioning [Steinbuch (1961, 1971)]. Later this model was studied under biological and mathematical aspects mainly by Willshaw [Willshaw *et al.* (1969)] and Palm [Palm (1982, 1990)].

Associative memory is composed of a cluster of units. Each unit represents a simple model of a real biological neuron. The Lernmatrix was invented by Steinbuch, whose goal was to produce a network that could use a binary version of Hebbian learning to form associations between pairs of binary vectors, for example each one representing a cognitive entity. Each unit is composed of binary weights, which correspond to the synapses and dendrites in a real neuron (see Figure. 4.16).

They are described by $w_{ij} \in \{0, 1\}$ in Figure 4.17. T is the threshold of the unit. The Lernmatrix is simply called *associative memory* if no confusion with other models is possible [Anderson (1995a); Ballard (1997)].

The patterns, which are stored in the Lernmatrix, are represented by binary vectors. The presence of a feature is indicated by a 'one' component of the vector, its absence through a 'zero' component of the vector. A pair of

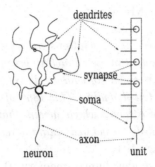

Fig. 4.16   A unit is an abstract model of a biological neuron [McClelland and Kawamoto (1986); Palm (1990); Hertz *et al.* (1991); OFTA (1991); Schwenker (1996)].

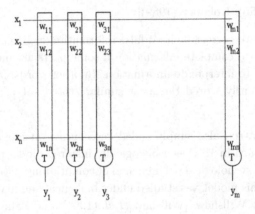

Fig. 4.17   The Lernmatrix is composed of a set of units which represent a simple model of a real biological neuron. The unit is composed of weights, which correspond to the synapses and dendrites in the real neuron. In this Figure they are described by $w_{ij} \in \{0, 1\}$ where $1 \leq i \leq m$ and $1 \leq j \leq n$. T is the threshold of the unit.

these vectors is associated and this process of association is called learning. The first of the two vectors is called the *question vector* and the second, the *answer vector*. After learning, the question vector is presented to the associative memory and the answer vector is determined by the retrieval rule.

Learning   Initially, no information is stored in the associative memory. Because the information is represented in weights, all unit weights are initially set to zero. In the learning phase, pairs of binary vector are associated.

Let $\vec{x}$ be the question vector and $\vec{y}$ the answer vector, the learning rule is:

$$w_{ij}^{new} \begin{cases} 1 & if \ y_i \cdot x_j = 1 \\ w_{ij}^{old} & \text{otherwise.} \end{cases} \qquad (4.36)$$

This rule is called the binary Hebbian rule [Palm (1982)]. Every time a pair of binary vectors is stored, this rule is used.

Retrieval In the *one-step* retrieval phase of the associative memory, a fault tolerant answering mechanism recalls the appropriate answer vector for a question vector $\vec{x}$. The retrieval rule for the determination of the answer vector $\vec{y}$ is:

$$y_i = \begin{cases} 1 & \sum_{j=1}^{n} w_{ij}x_j = T \\ 0 & \text{otherwise} \end{cases} \qquad (4.37)$$

where T is the threshold of the unit. The threshold T is set to the number of "one" components in the question vector $\vec{x}$, $T := |\vec{x}|$. It is quite possible that no answer vector is determined (zero answer vector). This happens when the question vector has a subset of components that was not correlated with the answer vector. A solution to this problem is the soft threshold strategy. In this strategy, the threshold is set to the maximum sum:

$$T :=_{max} i \sum_{j=1}^{n} \delta(w_{ij}x_j) \qquad (4.38)$$

with

$$\delta(x) = \begin{cases} 1 \text{ if } x > 0 \\ 0 \text{ if } x = 0 \end{cases} \qquad (4.39)$$

and the retrieval rule for the determination of the answer vector $\vec{y}$ is:

$$y_i = \begin{cases} 1 & \sum_{j=1}^{n} w_{ij}x_j \geq T \\ 0 & \text{otherwise.} \end{cases} \qquad (4.40)$$

This retrieval is called:

- association provided that the answer vector represents the reconstruction of the disturbed question vector;
- hetero-assocation if both vectors are different.

Example In Figure 4.18 the vector pair $\vec{x}_1 = (1,0,0,0,1)$ and $\vec{y}_1 = (0,1,1,1,0)$ is learned. The corresponding binary weights of the associated pair are indicated by a black square. In the next step the vector pair $\vec{x}_2 = (0,1,1,0,1)$ and $\vec{y}_2 = (1,1,0,0,1)$ is learned. The corresponding binary weights of the associated pair are indicated by a black circle. In third step the retrieval phase is preformed. The question vector $\vec{x}_* = (0,1,0,0,1)$ differs by one bit to the learned question vector $\vec{x}_2 = (0,1,1,0,1)$. The threshold T is set to the number of "one" components in the question vector $\vec{x}_*$, $T = 2$. The retrieved vector is the vector $\vec{y}_2 = (1,1,0,0,1)$ that was stored. A backward projection can be preformed in the fourth step. The synaptic matrix is a transpose of the matrix W, which is used for the forward projection. The similarity between the stored vector pair and the presented can be computed.

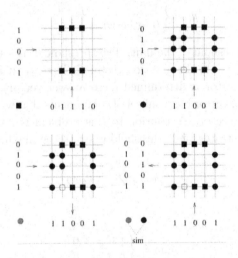

Fig. 4.18 The vector pair $\vec{x}_1 = (1,0,0,0,1)$ and $\vec{y}_1 = (0,1,1,1,0)$ is learned. The corresponding binary weights of the associated pair are indicated by a black square. In the next step the vector pair $\vec{x}_2 = (0,1,1,0,1)$ and $\vec{y}_2 = (1,1,0,0,1)$ is learned. The corresponding binary weights of the associated pair are indicated by a black circle. In third step the retrieval phase is preformed. The question vector $\vec{x}_* = (0,1,0,0,1)$ differs by one bit to the learned question vector $\vec{x}_2 = (0,1,1,0,1)$. The threshold T is set to the number of "one" components in the question vector $\vec{x}_*$, $T = 2$. The retrieved vector is the vector $\vec{y}_2 = (1,1,0,0,1)$ that was stored. A backward projection can be preformed in the fourth step. The synaptic matrix is a transpose of the matrix W, which is used for the forward projection. The similarity between the stored vector pair and the presented can be computed.

Storage capacity For an estimation of the asymptotic number L of vector pairs $(\vec{x}, \vec{y})$ that can be stored in an associative memory before it begins to make mistakes in the retrieval phase, it is assumed that both vectors have the same dimension n. It is also assumed that both vectors are composed of k ones, which are equally likely to be in any coordinate of the vector. In this case it was shown [Palm (1982); Hecht-Nielsen (1989); Sommer (1993)] that the optimum value for k is approximately

$$k \doteq \log_2(n/4). \tag{4.41}$$

For example for a vector of the dimension n=1000000 only $k = 18$ ones should be used to code a pattern according to the Equation 4.41. For an optimal value for k according to the Equation 4.41 with ones equally distributed over the coordinates of the vectors, approximately L vector pairs can be stored in the associative memory [Palm (1982); Hecht-Nielsen (1989)]. L is approximately

$$L \doteq (\ln 2)(n^2/k^2). \tag{4.42}$$

This value is much greater than n. The estimate of L is very rough because Equation 4.42 is only valid for very large networks. Equation 4.42 does not apply for networks of reasonable size, however the capacity increase is still considerable. For realistic values please consult Table 2 in [Knoblauch *et al.* (2010)]. Small deviation from the logarithmic sparseness reduces the network capacity. It is very difficult to find coding schemas that represent the information by logarithmic sparse codes [Knoblauch *et al.* (2010)].

It should be noted that the Lernmatrix system allows high capacity and fast access when working in parallel, each unit represents a neuron that performs calculations. On a conventional Von Neumann architecture, compressed look-up tables are more efficient [Knoblauch *et al.* (2010)]. However a Von Neuman architecture is not biologically plausible.

Information and storage capacity We indicate a sketch of a proof for Equation 4.41 and 4.42 [Hecht-Nielsen (1989)]. There are $C(n, k)$ different binary vectors of the dimension n with k ones,

$$C(n, k) = \frac{n!}{(n - k)! \cdot k!} \tag{4.43}$$

for example

$$C(3, 2) = \frac{3!}{(1)! \cdot 2!} = 3,$$

$$(1, 1, 0), \quad (1, 0, 1), \quad (0, 1, 1).$$

We can determine for each vector the probability the presence of a one

$$p_{C(n,k)} = \frac{1}{C(n,k)}.$$ (4.44)

The entropy of L vectors is

$$H(F) = -\sum_i p_i \log_2 p_i = -L \cdot p_{C(n,k)} \log_2 p_{C(n,k)}$$ (4.45)

and we can rewrite it as

$$H(F) = L \cdot \frac{1}{C(n,k)} \log_2 C(n,k).$$ (4.46)

The self-information or the information content associated with the outcome of a random variable ω_i is defined as

$$I(\omega_i) = -\log_2 P(\omega_i).$$ (4.47)

The information content of L vectors is

$$I = -L \cdot \log_2 p_{C(n,k)} = L \cdot \log_2 C(n,k) = L \cdot \log_2 \left(\frac{n!}{(n-k)! \cdot k!} \right).$$ (4.48)

We want to maximize the information I in correspondence to the size of the associative memory n,

$$Maximize \longrightarrow \frac{I}{n^2}.$$ (4.49)

Depending on the size n, we have to find optimal values for k and L.

- We need to determine the probability p after storing L binary vectors in the associative memory, that a weight w_{ij} at a certain position (ij) is one.
- We need to determine the probability $p-1$ after storing L binary vectors in the associative memory, that a weight w_{ij} at a certain position (ij) is zero.

The probability p depends on the probability $1 - p$. For L pairs the probability that a weight is zero is

$$(1 - p) = \left(\frac{n^2 - k^2}{n^2} \right)^L$$ (4.50)

since the probability of a sequence of n independent events is its product. For L pairs the probability that a weight is one is

$$p = 1 - \left(1 - \frac{k^2}{n^2} \right)^L.$$ (4.51)

We try to determine the probability of obtaining an extra 1 during recall of $\vec{y}_q$. We know that the vector $\vec{x}_q$ has k ones and the probability of a weight being 1 is p. Let us demand that the number of wrong ones on each $\vec{y}_q$ vector recall be 1. The product of $(n-k)$, the number of 0 in $\vec{y}_q$ and the probability of each 0 being wrongly set to one (p^k) will be equal to one

$$1 = (n-k) \cdot p^k. \tag{4.52}$$

Combining the Equations 4.51 and 4.52 yields

$$(n-k) \cdot \left(1 - \left(1 - \frac{k^2}{n^2}\right)^L\right)^k = 1, \tag{4.53}$$

$$1 - \left(1 - \frac{k^2}{n^2}\right)^L = (n-k)^{-\frac{1}{k}}, \tag{4.54}$$

$$\left(1 - \frac{k^2}{n^2}\right)^L = 1 - (n-k)^{-\frac{1}{k}}, \tag{4.55}$$

$$L \cdot \log\left(1 - \frac{k^2}{n^2}\right) = \log\left(1 - (n-k)^{-\frac{1}{k}}\right), \tag{4.56}$$

$$L = \frac{\log\left(1 - (n-k)^{-\frac{1}{k}}\right)}{\log\left(1 - \frac{k^2}{n^2}\right)}. \tag{4.57}$$

Combining the Equations 4.48

$$I = L \cdot \log_2 C(n,k) = \frac{\log\left(1 - (n-k)^{-\frac{1}{k}}\right)}{\log\left(1 - \frac{k^2}{n^2}\right)} \cdot \log_2\left(\frac{n!}{(n-k)! \cdot k!}\right) \tag{4.58}$$

and

$$\log_2\left(\frac{n!}{(n-k)! \cdot k!}\right) = \log_2(n!) - \log_2((n-k)!) - \log_2(k!). \tag{4.59}$$

We can use the logarithmic version of Sterling's formula. The Sterling's formula is given by

$$\log(n!) = \frac{n+1}{2} \cdot \log(n) - n + \frac{1}{2} \cdot \log(2 \cdot \pi), \tag{4.60}$$

$$\log_2(n!) = \frac{n+1}{2} \cdot \log_2(n) \cdot log(2) - n + \frac{1}{2} \cdot \log_2(2 \cdot \pi) \cdot \log(2),$$

$$\log_2(n!) = \frac{n+1}{2} \cdot \log_2(n) \cdot log(2) - n + 0.92. \tag{4.61}$$

All together yields

$$I = L \cdot \log_2 C(n, k) = \frac{1}{\log(2)} \cdot \left(\frac{\log\left(1 - (n-k)^{-\frac{1}{k}}\right)}{\log\left(1 - \frac{k^2}{n^2}\right)} \right) \cdot$$

$$\left(n + \frac{1}{2} \cdot (log(n) - log(n-k)) + k \cdot log(n-k) - log(k) \cdot \left(k + \frac{1}{2} \right) - 0.92 \right)$$

$$(4.62)$$

Using computer simulation we can determine the corresponding values k that maximize I

$$Maximize \longrightarrow \frac{I}{n^2}$$

depending on n, $n = 10^2, 10^3, \cdots, 10^{100}$, see Figure 4.19. We find the

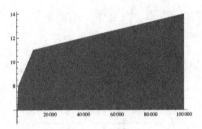

Fig. 4.19   Values k that maximizes I for $n = 10^2, 10^3, 10^4, 10^5$.

optimum value for k to be

$$k \doteq \log_2(n) - 2 = \log_2(n/4) \qquad (4.63)$$

and

$$L \doteq (\ln 2)(n^2/k^2).$$

Substituting Equation 4.63 into Equation 4.62 we get the upper bound for large n

$$I = n^2 \log 2 = n^2 \cdot 0.693 \qquad (4.64)$$

the asymptotic capacity is 69.31 percent with allowed error rate of one additional one per $\vec{y}_q$ as expressed by Equation 4.52. This capacity is only valid for sparse equally distributed ones [Palm (1982)].

Weight matrix diagram   The diagram of the weight matrix illustrates the weight distribution which results from the distribution of the stored patterns [Marcinowski (1987); Freeman (1994)]. Useful associative properties result from equally distributed weights over the whole weight matrix. Clusters in the diagram indicate strong correlation between parts of stored patterns. The load of the associative memory is indicated by the percentage of weights which are not zero. A high percentage indicates an overload and the loss of its associative properties. Figure 4.20 represents a diagram of a high loaded matrix with equally distributed weights.

Structure of weight matrix   The structure of the weight matrix indicates the elementary blocks which compose an associative memory. It is represented by the frequency of different sum values of the weights of rows or columns [Marcinowski (1987)]. The sum over column i is,

$$\mu_i = \sum_{j=1}^{n} w_{ij}$$

The μ_i are sorted with a new index $\pi = \iota(i)$,

$$\mu_1 \leq \mu_2 \leq \mu_3 \leq \mu_\pi \leq \ldots \leq \ldots \leq \mu_m.$$

The number ζ of groups with different μ values and the number of their elements is determined,

$$\underbrace{\mu_1 = \mu_2 = \mu_3}_{\tau_1 = 3} < \underbrace{\mu_\pi = \ldots}_{\tau_2} < \underbrace{\ldots = \mu_m.}_{\tau_\zeta}$$

This can be represented as a procedure:

$\Phi = 1$
$\tau_\Phi = 1$
FOR $\pi = 1$ TO m-1 STEP 1
    DO
      IF $\mu_\pi = \mu_{\pi+1}$ THEN $\tau_\Phi = \tau_\Phi + 1$
            ELSE DO $\Phi = \Phi + 1$; $\tau_\Phi = 1$ OD
    OD
$\zeta = \Phi.$

The ζ sorted different τ_Φ values are represented by a diagram. The x axis represents the $\Phi \in [1, 2, \ldots, \zeta]$ values and y axis the corresponding frequency of sum values τ_Φ. The relationship between the x axis ordinate and corresponding value μ_π is represented additionally, for example, by an additional plot. If the associative memory performs hetroassocative recalls, the associative matrix is not symmetric and the diagrams for the sum of rows and columns are different. The sum over row j is

$$\mu_j = \sum_{i=1}^{n} w_{ij}.$$

There are n μ_j values (see Figure 4.17). In Figure 4.21 the structure of the weight matrix of Figure 4.20 is represented. The plot illustrates that the weight matrix is composed of approximately 300 elementary blocks which represent a nearly gausian correlation between the stored pattern parts. Figure 4.20 shows the distribution results of the ten randomly set ones in the 2000 dimensional, 20000 learned vector pairs.

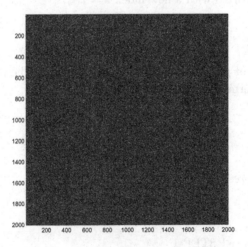

Fig. 4.20   The weight matrix after learning of 20000 test patterns, in which ten ones were randomly set in a 2000 dimensional vector represents a high loaded matrix with equally distributed weights. This example shows that weight matrix diagram often contains nearly no information. Information about the weight matrix can be extracted by the structure of weight matrix. (White color represents weights.)

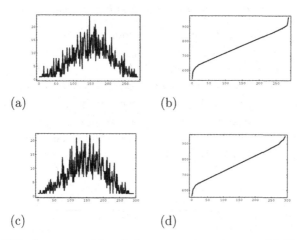

(a) (b)

(c) (d)

Fig. 4.21 38% of synapses of associative memory are not zero. (a) The frequency of different sum values of columns. (b) The corresponding sum values of columns. (c) The frequency of different sum values of rows. (d) The corresponding sum values of rows.

4.5 Sparse code for Sub-symbols

Usually suboptimal sparse codes are used. An example of a suboptimal sparse code is the representation of words by context-sensitive letter units [Wickelgren (1969, 1977); Rumelhart and McClelland (1986); Bentz *et al.* (1989)]. The ideas for the used robust mechanism come from psychology and biology [Wickelgren (1969, 1977); Rumelhart and McClelland (1986); Bentz *et al.* (1989)]. Each letter in a word is represented as a triple, which consists of the letter itself, its predecessor, and its successor. For example, six context-sensitive letters encode the word *desert*, namely: *_de, des, ese, ser, ert, rt_*. The character "*_*" marks the word beginning and ending. Because the alphabet is composed of 26+1 characters, 27^3 different context-sensitive letters exist. In the 27^3 dimensional binary vector each position corresponds to a possible context-sensitive letter, and a word is represented by indication of the actually present context-sensitive letters.

A set of features can be represented by a binary vector and represent a category. A position in the corresponding vector corresponds to a feature. To be sparse, the set of features that describes a category compared to the dimension of the vector has to be sufficiently small. This is because, of all possible features, only some should define categories. This can be achieved by sparsification based on unary sub-vector representation.

4.5.1 *Sparsification based on unary sub-vectors*

A binary representation of a number h would require a vector of length $d = \lfloor log_2 h + 1 \rfloor$. However if we represent the number h in unary, we require h positions. One unary representation of $h \neq 0$ is a string of $h - 1$ zeros with a one at h-th postion [Wichert (2013)]. A binary number of length d is represented by a unary number of 2^d positions, which is exponential in the size of input. A binary vector $\vec{x}$ of dimension t is split into f distinct sub vectors of dimension $p = dim(t/f)$. The binary sub vectors $u_i(\vec{x})$ of dimension $p = dim(t/f)$ are represented as unary vectors of dimension 2^p :

$$\vec{x} = \underbrace{x_1,, x_2, \cdots, x_p}_{u_1(\vec{x})}, \cdots, \underbrace{x_{m-p+1}, \cdots, x_m}_{u_f(\vec{x})} \qquad (4.65)$$

The resulting binary vector is composed out of the unary vectors and has the dimension $f \cdot 2^p$. In the following example a binary vector of dimension 6 is split into 2 distinct sub vectors of dimension 3. The binary sub vectors $u_i(\vec{x})$ of dimension 3 are represented as unary vectors of dimension 2^3 :

$$\vec{x} = \underbrace{1, 0, 1}_{u_1(1,0,1)}, \underbrace{0, 0, 1}_{u_2(0,0,1)} \qquad (4.66)$$

$$u_1(1, 0, 1) = (0, 0, 0, 0, 1, 0, 0, 0); \quad (h = 5)$$

$$u_2(0, 0, 1) = (1, 0, 0, 0, 0, 0, 0, 0); \quad (h = 1)$$

$$u(\vec{x}) = (0, 0, 0, 0, 1, 0, 0, 0, 1, 0, 0, 0, 0, 0, 0, 0), \qquad (4.67)$$

resulting in a new vector of dimension $16 = 2 * 2^3$ with 2 ones. The resulting vector is more sparse, however some information related to correlation is lost [Wichert (2013)]. These ideas are related to the Wilshaw model of associative memory with local inhibition [Shim *et al.* (1990)] and [Kropff and Treves (2005)].

4.6 Deduction Systems and Associative Memory

In this section we will present a straightforward transformation from symbolic rules into a representation by associative memory. We will indicate that deduction systems may be represented by an associative memory with feedback connections [Wichert (2005b)], [Wichert (2006)], [Wichert (2012)].

Binary vectors can represent features. A 'one' represents a feature at the corresponding position of a binary vector; its absence is denoted by a 'zero'. The feature set $A, B, C, D, E, F, G, H, I, J, K$ (defined in the preceding section) is represented by a binary vector of dimension 11, no distinction between categories and features is made. The presence of features C and E is represented by the binary vector $[0\ 0\ 1\ 0\ 1\ 0\ 0\ 0\ 0\ 0\ 0]$.

The associative memory represents the long-term memory of our deduction system in which the rules are stored. In the initialization phase of the associative memory, no information is stored. Because the information is represented in the weights, they are all initially set to zero. In the learning phase, binary vector pairs are associated. In the first vector $\vec{x}$ we store the feature set; the category itself is indicated by the second vector $\vec{y}$. For example, the rule $D \wedge F$ then B is represented in the vectors $x = [0\ 0\ 0\ 1\ 0\ 1\ 0\ 0\ 0\ 0\ 0]$ and $y = [0\ 1\ 0\ 0\ 0\ 0\ 0\ 0\ 0\ 0\ 0]$.

We demonstrate this procedure with the example that was introduced in the section about the deduction systems (see Section 3.2.1). For clarity we can replace the names of features and categories by symbols, each symbol representing a name, for example B representing "oil lamp lights during driving round a bend":

(1) $B \vee C$ then A
(2) $D \wedge F$ then B
(3) $E \wedge F$ then C
(4) $H \wedge F \wedge I$ then G
(5) $F \wedge I$ then J
(6) K then F

In Figure 4.22 we see the associative memory after learning of the six rules. The 'or' rules are indicated by a one in the threshold. For example, the 'or' rule $B \vee C$ then A is represented by the first unit, and the rule $D \wedge F$ then B is represented by the second unit (see Figure 4.22).

After learning the categories can be determined by the inference with the aid of associative memory. The present features represented by the question vector $\vec{x}$ are presented to the associative memory and the categories are identified by the retrieval rule which determines the answer vector $\vec{y}$ with the aid of the following adapted retrieval rule:

$$y_i = \mu(z_i) \tag{4.68}$$

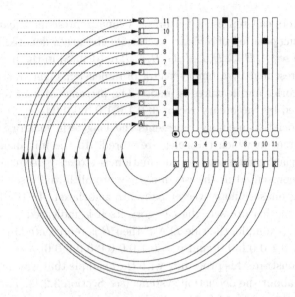

Fig. 4.22 The architecture of our inference system is composed of associative memory with feedback connections [Palm (1990); Palm *et al.* (1992)]. The rule $B \vee C$ then A is represented by the first unit; that it is an 'or' rule is indicated by a one in its threshold (represented in this Figure by a black dot). The associative memory forms the long-term memory; the short-term memory that is initialized with the initial state description is represented by the row buffer on the left side of the associative memory. The features of the short-term memory are presented to the associative memory, which determines the categories by using the retrieval rule. The determined categories are transported from the buffer below the units (column buffer) via the feedback connections to the short-term memory.

with

$$z_i = \frac{\sum_{j=1}^{n} w_{ij} x_j - 1}{\sum_{j=1}^{n} w_{ij}} \tag{4.69}$$

and

$$\mu(z_i) = \begin{cases} 1 \ if \begin{cases} z_i > 0 & \text{for or rules} \\ z_i = 1 & \text{for and rules} \end{cases} \\ 0 \ else \end{cases} \tag{4.70}$$

The short-term memory, which is initialized with the initial state description, is represented by the row buffer (short-term memory) on the

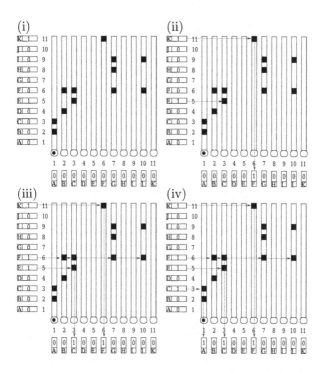

Fig. 4.23   (i) The features 'oil lamp lights up' and 'braking' are represented in our symbol notation by K and E respectively. The short-term memory is initialized with /K, E/. (ii) In the first inference step, F is deduced. The activation of the units is indicated by the buffer below the units and should be not confused with the 'or' rule indication of a one in the threshold (represented by a black dot). iii) The short-term memory is now /K, E, F/. The features of the short-term memory are presented to the associative memory, and C and F are deduced in the following inference. (iv) The short-term memory is now updated to /K, E, F, C/. In the next inference step, C, F and A are deduced. A is deduced, because $A \Rightarrow B \vee C$ is an 'or' rule as indicated by the threshold value *one* of the corresponding unit (represented by a black dot

left side of the associative memory, see Figure 4.22. The features of the short-term memory are presented to the associative memory, which determines the categories by using the retrieval rule to perform an inference step. The determined categories are transported from the buffer below the units (column buffer) via the feedback connections to the short-term memory. The short-term memory is updated and the procedure is repeated until the short-term memory does not change, i.e. the number of features in it does not grow.

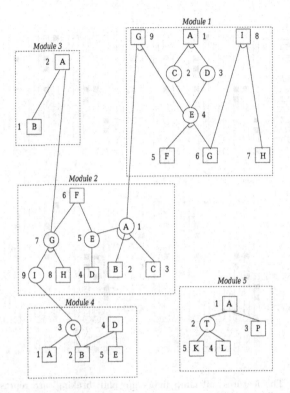

Fig. 4.24   Representation of 16 rules arranged in five modules by two directed AND/OR graphs. A name and a number in the context of a module indicate each feature. Each module is represented by an associative memory. The number of a feature indicates the position in the corresponding vector. A disorder that is defined in a certain module can cause a manifestation in other modules. This relation corresponds to connections between modules. The 'and' rules are indicated by an arc between the links connecting the nodes, which indicate the manifestations.

The features 'oil lamp lights up' and 'braking' are present (represented in our symbol notation by K and E). The short-term memory is initialized with $/K, E/$ (see Figure 4.23 (i)). In the first inference step, F is deduced; the short-term memory is now $/K, E, F/$ (see Figure 4.23 (ii)). The features of the short-term memory are presented to the associative memory and, in the following inference, C and F are deduced (see Figure 4.23 (iii)). The short-term memory is then updated to $/K, E, F, C/$. In the next inference steps, C, F and A are deduced. A is deduced, because $A \Rightarrow B \vee C$ is an 'or' rule as indicated by the threshold value of the corresponding unit (see Figure 4.23 (iv)). The inference procedure is completed because no new features are determined in the following inference step. In our example the category A would correspond to "the cable of the oil pressure lamp is loose."

The representation of directed AND/OR graphs by associative memory with feedback are summarized in the following points:

- The inference in the AND/OR graphs corresponds to breadth-first search.
- The number of cycles performed by the associative memory with the feedback correspond to the maximum depth of the represented graphs.
- The directed AND/OR graph can contain cycles, because only new, not yet present disorders are added to the short term memory, and the feedback is done until the number of features in the short term memory does not grow.

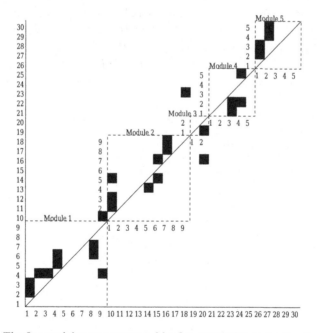

Fig. 4.25   The five modules are represented by five associative memories. By arranging them diagonal, we compose a global associative memory. An associative memory of dimension 30 evolves. In this global context, connections between modules can be easily indicated by weights depicted outside the modules. Connection from the first to the second module is indicated by the weights in the column of the first module and the row of the second module. In this Figure we can see three connections between the modules.

- The number of represented disorders is correlated with the size of the associative memory; this number is only limited by the size of the expandable associative memory.

4.6.1 *Taxonomic knowledge organization*

For clarity, rules should be arranged in groups [Aikins (1986); Kahn *et al.* (1987)] that define taxonomy. A module could represent a group, each feature is indicated by a name in the context of a module and each module is represented by an associative memory [Wichert (2012)] (see Figure 4.24).

Each module (see Figure 4.24) could correspond to a different area of the human brain. How can we link this different areas of the brain? For example, 5 modules would be represented by 5 associative memories. From the 5 associative memories, we can compose a global associative memory by the arrangement on the diagonal. An associative memory of the dimension 30 evolves in which local feature addresses are translated into global feature addresses (see Figure 4.25). In this global context, connections between modules can be easily indicated by weights outside the modules, in the column of the first module and the row to the second module (connection from the first module to the second module). In Figure 4.25 we can see three connections between the modules corresponding to our rule base [Wichert (2012)].

Chapter 5

Reversible Algorithms

5.1 Reversible Computation

Energy is negligible when using the Turing machine model, because the Turing machine itself constitutes an infinitely long tape and does not require any energy resources. However, what is the relation between energy and information that is processed by a Turing machine? In the thermodynamic Maxwell paradox, there is a demon that observes the gas molecules. Between the chambers, there is a small door. The demon can open and close the small door, passing only one molecule into a chamber. The negative of the demon's entropy increments as the measure of the quantity of the information that it has used. Information increments when entropy decrements. The information must be stored in a demon's memory. Given the fact that the memory is finite, the demon must erase some information. The erasing of information increases the entropy represented by energy. Bennett (1973) showed [Bennett (1973)] that irreversible overwriting of one bit causes at least $k \cdot T \cdot log2$ joules of energy dissipation, where k is Boltzmann's constant and T is the absolute temperature. Bennett also indicated that this lower bound can be ignored when using reversible computation. Reversible computing is a model of computing in which the computational process is reversible. For example, a NOT gate is reversible in the sense that one can infer the output from the input. However, neither the AND or OR gates are reversible in the sense that one cannot infer the output from the input. For example, $(1\ AND\ 0) = (0\ AND\ 1) = (0\ AND\ 0) = 0$ [Bennett (1982)]. Reversibility is obtained by Bennett by the storage of all of the computational steps. A three-tape Turing machine is used, with an input tape, history tape and output tape. The computation is performed on the input tape, and all steps are stored on the history tape. Without the history tape, the computational history would be forgotten. When the computation stops, the results are copied to the output tape, and the computation is run backward to erase the history tape for feature usage. Any Turing machine can be simulated by a reversible Turing machine [Bennett (1988)], [Bennett (1989)]. For a reversible production system, the sequence of productions at each step must be remembered. This requirement is usually met for any production system. A computation of a production system is specified by the initial and the goal state, the set of productions. The solution is represented by the sequence of productions at each step.

5.2   Reversible Circuits

5.2.1   *Boolean gates*

The sets of truth functions can be computed using Boolean circuits, which are composed of Boolean gates. An algorithm can be described by such a circuit; however, the AND and OR gates are not reversible; each one of them erases one bit and generates approximately $k \cdot T \cdot log2$ joules of energy dissipation [Landauer (1961)], [Landauer (1992)]. During the computation, information is lost; however, at the same time, the entropy grows [Landauer (1992)], [Bennett (2003)]. For this reason, processors generate waste heat and must be cooled to keep them within permissible operating temperature limits. A solution to the generation of waste heat is reversible Boolean gates. However, reversible Boolean gates require additional *waste* bits.

5.2.2   *Reversible Boolean gates*

To make a circuit reversible, we must make each of the gates reversible. A necessary condition for a reversible gate is that of a bijective transition function with m inputs and m outputs. No injective transition function can be used, if n is the input and m the output; if $n > m$, then some information is lost. Such a bijective function is a permutation of m inputs and m outputs. For m bits, there are $c = 2^m$ different combinations. For c different combinations, there are $c!$ possible permutations between the input and output. A reversible gate is such a permutation. For the NOT gate, there are two possible combinations of one bit, $c = 2^1$. Either the bit is 1 or 0. There are also two possible permutations, which means two different gates, which are both reversible. One gate is the identity gate, and the other gate is the NOT gate. Both of them are reversible. For the

Table 5.1 Truth table of the Toffoli gate.

dec.	inputs x_1, x_2, x_3	outputs y_1, y_2, y_3	dec.
0	0,0,0	0,0,0	0
1	0,0,1	0,0,1	1
2	0,1,0	0,1,0	2
3	0,1,1	0,1,1	3
4	1,0,0	1,0,0	4
5	1,0,1	1,0,1	5
6	*1,1,0*	*1,1,1*	*7*
7	*1,1,1*	*1,1,0*	*6*

identity gate, the input is equal to the output. For gates with two bits, there are altogether four combinations of two bits, $c = 2^2$ and $24 = 4!$ possible permutations, which means 24 different gates. However, none of the 24 gates solves the AND or OR problem.

5.2.3 Toffoli gate

The AND gate can be only computed by a reversible gate, which operates on three bits. On there bits, $c = 2^3$ and $40320 = 8!$ possible permutations. One of the possible permutations corresponds to the truth table of the Toffoli gate [Toffoli (1980a)], [Toffoli (1980b)], [Toffoli (1980c)] Each value of Table 5.1 corresponds to three input bits x_1, x_2, x_3 and three output bits y_1, y_2, y_3. The permutation is defined by the exchange of the values $1, 1, 0$ with $1, 1, 1$ (decimal $6, 7$).

The Toffoli gate does not change the first input bits x_1 and x_2. The operation is described by the following mapping on three input bits x_1, x_2, x_3 with $\mathbf{B} = \{0, 1\}$

$$T : \mathbf{B}^3 \to \mathbf{B}^3 :, T(x_1, x_2, x_3) = (x_1, x_2, (x_1 \wedge x_2) \oplus x_3)$$

A Toffoli gate is a universal reversible gate it performs following operations.

- It computes the AND operation, the ancilla (fixed) bit x_3 is set to 0

$$T : \mathbf{B}^3 \to \mathbf{B}^3 :, T(x_1, x_2, 0) = (x_1, x_2, x_1 \wedge x_2)$$

- It computes the NOT operation on x_3

$$T : \mathbf{B}^3 \to \mathbf{B}^3 :, T(1, 1, x_3) = (1, 1, \neg x_3)$$

- It computes the $NAND$ operation, the ancilla (fixed) bit x_3 is set to 1

$$T : \mathbf{B}^3 \to \mathbf{B}^3 :, T(x_1, x_2, 1) = (x_1, x_2, \neg(x_1 \wedge x_2))$$

- It computes the $FANOUT$ operation (the value of bit x_2 is copied into x_3)

$$T : \mathbf{B}^3 \to \mathbf{B}^3 :, T(1, x_2, 0) = (1, x_2, x_2)$$

The OR operation follows from the De Morgan's laws

$$x_1 \lor x_2 = \neg(\neg x_1 \land, \neg x_2)$$

Because $NAND$ and $FANOUT$ are together universal, we can implement any reversible circuit using the Toffoli gate.

5.2.4   Circuit

A reversible circuit can be built using Toffoli gates and NOT gates. This construct represents a permutation on m bits, defining an injective mapping $\mathbf{B}^m \to \mathbf{B}^m$. Out of m bits, several bits act as control bits (ancilla bits) and others are not changed during the computation. For each AND operation, one ancilla bit is required. A reversible circuit performs a permutation of the input bits. The output is a permutation of the input bits. Each reversible circuit can be represented by a permutation matrix. As stated before, a circuit is not an algorithmic device; by itself, it does not correspond to a universal reversible Turing machine. This arrangement also applies to any reversible circuit.

Chapter 6

Probability

6.1 Kolmogorovs Probabilities

Probability theory is built around Kolmogorov's axioms (first published in 1933, [Kolmogorov (1933)]). All probabilities are between 0 and 1. For any proposition a,

$$0 \leq P(a) \leq 1$$

and

$$P(true) = 1, \quad P(false) = 0.$$

To each sentence, a numerical degree of belief between 0 and 1 is assigned, which provides a way of summarizing the uncertainty. The last axiom expresses the probability of disjunction and is given by

$$P(a \vee b) = P(a) + P(b) - P(a \wedge b)$$

Where do these numerical degrees of belief come from?

- Humans can believe in a subjective viewpoint, which can be determined by some empirical psychological experiments. This approach is a very subjective way to determine the numerical degree of belief.
- A more objective method results from physical experiments or from some databases describing market behavior: for any finite sample, we can estimate the true fraction and also calculate how accurate our estimation is likely to be. By using samples, as in most physical measurements, we estimate the values. This approach is called frequentist. We approach the true value by counting the frequency of an event but do not reach the true value because we cannot access the whole population of events.

- It appears that the true values can be determined from the true nature of the universe, for example, for a fair coin, the probability of heads is 0.5. This approach is related to the Platonic world of ideas. However, we can never verify whether a fair coin exists. To accomplish such a verification, we would have to follow the frequentist approach.

6.1.1 Conditional probability

The degree of belief $P(a)$ is attached to a sentence a before any evidence about the nature of the sentence is obtained; we call this probability the prior (before) probability. Arising from the frequentist approach, one can determine the probability of an event a by counting. If Ω is the set of all possible events, $P(\Omega) = 1$, then $a \in \Omega$. The cardinality determines the number of elements of a set, $card(\Omega)$ is the number of elements of the set Ω, $card(a)$ is the number of elements of the set a and

$$P(a) = \frac{card(a)}{card(\Omega)}. \tag{6.1}$$

Now we can define the posterior probability, the probability of a after the evidence b is obtained

$$P(a|b) = \frac{card(a \wedge b)}{card(b)}. \tag{6.2}$$

The posterior probability is also called the conditional probability. From

$$P(a \wedge b) = \frac{card(a \wedge b)}{card(\Omega)} \tag{6.3}$$

and

$$P(b) = \frac{card(b)}{card(\Omega)} \tag{6.4}$$

we get

$$P(a|b) = \frac{P(a \wedge b)}{P(b)} \tag{6.5}$$

and

$$P(b|a) = \frac{P(a \wedge b)}{P(a)}. \tag{6.6}$$

6.1.2 *Bayes's rule*

The Bayes's rule follows from both equations

$$P(b|a) = \frac{P(a|b) \cdot P(b)}{P(a)}. \tag{6.7}$$

For mutually exclusive events $b_1, ..., b_n$ with

$$\sum_{i=1}^{n} P(b_i) = 1 \tag{6.8}$$

the law of total probability is represented by

$$P(a) = \sum_{i=1}^{n} P(a) \wedge P(b_i), \tag{6.9}$$

$$P(a) = \sum_{i=1}^{n} P(a|b_i) \cdot P(b_i). \tag{6.10}$$

Bayes rule can be used to determine the prior total probability $P(h)$ of hypothesis h to given data D.

- $P(D|h)$ is the probability that a hypothesis h generates the data D. $P(D|h)$ can be easily estimated. For example, what is the probability that some illness generates some symptoms?
- The probability that an illness is present given certain symptoms, can be then determined by the Bayes rule

$$P(h|D) = \frac{P(D|h) \cdot P(h)}{P(D)}. \tag{6.11}$$

The most probable hypothesis h_i out of a set of possible hypothesis $h_1, h_2, \cdots$ given some present data is according to the Bayes rule

$$P(h_i|D) = \frac{P(D|h_i) \cdot P(h_i)}{P(D)}. \tag{6.12}$$

To determine the maximum posteriori hypothesis h_{MAP} we maximize

$$h_{map} = argmax_{h_i} \frac{P(D|h_i) \cdot P(h_i)}{P(D)}. \tag{6.13}$$

The maximization is independent of $P(D)$, it follows

$$h_{map} = argmax_{h_i} P(D|h_i) \cdot P(h_i). \tag{6.14}$$

Given the scores x and y

$$x = P(D|h) \cdot P(h), \quad z = P(D|\neg h) \cdot P(\neg h)$$

the probabilities $P(h|D)$ and $P(\neg h|D)$ can be determined by normalization, talking into account $1 = P(h|D) + P(\neg h|D)$.

6.1.3   *Joint distribution*

The joint distribution for n possible variables is described by 2^n possible combinations. The probability distribution $d_1 \times d_2 \times \cdots \times d_n$ corresponds to a vector of length 2^n. For a joint distribution of n possible variables, the exponential growth of combinations being true or false becomes an intractable problem for large n. For

$$P(h_i|d_1, d_2, d_3, .., d_n) = \frac{P(d_1, d_2, d_3, ..., d_n|h_i) \cdot P(h_i)}{P(d_1, d_2, d_3, ..., d_n)} \qquad (6.15)$$

all $2^n - 1$ possible combinations must be known. There are two possible solutions to this problem.

- The first solution is the decomposition of large probabilistic domains into weakly connected subsets via conditional independence,

$$P(d_1, d_2, d_3, ..., d_n|h_i) = \prod_{j=1}^{n} P(d_j|h_i). \qquad (6.16)$$

This approach is known as the Naïve Bayes assumption and is one of the most important developments in the recent history of Artificial Intelligence. It assumes that a single cause directly influences a number of events, all of which are conditionally independent,

$$h_{map} = argmax_{h_i} \prod_{j=1}^{n} P(d_j|h_i) \cdot P(h_i). \qquad (6.17)$$

However, this conditional independence is very restrictive. Often, it is not present in real life events. Dependence between some events is always present.

- Bayesian networks represent the second and more realistic solution. Bayesian networks can describe a probability distribution of a set of variables by combining conditional independence assumptions with conditional probabilities. Unlike the Naïve Bayes assumption, which states that all of the variables are conditionally independent given the value of the target variable, Bayesian networks enable these conditional independence assumptions to be applied to subsets of variables, providing a model with fewer constraints than the Bayes assumption [Mitchell (1997)].

6.1.3.1   *Example*

Cancer screening aims to detect cancer before symptoms appear. This may involve for example a blood tests. Suppose a result of one *secure* test is positive [Mitchell (1997)]. The test is secure because in 99 percent of the cases the test returns a correct positive result $(= p)$ in which a rare form of cancer is actually present. Should the doctor tell the patient, that he has cancer?

He should not do it. It is quite probable that a false positive error occurs. A consequence of the Bayesian inference is that such false positive errors occur when the prior probability is very low. In our case it is the rare form of cancer. The test has correct negative result $(= n)$ in 99 percent of the cases when rare form of cancer is not present. It is also known that 0.001 of the entire population have rare form of cancer $(= c)$.

$$P(c) = 0.001, \quad P(\neg c) = 0.999,$$

$$P(p|c) = 0.99, \quad P(n|c) = 0.01,$$

$$P(p|\neg c) = 0.01, \quad P(n|\neg c) = 0.99.$$

We determine h_{map},

$$P(c|p) = \alpha \cdot P(p|c) \cdot P(c) = \alpha \cdot 0.99 \cdot 0.001 = \alpha \cdot 0.00099, \quad (6.18)$$

$$P(\neg c|p) = \alpha \cdot P(p|\neg c) \cdot P(\neg c) = \alpha \cdot 0.01 \cdot 0.999 = \alpha \cdot 0.00999, \quad (6.19)$$

it follows

$$h_{map} = \neg c.$$

By normalization we get the actual probabilities

$$P(c|p) = \frac{0.00099}{0.00099 + 0.00999} = 0.0901639,$$

and

$$P(\neg c|p) = \frac{0.00999}{0.00099 + 0.00999} = 0.909836.$$

However if we repeat the test again according to the the Naïve Bayes assumption

$$P(c|p) = \alpha \cdot P(p|c) \cdot P(c) = \alpha \cdot 0.99 \cdot 0.99 \cdot 0.001 = \alpha \cdot 0.00098, \quad (6.20)$$

$$P(\neg c|p) = \alpha \cdot P(p|\neg c) \cdot P(\neg c) = \alpha \cdot 0.01 \cdot 0.01 \cdot 0.999 = \alpha \cdot 0.0000999, \quad (6.21)$$

$$h_{map} = c.$$

To rule out false positive error the doctor has to repeat the test.

6.1.4   *Naïve Bayes and counting*

The Naïve Bayes approach is related to simple counting if we follow the frequentist approach. For maximum a posteriori hypothesis h_{map}

$$h_{map} = argmax_{h_i} \prod_{j=1}^{n} P(d_j|h_i) \cdot P(h_i) \tag{6.22}$$

Ω is a set of all possible events

$$P(h_i) = \frac{card(h_i)}{card(\Omega)} \tag{6.23}$$

and

$$P(d_j|h_i) = \frac{card(d_j \wedge h_i)}{card(h_i)}, \tag{6.24}$$

$$h_{map} = argmax_{h_i} \prod_{j=1}^{n} \frac{card(d_j \wedge h_i)}{card(h_i)} \cdot \frac{card(h_i)}{card(\Omega)}. \tag{6.25}$$

Because Ω is a set of all possible events it does not play a role in the process maximization of h_{map}

$$h_{map} = argmax_{h_i} \prod_{j=1}^{n} card(d_j \wedge h_i) \tag{6.26}$$

we can apply *log*

$$h_{map} = argmax_{h_i} \log \left(\prod_{j=1}^{n} card(d_j \wedge h_i) \right), \tag{6.27}$$

$$h_{map} = argmax_{h_i} \sum_{j=1}^{n} \log \left(card(d_j \wedge h_i) \right). \tag{6.28}$$

For the process of maximization h_{map} we can simply write

$$h_{map} = argmax_{h_i} \sum_{j=1}^{n} card(d_j \wedge h_i). \tag{6.29}$$

The result is related to categorial representation based the contrast model of Tversky [Tversky (1977)].

6.1.5 Counting and categorization

An object is judged to belong to a verbal to the extent that its features are predicted by the verbal category [Osherson (1987)]. The sets of prototypical features defines a category. If Ca is a category and B the features set, so only $Ca \cap B$ features are considered [Wichert (1998)], [Wichert (2000)]. Then

$$card(Ca \wedge B) = |Ca \cap B|, \tag{6.30}$$

we normalize the result, in our case we normalize to the interval $[-1, 1]$ and define the $Sim(Ca, B)$ function as

$$Sim(Ca, B) = \frac{2}{|Ca|} \cdot |Ca \cap B| - 1 \in [-1, 1] \tag{6.31}$$

$|Ca|$ is the number of the prototypical features that define the category Ca. This function corresponds to the simplified normalized contrast model of Tversky [Tversky (1977)]

$$Sim(Ca, B) = \alpha|Ca \cap B| - \beta|Ca - B| \tag{6.32}$$

in which only $Ca \cap B$ features are considered

$$Sim(Ca, B) = \alpha|Ca \cap B| - \beta(|Ca - (Ca \cap B)| \tag{6.33}$$

it is supposed that the similarity value should be from the interval $[-1, 1]$ so $\alpha = 1/|Ca|$ and $\beta = 1/|Ca|$ and

$$Sim(Ca, B) = \frac{|Ca \cap B|}{|Ca|} - \frac{|(Ca - (Ca \cap B)|}{|Ca|}. \tag{6.34}$$

The present features are counted and normalized so that the value can be compared. For example, the category **bird** is defined by the following features: flies, sings, lays eggs, nests in trees, eats insects. The category **bat** is defined by the following features: flies, gives milk, eat insects. The following features are present: flies and gives milk.

$$Simc(\mathbf{bird}, present features) = \frac{1}{5} - \frac{4}{5} = \frac{2}{5} \cdot 1 - 1 = -\frac{3}{5}, \tag{6.35}$$

$$Simc(\mathbf{bat}, present features) = \frac{2}{3} - \frac{1}{3} = \frac{2}{3} \cdot 2 - 1 = \frac{1}{3}. \tag{6.36}$$

Features that discriminate among relevant facts should have a higher salience than those that do not [Smith (1995)]. The features of an equal salience have a unary representation, they can only be represented as existent or nonexistent. A category that is described as a set of features can be present with different grades of vagueness corresponding to the cardinal number of the set. A set of features that describes a category can be sometimes divided into subsets that represent some subcategories. Each feature can be also regarded as a kind of subcategory. If this subcategory cannot be described by other features, but, nevertheless, should have the properties of variable salience and vagueness, it is described by invisible features. To each feature a number of invisible features is assigned dependent on its salience. An example of two old sayings from country folklore:

(1) If it is April and it snows much then probably the apple harvest will be bad.

(2) If it is April and it rains a lot and it is very cold then the vintage will be good.

The number of invisible features as determined by the observer:

- **April** is represented by one invisible feature, as it can be present or absent.
- **Snows much** is described by two invisible features because the observer thinks that it has a higher salience than **April**. It can be either present, maybe present, or absent.
- The observer thinks that **rains a lot** has the same salience as **snows much**.
- The observer thinks that **very cold** has the greatest salience, as it is described by three invisible features. It can be either present, maybe present, maybe absent or absent.

With this approach hierarchical categorization can be preformed in analogy to the Naïve Bayes approach. Categories can be divided into subcategories, so that a taxonomy can be constructed and represented by an acyclic graph. The nodes in this graph correspond to categories and the links indicate the "is a subcategory" relation between them. The process of the hierarchical categorization can be performed by moving from more general categories to more specific categories until the desired categories are reached. Several expert systems were build based on this approach [Wichert (2000)], [Wichert (2004)].

6.1.6 *Bayesian networks*

Bayesian networks also provide a natural representation for (causally induced) conditional independence. Bayesian networks also called belief networks because they represent our beliefs. They represent a set of conditional independence assumptions, by the topology of an acyclic directed graph and sets of conditional probabilities. In the network each variable is represented by a node and the links between them represents the conditional independence of the variable towards its non descendants and its immediate predecessors. Bayesian networks represent for each variable a conditional probability table which describes the probability distribution of a specific variable given the values of its immediate predecessors. A conditional distribution for each node x_i given its parents is

$$P(x_i|Parent_1(x_i), Parent_2(x_i), .., Parent_k(x_i))$$

with k usually between 1 and 4 for nodes x_i. Full joint distribution is given by

$$P(x_1, .., x_n) = \prod_{i=1}^{n} P(x_i|Parent_1(x_i), Parent_2(x_i), .., Parent_k(x_i)). \quad (6.37)$$

Given the x query variable which value has to be determined and e evidence variable which is known and the remaining unobservable variables we preform a summation over all possible y (all possible values of the unobservable variables y according to the law of total probability)

$$P(x|e) = \alpha \sum_y P(x, e, y). \quad (6.38)$$

The values $P(x|e), P(\neg x|e)$ can be determined by normalization

$$1 = \alpha \cdot \left(\sum_y P(x, e, y) + \sum_y P(\neg x, e, y) \right).$$

Cooper [Cooper and Herskovits (1990)] has found that the exact inference of probabilities is a $NP - hard$ problem.

6.1.6.1 *Example*

The network topology reflects our belief in the associated causal knowledge. Consider the well-known example of Judea Perl [Pearl (1989)], [Russell and Norvig (2010)]. I am at work in Los Angeles, and neighbor John calls to say that the alarm of my house is ringing, but neighbor Mary does not call. Sometimes minor earthquakes set off the alarm. Is there a burglary? Constructing a Bayesian network is difficult because each variable should be directly influenced by only a few other variables. In the example, there are five variables, namely, $Burglary(= b)$, $Earthquake(= e)$, $Alarm(= a)$, $JohnCalls(= j)$, and $MaryCalls(= m)$. The corresponding network topology is indicated in Figure 6.1 and reflects the following "causal" knowledge:

- A burglar can set the alarm off.
- An earthquake can set the alarm off.
- The alarm can cause Mary to call.
- The alarm can cause John to call.

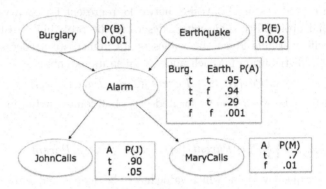

Fig. 6.1   A Bayesian network and the corresponding conditional probability tables. Each row requires one number p for $P(X) = true$ ($P(X) = false$ is $1 - p$).

If all values are observed, for example we know that

$$j = true, m = true, a = true, b = false, e = false$$

then

$$P(j \wedge m \wedge a \wedge \neg b \wedge \neg e) = P(j, m, a, \neg b, \neg e)$$

$$P(j, m, a, \neg b, \neg e) = P(j|a) \cdot P(m|a) \cdot P(a|\neg b \wedge \neg e) \cdot P(\neg b) \cdot P(\neg e)$$

$$P(j, m, a, \neg b, \neg e) = 0.9 \cdot 0.7 \cdot 0.001 \cdot 0.999 \cdot 0.998 = 0.00062.$$

There are three types of variables: x query variable, e evidence variables and unobservable variables y. An unobservable variable y is irrelevant unless y is ancestor of x or e. We want to determine the probability of *Alarm* if *Burglary* , *Earthquake, JohnCalls, MaryCalls* are unknown. In this example *JohnCalls* and *MaryCalls* are irrelevant [Russell and Norvig (2010)]. We want to determine the probability of

$$P(A|b, e, j, m) = \alpha \sum_b \sum_e \sum_j \sum_m P(A, b, e, j, m). \qquad (6.39)$$

Small letters indicate instantiationed variables,

$$P(A|b, e, j, m)$$

$$= \alpha \sum_b \sum_e \left(P(A|b, e) \cdot P(b) \cdot P(e) \cdot \sum_j P(j|A) \cdot \sum_m P(m|A) \right) \quad (6.40)$$

JohnCalls and *MaryCalls* are irrelevant, because the sum over j and m are one

$$\sum_j P(j|a) = \sum_j P(j|\neg a) = \sum_m P(m|a) = \sum_m P(m|\neg a) = 1,$$

for example

$$\sum_j P(j|a) = 0.9 + 0.1 = 1.$$

It follows that

$$P(A|b, e, j, m) = \alpha \cdot \sum_b \sum_e P(A|b, e) \cdot P(b) \cdot P(e) \cdot 1 \cdot 1 \quad (6.41)$$

and

$$P(A|b, e, j, m)$$

$$= \alpha \cdot \sum_b \left(P(A|b, e) \cdot P(b) \cdot P(\neg e) + P(A|b, \neg e) \cdot P(b) \cdot P(\neg e) \right) \quad (6.42)$$

$$P(A|b, e, j, m) = \alpha \cdot \left(P(A|b, e) \cdot P(b) \cdot P(\neg e) + P(A|b, \neg e) \cdot P(b) \cdot P(\neg e) \right.$$

$$\left. + P(A|\neg b, e) \cdot P(\neg b) \cdot P(\neg e) + P(A|\neg b, \neg e) \cdot P(\neg b) \cdot P(\neg e) \right) \quad (6.43)$$

with the values from conditional probability table

$$P(a|b, e, j, m) = \alpha(0.95 \cdot 0.001 \cdot 0.002 + 0.94 \cdot 0.01 \cdot 0.998$$

$$+ 0.29 \cdot 0.999 \cdot 0.002 + 0.001 \cdot 0.999 \cdot 0.998)$$

and

$$P(\neg a|b, e, j, m) = \alpha(0.05 \cdot 0.001 \cdot 0.002 + 0.06 \cdot 0.01 \cdot 0.998$$

$$+ 0.71 \cdot 0.999 \cdot 0.002 + 0.999 \cdot 0.999 \cdot 0.998),$$

$$P(a|b, e, j, m) = \alpha \cdot 0.010960, \quad P(\neg a|b, e, j, m) = alpha \cdot 0.99802, \quad (6.44)$$

$$\alpha = \frac{1}{0.010960 + 0.99802}. \quad (6.45)$$

The probability of *Alarm* being present or not is

$$P(a|b, e, j, m) = 0.010862, \quad P(\neg a|b, e, j, m) = 0.98914. \quad (6.46)$$

6.2   Mixed Distribution

Suppose that the variable d_1 represents whether a person likes mathematics or not. The truth-values are represented by 0 and 1, so $d_1 = 0$ means that the person does not like mathematics. The next variable d_2 represents whether the person studies philosophy or not, and d_3 represents if the person knows how to play chess or not. If we introduce positional notation for the variables, then $d_1, d_2, d_3 = 101$ would mean that the person likes mathematics and does not study philosophy and knows how to play chess. The probability of $P(d_1 = 1, d_2 = 0, d_3 = 1)$ is written in short as p_{101}. In this case, the distribution $d_1 \times d_2 \times d_3$ is represented by a vector of length 8 [Rieffel and Polak (2011)]:

$$\vec{p} = (p_{000}, p_{001}, p_{010}, p_{011}, p_{100}, p_{101}, p_{110}, p_{111}). \qquad (6.47)$$

Suppose that we do not know anything about a person; in this case, the probability distribution is a mixed distribution and is represented by the vector

$$\vec{p} = (1/8, 1/8, 1/8, 1/8, 1/8, 1/8, 1/8, 1/8).$$

The vector p represents the mixed distribution on uncertainty before knowing the facts about the person. Every possible combination has the same probability. Before we know the facts, the distribution is mixed, with 2^3 states. After learning the fact that the person studies philosophy, $d_2 = 1$, we know for certain that four possible combinations are not present, namely those combinations in which $d_2 = 0$, which are $p_{000}, p_{001}, p_{100}$ and p_{101}. The mixed distribution represented by the vector $\vec{p}$ must be re-normalized,

$$\vec{p} = (0, 0, 1/4, 1/4, 0, 0, 1/4, 1/4).$$

After learning the fact that the person does like mathematics, $d_1 = 1$, the mixed distribution represented by the vector $\vec{p}$, must be re-normalized again

$$\vec{p} = (0, 0, 0, 0, 0, 0, 1/2, 1/2).$$

Finally, after learning that the person plays chess $d_3 = 1$, the mixed distribution becomes pure; in this case, there is no uncertainty that the vector $\vec{p}$ is a unary vector with a one at the position that corresponds to p_{111}

$$\vec{p} = (0, 0, 0, 0, 0, 0, 0, 1).$$

6.3 Markov Chains

A physical system is described by the state of the system. The state of the system can be represented by a vector $\vec{x}$. A single object can be described in classical mechanics by its position and momentum. Momentum is the product of the mass and velocity of an object. The corresponding vector is $\vec{x} = (x_1, x_2, x_3, p_1, p_2, p_3) \in R^6$, where (x_1, x_2, x_3) describes the position and (p_1, p_2, p_3) describes the momentum of the object. As the object moves, the state of the system changes over time $\vec{x}(t)$. Classical mechanics describes the time evolution of the state by the Hamiltonian equation of motion represented by differential equations [Hirvensalo (2004)], [Ross (2009)].

If we do not know the states of the system, we can attempt to describe the probability distribution of the system. We know that a system is in states $x_1, ..., x_n$ with probabilities $p_1, ..., p_n$ and that they sum up to 1. The probability distribution over state x_i is represented by the mixed state

$$p_1[x_1] + p_2[x_2] + ... + p_n[x_n]. \tag{6.48}$$

Tossing a fair coin with a head and a tail is represented by the mixed state

$$0.5[h] + 0.5[t].$$

The time evolution of a system is a non-deterministic procedure. It develops each state x_i into a distribution

$$p_{1i}[x_1] + p_{2i}[x_2] + ... + p_{ni}[x_n]$$

where p_{ij} is the probability that the system state x_i evolves into x_j. A simplification can be reached by using discrete time. Another simplification is the one-level dependence of the state, which is also called the Markov property. Each state is dependent on the preceding state. The discrete probabilistic time evolution represents a Markov chain that can be described by linear mapping. Transition probabilities between states are represented by conditional probabilities

$$p_{ij} = P(x_j(t+1)|x_i(t)). \tag{6.49}$$

We represent

$$p_1[x_1] + p_2[x_2] + ... + p_n[x_n]$$

by a stochastic vector

$$\vec{p} = (p_1, p_2, .., p_n).$$

For a state x_i the mapping is represented by

$$p_i' = p_{i1}p_1 + p_{i2}p_2 + ... + p_{ini}p_n. \qquad (6.50)$$

The vector is defined by an $n \times n$ stochastic matrix $P = [p_{ij}]$ that is also called a Markov matrix or a stochastic matrix, and it has the following properties:

$$(i) \; p_{ij} \geq 0 \; for \; 1 \leq i, j \leq n;$$

$$(ii) \sum_{i=1}^{n} p_{ij} = 1 \; for \; 1 \leq j \leq n.$$

The probabilities are related by the linear mapping using the stochastic matrix P with

$$\begin{pmatrix} p_1' \\ p_2' \\ \vdots \\ p_n' \end{pmatrix} = \begin{pmatrix} p_{11} & p_{12} & \cdots & p_{1n} \\ p_{21} & p_{22} & \cdots & p_{2n} \\ \vdots & \vdots & \ddots & \vdots \\ p_{n1} & p_{n2} & \cdots & p_{nn} \end{pmatrix} \cdot \begin{pmatrix} p_1 \\ p_2 \\ \vdots \\ p_n \end{pmatrix}. \qquad (6.51)$$

Because all the columns sum to one we are guaranteed that

$$p_1' + p_2' + .. + p_n' = p_1 + p_2 + .. + p_n. \qquad (6.52)$$

A Markov chain is a mathematical system that undergoes transitions that are described by a stochastic matrix that moves from one stochastic vector to another [Markov (1954)]. The asymptotic behavior of Markov chains either converges to a fixed distribution or goes to a periodic sequence of distributions. Given that all of the entries of the stochastic matrix are larger than zero, which means that each state can be reached from another state, there is a fixed distribution $\vec{q}$. The distribution $\vec{q}$ is independent of the initial distribution $\vec{p}$. A fixed distribution is unchanged when it is transformed by P. The fixed distribution $\vec{q}$ is represented by the eigenvector of P, with the eigenvalue equal to 1.

$$\begin{pmatrix} q_1 \\ q_2 \\ \vdots \\ q_n \end{pmatrix} = \begin{pmatrix} p_{11} & p_{12} & \cdots & p_{1n} \\ p_{21} & p_{22} & \cdots & p_{2n} \\ \vdots & \vdots & \ddots & \vdots \\ p_{n1} & p_{n2} & \cdots & p_{nn} \end{pmatrix} \cdot \begin{pmatrix} q_1 \\ q_2 \\ \vdots \\ q_n \end{pmatrix} \qquad (6.53)$$

because $\vec{q}$ is a probability vector, it follows that

$$\sum_{i=1}^{n} q_i = 1.$$

P describes the transition of the states of the weather, such as sunny, cloudy and rainy (see Figure 6.2). Each state of the weather can be reached from another state, and the prediction over several days is increasingly inaccurate. The prediction tends toward a steady state vector that represents the probabilities of sunny, cloudy and rainy, independent of the initial weather state. The information about the initial weather is lost and cannot be reconstructed. The evolution of a stochastic matrix does not lead to a loss of

Fig. 6.2 Transition of for the states of the weather, such as sunny, cloudy and rainy represented by the symbol "sun", "cloud" and "rain". Each state of the weather can be reached from another state.

information if the matrix is orthogonal. An example orthogonal stochastic matrix is the permutation matrix. A permutation matrix is a square binary matrix that has exactly one entry 1 in each row and each column and is 0 elsewhere. As a consequence, each state cannot be reached from another state.

Chapter 7

Introduction to Quantum Physics

7.1 Unitary Evolution

Physical measurements have an intrinsically probabilistic character. Repetitions of an observation using the same experimental apparatus with the same initial conditions will generally yield different measurements of the observed variable. Statistical laws govern the totality of large observations. An object can be described in classical mechanics by a vector $\vec{x} = (x_1, x_2, x_3, p_1, p_2, p_3) \in R^6$, which describes its position (x_1, x_2, x_3) and its momentum (p_1, p_2, p_3). The changes in the position and the momentum of the object over time are described by the Hamiltonian equation of motion

$$\frac{d}{dt}x_i = \frac{\partial}{\partial p_i}H, \frac{d}{dt}p_i = \frac{\partial}{\partial x_i}H. \tag{7.1}$$

The state of the object is described by the Hamiltonian function

$$H = H(x_1, x_2, x_3, p_1, p_2, p_3).$$

The wavefunction in quantum mechanics, if unobservable, evolves in a smooth and continuous way according to the Schrödinger equation, which is related to the Hamiltonian equation of motion. This equation describes a linear superposition of different states at time t, which is represented by the vector $\mathbf{x}(t)$,

$$i \cdot h \cdot \frac{d}{dt}\mathbf{x}(t) = H \cdot \mathbf{x}(t) \tag{7.2}$$

with $i = \sqrt{-1}$ and h being the Planck's constant. For simplification we set $h = 1$. H is the Hamiltonian operator, which is related to the total energy of the system. A general solution of the Schroedinger equation (for the time-independent Hamiltonian) represents the unitary evolution with

$$\mathbf{x}(t) = e^{-i \cdot t \cdot H} \cdot \mathbf{x}(0) = U_t \cdot \mathbf{x}(0) \tag{7.3}$$

95

where $U_t = e^{-i \cdot t \cdot H}$ is the evolutionary operator, which can be represented by a unitary matrix. Unitary evolution is deterministic and reversible. The vector $\mathbf{x}(t)$ describes the probability of the presence of certain states. A dimension represents each state, and the value of the vector is related to the probability of the state being present. However, measurements always find the physical system to be in a definite state, which does something to the wavefunction represented by the vector $\mathbf{x}(t)$. This something is not explained by quantum theory.

7.1.1 Schrödinger's cat paradox

The best known example of this type kind of this 'something' is the Schrödinger's cat paradox [Schrödinger (1935)]. "When I hear about Schrödinger's cat, I reach for my gun," is a quote from Stephen Hawking. In our description of the paradox we will replace the cat with a rabbit...

A rabbit is apparently evolving into a superposition of two states that can be characterized as an alive rabbit and a dead rabbit. A Geiger counter measures the decay of a radioactive substance. There is a fifty percent chance that, in a given time frame, decay is measured. The Geiger counter is connected to a device that kills the rabbit, if decay is measured. Because the rabbit and the Geiger counter are in a closed room, we do not know whether the rabbit is dead or alive. Each of these possibilities is associated with a specific fifty percent probability. The rabbit is in a mixed state, and the two states are "really" present at the same time. A measurement always finds either an alive rabbit or a dead rabbit with a probability of fifty percent.

7.1.2 Interpretations of quantum mechanics

As long as we make no measurements, there are no random effects. The behavior of the system is strictly deterministic. The randomness is only present during the measurement. Randomness is an effect of measurement. Different interpretations of quantum mechanics propose different solutions of the measurement problem. We present the two most influential explanations:

- The most popular interpretation, the Copenhagen interpretation, claims that quantum mechanics is a mathematical tool that is used in the calculation of probabilities and has no physical existence; all other questions are metaphysical. This popular unscientific interpretation delayed for many years the development of quantum computation [Heisenberg (1949)].

- The many-worlds theory led to the development of the first quantum algorithms; this approach is less popular due to some philosophical difficulties. The many-worlds theory views reality as a many-branched tree in which every possible quantum outcome is realized [Everett (1959)], [Byrne (2007)]. The subjective appearance of the wave function collapse is explained by the mechanism of quantum decoherence. Every possible outcome to every event exists in its own world. In one world, randomness exists, but not in the universe (multiverse) that describes all possible worlds [Deutsch (1997)].

7.2 Quantum Mechanics

A bit can be represented by the state of a simple 2-state quantum system such as the spin state of a particle. When measured, the spin is always in one of two possible states: spin-up or spin-down. A quantum mechanical description of a physical system is related to a probabilistic representation; it is described by a vector in Hilbert space. This description extends the two- or three-dimensional Euclidean space into spaces that have any finite or infinite number of dimensions. In such a space, the Euclidean norm is induced by the inner product

$$\|\mathbf{x}\| = \sqrt{\langle \mathbf{x} | \mathbf{x} \rangle}. \tag{7.4}$$

A basis of n dimensional Hilbert space H_n is chosen. A 2-state system is described by a two dimensional Hilbert space H_2. For the basis

$$\mathbf{e}_1 = \begin{pmatrix} 1 \\ 0 \end{pmatrix}, \mathbf{e}_2 = \begin{pmatrix} 0 \\ 1 \end{pmatrix} \tag{7.5}$$

the system is described by a vector $\mathbf{x}$ with complex numbers ω_1, ω_2 that represent the amplitude of each dimension

$$\mathbf{x} = \omega_1 \cdot \mathbf{e}_1 + \omega_2 \cdot \mathbf{e}_2 = \begin{pmatrix} \omega_1 \\ \omega_2 \end{pmatrix}. \tag{7.6}$$

The probabilities are real numbers between 0 and 1. The probability that the system is in e_1 and e_2 is $|\omega_1|^2$ and $|\omega_2|^2$. This is because the product of complex number with is conjugate is always a real number

$$\omega^* \cdot \omega = (x - y \cdot i) \cdot (x + y \cdot i) = x^2 + y^2 = |\omega|^2. \tag{7.7}$$

The vector representing a state is normalized. Its length is one. The amplitudes correspond to the probability with

$$|\omega_1|^2 + |\omega_2|^2 = 1.$$

Paul Dirac introduced the following notation for a vector $\mathbf{x}$ describing a state

$$|x\rangle = \omega_1 \cdot |e_1\rangle + \omega_2 \cdot |e_2\rangle = \omega_1 \cdot |x_1\rangle + \omega_2 \cdot |x_2\rangle = \begin{pmatrix} \omega_1 \\ \omega_2 \end{pmatrix} \qquad (7.8)$$

with

$$|e_1\rangle = |x_1\rangle, |e_2\rangle = |x_2\rangle.$$

It is a shorthand notation for a column vector. Related to the scalar product $\langle x|x \rangle$ row vector are $\langle x|$ "bra" and and column vectors are $|x\rangle$ "kets" from bra(c)kets. A state vector is just a particular instance of a ket vector. It is specified by a particular choice of basis and refers to observable that can have some system properties.

Operators represented by a square matrix give mathematical description how something changes in the quantum world. For a 2-state quantum system an operator that acts on the memory register would be represented by a 2×2 dimensional unitary matrix. In Unitary matrices, its conjugate transpose is equal to its inverse.

$$U^* = U^{-1}. \qquad (7.9)$$

7.2.1 *Stochastic Markov evolution and unitary evolution*

To indicate the difference to a Markov chain we introduce the example of a quantum coin, a system with two states 0 and 1 with

$$|0\rangle = \begin{pmatrix} 1 \\ 0 \end{pmatrix}, |1\rangle = \begin{pmatrix} 0 \\ 1 \end{pmatrix}. \qquad (7.10)$$

The mapping is represented as

$$|0\rangle \rightarrow \frac{1}{\sqrt{2}} \cdot |0\rangle + \frac{1}{\sqrt{2}} \cdot |1\rangle \qquad (7.11)$$

and

$$|1\rangle \rightarrow \frac{1}{\sqrt{2}} \cdot |0\rangle - \frac{1}{\sqrt{2}} \cdot |1\rangle. \qquad (7.12)$$

The corresponding operator is indicated by the following unitary matrix,

$$W = \begin{pmatrix} \frac{1}{\sqrt{2}} & \frac{1}{\sqrt{2}} \\ \frac{1}{\sqrt{2}} & -\frac{1}{\sqrt{2}} \end{pmatrix} = \frac{1}{\sqrt{2}} \cdot \begin{pmatrix} 1 & 1 \\ 1 & -1 \end{pmatrix}. \qquad (7.13)$$

If the system starts in state $|0\rangle$ and undergoes the time evolution, the probability of observing 0 or 1 is $\left|\frac{1}{\sqrt{2}}\right|^2 = \frac{1}{2}$. If we do not preform a measurement and repeat the mapping, the probability of observing 0 becomes 1 and observing 1 becomes zero. This is due to the fact, that the amplitudes of $|1\rangle$ cancel each other. This effect is called destructive interference and cannot occur in the probability distribution since all its coefficients are non-negative real numbers.

Stochastic Markov evolution The behavior of a fair coin can be modeled by a Markov chain described by a stochastic matrix. The behavior of the system is independent from initial distribution $\vec{p}$. The information about the initial state is lost. The fixed distribution is reached after one step.

$$\begin{pmatrix} \frac{1}{2} \\ \frac{1}{2} \end{pmatrix} = \begin{pmatrix} \frac{p_1+p_2}{2} \\ \frac{p_1+p_2}{2} \end{pmatrix} = \begin{pmatrix} \frac{1}{2} & \frac{1}{2} \\ \frac{1}{2} & \frac{1}{2} \end{pmatrix} \cdot \begin{pmatrix} p_1 \\ p_2 \end{pmatrix}. \tag{7.14}$$

If constantly observed the quantum coin has the same behavior as a fair coin described by a stochastic matrix. The probability of being in one of the states is 0.5. Each time the coin is tossed the "random" effect is observed.

Unitary evolution During unitary evolution of a (not observed) quantum coin the information about the initial state is not lost, the system is reversible and deterministic. Each of the two state is present. The loss of information about its history occurs during the measurement.

In the next section we demonstrate the relation between the unitary matrices and evolutionary operator $U_t = e^{-i \cdot t \cdot H}$.

7.3 Hilbert Space

Amplitude distribution corresponds to a unit-length vector of a finite dimensional Hilbert space over complex numbers of dimension n denoted as H_n. The inner product is defined as by the inner product

$$\langle x|y \rangle = \langle y|x \rangle^*$$

$$\langle x|x \rangle \geq 0, \langle x|x \rangle = 0 \Leftrightarrow x = 0$$

$$\langle x|c_1 \cdot y + c_2 \cdot z \rangle = c_1 \cdot \langle x|y \rangle + c_2 \cdot \langle x|z \rangle$$

with

$$x, y, z \in H_n, c_1, c_2 \in C.$$

With a fixed basis we will use the the coordinate representation that will induce the inner prouduct by

$$\langle x|y \rangle = x_1^* \cdot y_1 + x_2^* \cdot y_2 + \cdots + x_n^* \cdot y_n$$

and the Euclidean vector norm. Is is a vector space with and Euclidean norm. If W is a subspace of a V, then the orthogonal complement of W is also a subspace of V. The orthogonal complement $W^\perp$ is the set of vectors

$$W^\perp = \{ \mathbf{y} \in V | \langle \mathbf{y}|\mathbf{x} \rangle = 0 \ \ \mathbf{x} \in V \} \tag{7.15}$$

and ach vector $\mathbf{x} \in V$ can be represented as $\mathbf{x} = \mathbf{x}_W + \mathbf{x}_{W^\perp}$ with $\mathbf{x}_W \in W$ and $\mathbf{x}_{W^\perp} \in W^\perp$. The mapping $P \cdot \mathbf{x} = \mathbf{x}_W$ is an orthogonal projection. Such projection is always a linear transformation and can be represented by a projection matrix P. The matrix is self-adjoint $P = P^*$ with $P = P^2$. An orthogonal projection can never increase a norm

$$\|P \cdot \mathbf{x}\|^2 = \|\mathbf{x}_W\|^2 \le \|\mathbf{x}_W\|^2 + \|\mathbf{x}_{W^\perp}\|^2 = \|\mathbf{x}_W + \mathbf{x}_{W^\perp}\|^2 = \|\mathbf{x}\|^2. \tag{7.16}$$

P can be generated by the normalized vector $|x\rangle$ indicating the direction of the bisecting line

$$|x\rangle = \frac{1}{\sqrt{n}} \cdot |x_1\rangle + \frac{1}{\sqrt{n}} \cdot |x_2\rangle + \cdots + \frac{1}{\sqrt{n}} \cdot |x_n\rangle = \begin{pmatrix} \frac{1}{\sqrt{n}} \\ \vdots \\ \frac{1}{\sqrt{n}} \end{pmatrix} \tag{7.17}$$

and the row representation

$$\langle x| = \left(\frac{1}{\sqrt{n}}, \frac{1}{\sqrt{n}}, \cdots, \frac{1}{\sqrt{n}} \right). \tag{7.18}$$

The projection matrix is

$$P = |x\rangle\langle x| = \begin{pmatrix} \frac{1}{n} & \frac{1}{n} & \cdots & \frac{1}{n} \\ \frac{1}{n} & \frac{1}{n} & \cdots & \frac{1}{n} \\ \vdots & \vdots & \ddots & \vdots \\ \frac{1}{n} & \frac{1}{n} & \cdots & \frac{1}{n} \end{pmatrix}. \tag{7.19}$$

The projection P computes for each dimension described by the fixed basis, for example $|x_i\rangle = |e_i\rangle$, the mean value of all dimensions. An example of such a projection in the two dimensional Hilbert space is the stochastic matrix describing the behavior of a fair coin.

7.3.1 Spectral representation*

A linear mapping $H_n \to H_n$ is called an operator. An operator A is self-adjoint if

$$\langle x \,|A \cdot y\rangle = \langle A^* \cdot x|y\rangle. \tag{7.20}$$

For a fixed basis a matrix can represent an operator. A self-adjoint operator is represented by a Hermitian matrix $A^* = A$ with $a_{ij} = \overline{a_{ji}}$. For real values the Hermitian matrix is a symmetrical matrix with $A^T = A$. Hermitian matrices have real eigenvalues and corresponding eigenvectors are orthogonal. From the definition of eigenvalues and eigenvectors

$$A \cdot x = \lambda \cdot x$$

consequently

$$\lambda^* \cdot \langle x|x\rangle = \langle \lambda \cdot x|x\rangle = \langle A \cdot x|x\rangle = \langle x|A \cdot x\rangle = \lambda \cdot \langle x|x\rangle.$$

The eigenvectors of different eigenvalues $\lambda_1 \neq \lambda_2$ are orthogonal,

$$\lambda_1 \cdot \langle x_1|x_2\rangle = \langle A \cdot x_1|x_2\rangle = \langle x_1|A \cdot x_2\rangle = \lambda_2 \cdot \langle x_1|x_2\rangle$$

hence the two different eigenvectors are orthogonal

$$\lambda_1 \cdot \langle x_1|x_2\rangle = \lambda_2 \cdot \langle x_1|x_2\rangle \Rightarrow \langle x_1|x_2\rangle = 0.$$

A Hermitian matrix can be represented by a sum of projections of its orthonormal eigenvectors (normalized eigenvectors) $x_1, \cdots, x_n$ weighted by its eigenvalues. The projections are defined by the matrix $|x_i\rangle\langle x_i|$ with $|x_i\rangle\langle x_i| = (|x_i\rangle\langle x_i|)^2$. The set of the eigenvalues is called the spectrum and the corresponding representation a spectral representation

$$A = \lambda_1 \cdot |x_1\rangle\langle x_1| + \lambda_2 \cdot |x_2\rangle\langle x_2| + \cdots + \lambda_n \cdot |x_n\rangle\langle x_n|. \tag{7.21}$$

The function $e^{i \cdot A}$ with a self-adjoint operator A is unitary

$$e^{i \cdot A} = e^{i \cdot \lambda_1} \cdot |x_1\rangle\langle x_1| + e^{i \cdot \lambda_2} \cdot |x_2\rangle\langle x_2| + \cdots + e^{i \cdot \lambda_n} \cdot |x_n\rangle\langle x_n|. \tag{7.22}$$

An operator U is unitary, if $U^* = U^{-1}$,

$$\left(e^{i \cdot A}\right)^* = \left(e^{i \cdot A}\right)^{-1}, \tag{7.23}$$

$$\left(e^{i \cdot A}\right)^{-1} = e^{-i \cdot \lambda_1} \cdot |x_1\rangle\langle x_1| + e^{-i \cdot \lambda_2} \cdot |x_2\rangle\langle x_2| + \cdots + e^{-i \cdot \lambda_n} \cdot |x_n\rangle\langle x_n|. \tag{7.24}$$

This representation is similar to the evolutionary operator $U_t = e^{-i \cdot t \cdot H}$ for $t = 1$ and $A = H$ is the Hamiltonian operator that is related to the total energy of the system. Mathematical description in a quantum world is given by operators represented by a unitary square matrix. For example the unitary matrix that describes the quantum coin is

$$W = \frac{1}{\sqrt{2}} \cdot \begin{pmatrix} 1 & 1 \\ 1 & -1 \end{pmatrix}. \tag{7.25}$$

What is the relation between a unitary matrix and the evolutionary operator? For simplicity we omit the minus sign and write instead of U^* simply

$$W = U = e^{i \cdot H}.$$

What is the corresponding Hamiltonian operator? A unitary operator U is not self-adjoint, the Matrix is unitary but not Hermitian. However it can be decomposed into two self-adjoint operators. As shown before each self-adjoint operators has a spectral representation

$$U = \frac{1}{2} \cdot (R + i \cdot I) \tag{7.26}$$

with

$$R = \frac{1}{2} \cdot (U + U^*), \quad I = \frac{1}{i \cdot 2} \cdot (U + U^*).$$

R and I are Hermitian matrices and their spectral representation is

$$R = \lambda_1 \cdot |x_1\rangle\langle x_1| + \lambda_2 \cdot |x_2\rangle\langle x_2| + \cdots + \lambda_n \cdot |x_n\rangle\langle x_n|$$

and

$$I = \mu_1 \cdot |x_1\rangle\langle x_1| + \mu_2 \cdot |x_2\rangle\langle x_2| + \cdots + \mu_n \cdot |x_n\rangle\langle x_n|.$$

U can be written as

$$U = (\lambda_1 + i \cdot \mu_1) \cdot |x_1\rangle\langle x_1| + \cdots + (\lambda_n + i \cdot \mu_n) \cdot |x_n\rangle\langle x_n|. \tag{7.27}$$

How can we represent U as $U = e^{i \cdot H}$?

For all eigenvalues of U

$$\langle x|x \rangle = \langle x|U \cdot U^*x \rangle = \langle U \cdot x|U \cdot x \rangle = \langle \lambda \cdot x|\lambda \cdot x \rangle = |\lambda|^2 \cdot \langle x|x \rangle$$

the absolute value is 1

$$1 = |\lambda_i + \mu_i|$$

all values of λ_i and μ_i are real values from the interval $[-1, 1]$. Therefore there exist a value θ_i for each i with

$$\lambda_i = \cos \theta_i, \quad \mu_i = \sin \theta_i, \tag{7.28}$$

and because $e^{i \cdot x} = \cos x + i \cdot \sin x$

$$\lambda_i + i \cdot \mu_i = \cos \theta_i + i \cdot \sin \theta_i, \tag{7.29}$$

$$\mu_i = e^{i \cdot \theta_i}. \tag{7.30}$$

We can now represent any unitary operator U by the spectral representation

$$U = e^{i \cdot H} = e^{i \cdot \theta_1} \cdot |x_1\rangle\langle x_1| + e^{i \cdot \theta_2} \cdot |x_2\rangle\langle x_2| + \cdots + e^{i \cdot \theta_n} \cdot |x_n\rangle\langle x_n|. \tag{7.31}$$

with the corresponding Hamilton operator H

$$H = \theta_1 \cdot |x_1\rangle\langle x_1| + \theta_1 \cdot |x_2\rangle\langle x_2| + \cdots \theta_n \cdot |x_n\rangle\langle x_n|. \tag{7.32}$$

Example   The unitary matrix that describes the quantum coin

$$W = \frac{1}{\sqrt{2}} \cdot \begin{pmatrix} 1 & 1 \\ 1 & -1 \end{pmatrix}$$

is as well Hermitian with $W^T = W$. Because of this the two eigenvalues are real, -1 and 1 . The corresponding eigenvectors are

$$|x_1\rangle = \frac{1}{\sqrt{4 - 2 \cdot \sqrt{2}}} \cdot \begin{pmatrix} 1 - \sqrt{2} \\ 1 \end{pmatrix}$$

and

$$|x_2\rangle = \frac{1}{\sqrt{4 + 2 \cdot \sqrt{2}}} \cdot \begin{pmatrix} 1 + \sqrt{2} \\ 1 \end{pmatrix}.$$

The Hermitian matrix W can be represented by the spectral representation

$$W = 1 \cdot |x_1\rangle\langle x_1| - 1 \cdot |x_2\rangle\langle x_2| \tag{7.33}$$

with

$$|x_1\rangle\langle x_1| = \begin{pmatrix} \frac{1-\sqrt{2}}{4} & \frac{-\sqrt{2}}{4} \\ \frac{-\sqrt{2}}{4} & \frac{1+\sqrt{2}}{4} \end{pmatrix}$$

and

$$|x_2\rangle\langle x_2| = \begin{pmatrix} \frac{1+\sqrt{2}}{4} & \frac{\sqrt{2}}{4} \\ \frac{\sqrt{2}}{4} & \frac{1-\sqrt{2}}{4} \end{pmatrix}.$$

We can now represent unitary operator W as (evolutionary operator)

$$U = e^{i \cdot H} = e^{i \cdot 0} \cdot |x_1\rangle\langle x_1| + e^{i \cdot \pi} \cdot |x_2\rangle\langle x_2| = |x_1\rangle\langle x_1| + e^{i \cdot \pi} \cdot |x_2\rangle\langle x_2| \tag{7.34}$$

with the corresponding Hamilton operator H

$$H = 0 \cdot |x_1\rangle\langle x_1| + \pi \cdot |x_2\rangle\langle x_2|. \tag{7.35}$$

A unitary matrix can be represented by the evolutionary operator with the Hamilton operator H.

7.4   Quantum Time Evolution

Quantum time Evolution is described by Schrödinger equation, its solution represents the unitary evolution described by the unitary operator U_t. The unitary operator is determined by the requirements for the time-evolution mapping

$$\mathbf{x}(t) = U_t \cdot \mathbf{x}(0).$$

Suppose U_t is a time-evolution mapping, then the following requirements should be fulfilled [Hirvensalo (2004)]

- U_t should preserve the norm,

$$\| U_t \cdot \langle x| \| = \| \langle x| \|.$$

The length of a vector is always one, before and after the mapping. It determines the probability of the presence of certain states represented by its dimensions. The vector itself describes the probability distribution.

- The mapping U_t is linear

$$U_t \cdot (\lambda_1 \cdot |x_1\rangle + \cdots + \lambda_n \cdot |x_n\rangle) = U_t \cdot \lambda_1 \cdot |x_1\rangle + \cdots + U_t \cdot \lambda_n \cdot |x_n\rangle.$$

For the basis

$$|e_1\rangle = |x_1\rangle, |e_2\rangle = |x_2\rangle, \cdots, |e_n\rangle = |x_n\rangle$$

the linearity corresponds to simple matrix operation

$$U \cdot \begin{pmatrix} \lambda_1 \\ \lambda_2 \\ \vdots \\ \lambda_n \end{pmatrix} = U \cdot \begin{pmatrix} \lambda_1 \\ 0 \\ \vdots \\ 0 \end{pmatrix} + U \cdot \begin{pmatrix} 0 \\ \lambda_2 \\ \vdots \\ 0 \end{pmatrix} + \cdots + U \cdot \begin{pmatrix} 0 \\ 0 \\ \vdots \\ \lambda_n \end{pmatrix}.$$

- For all t_1 and t_2

$$U_{t_2+t_1} = U_{t_2} U_{t_1}.$$

- The time evolution must be smooth. Even if we are interested in the state of the system a discrete time points, the evolution should be smooth and continuous

$$\lim_{t \to t_0} U_t \cdot \mathbf{x}(0) = \lim_{t \to t_0} \mathbf{x}(t) = \mathbf{x}(t_0).$$

Only a unitary operator can satisfy the first three requirements. It can be represented by a unitary matrix and by the evolutionary operator with the Hamilton self-adjoint operator H. If U_t satisfies all four requirements, there exists self-adjoint operator H with a relation to time t

$$U_t = e^{-i \cdot t \cdot H}$$

and

$$\mathbf{x}(t) = e^{-i \cdot t \cdot H} \cdot \mathbf{x}(0) = U_t \cdot \mathbf{x}(0).$$

The time evolution is continuous and reversible, however we will represent an algorithm as a sequence of one-length vectors in discrete time steps

$$t_0 \to t_1 \to t_2 \to t_3 \to \cdots$$

as

$$|x\rangle \to U_1 \cdot |x\rangle \to U_2 \cdot U_1 \cdot |x\rangle \to U_3 \cdot U_2 \cdot U_1 \cdot |x\rangle \to \cdots$$

This representation is motivated by the first and second requirement.

7.5 Compound Systems

A 2-state quantum system is described by a two dimensional Hilbert space H_2,

$$|x_1\rangle = \begin{pmatrix} 1 \\ 0 \end{pmatrix}, |x_2\rangle = \begin{pmatrix} 0 \\ 1 \end{pmatrix} \qquad (7.36)$$

is described by a vector $|x\rangle$ with complex numbers ω_1, ω_2 that represent the amplitude of each dimension.

$$|x\rangle = \omega_1 \cdot |x_1\rangle + \omega_2 \cdot |x_2\rangle = \begin{pmatrix} \omega_1 \\ \omega_2 \end{pmatrix}. \qquad (7.37)$$

Such a 2-state quantum system corresponds to a qubit with the basis

$$|0\rangle = |x_1\rangle, \quad |1\rangle = |x_2\rangle.$$

The qubit is described by a vector $|x\rangle$ with complex numbers ω_1, ω_2 that represent the amplitude of each dimension

$$|x\rangle = \omega_0 \cdot |0\rangle + \omega_1 \cdot |1\rangle. \qquad (7.38)$$

The vector has length one with

$$|\omega_0|^2 + |\omega_1|^2 = 1 \rightarrow \| |x\rangle \| = 1.$$

The unitary matrix W performs the following mapping in the ket notation

$$W \cdot |0\rangle = W \cdot 1 \cdot |0\rangle + W \cdot 0 \cdot |1\rangle = \frac{1}{\sqrt{2}} \cdot |0\rangle + \frac{1}{\sqrt{2}} \cdot |1\rangle$$

with the vector notation

$$\frac{1}{\sqrt{2}} \cdot \begin{pmatrix} 1 & 1 \\ 1 & -1 \end{pmatrix} \cdot \begin{pmatrix} 1 \\ 0 \end{pmatrix} = \begin{pmatrix} \frac{1}{\sqrt{2}} \\ \frac{1}{\sqrt{2}} \end{pmatrix}.$$

Applying W again results in

$$W \cdot \left(\frac{1}{\sqrt{2}} \cdot |0\rangle + \frac{1}{\sqrt{2}} \cdot |1\rangle \right) = W \cdot \frac{1}{\sqrt{2}} \cdot |0\rangle + W \cdot \frac{1}{\sqrt{2}} \cdot |1\rangle = |0\rangle$$

with the vector notation

$$\frac{1}{\sqrt{2}} \cdot \begin{pmatrix} 1 & 1 \\ 1 & -1 \end{pmatrix} \cdot \begin{pmatrix} \frac{1}{\sqrt{2}} \\ \frac{1}{\sqrt{2}} \end{pmatrix} = \begin{pmatrix} 1 \\ 0 \end{pmatrix}.$$

How can we represent a register composed of two qubits? Such a register would represent 2^2 possible states and would be represented in a Hilbert space H_4. The first qubit is represented by a two dimensional Hilbert space H_2,

$$|x\rangle = \omega_0 \cdot |0\rangle + \omega_1 \cdot |1\rangle = \begin{pmatrix} \omega_0 \\ \omega_1 \end{pmatrix}$$

and the second as

$$|y\rangle = \omega_0 \cdot |0\rangle + \omega_1 \cdot |1\rangle = \begin{pmatrix} \omega_0 \\ \omega_1 \end{pmatrix}.$$

The register of two qubits is represented as a direct product of $|x\rangle$ and $|y\rangle$

$$|x\rangle \otimes |y\rangle = |x\rangle |y\rangle = |xy\rangle = \begin{pmatrix} \omega_0 \\ \omega_1 \end{pmatrix} \otimes \begin{pmatrix} \omega_0 \\ \omega_1 \end{pmatrix} = \begin{pmatrix} \omega_0 \cdot \omega_0 \\ \omega_0 \cdot \omega_1 \\ \omega_1 \cdot \omega_0 \\ \omega_1 \cdot \omega_1 \end{pmatrix} = \begin{pmatrix} \omega_0 \\ \omega_1 \\ \omega_2 \\ \omega_3 \end{pmatrix} \quad (7.39)$$

or

$$|xy\rangle = (\omega_0 \cdot |0\rangle + \omega_1 \cdot |1\rangle) \otimes (\omega_0 \cdot |0\rangle + \omega_1 \cdot |1\rangle)$$

$$|xy\rangle = \omega_0 \cdot |00\rangle + \omega_1 \cdot |01\rangle + \omega_2 \cdot |10\rangle + \omega_3 \cdot |11\rangle \quad (7.40)$$

with the new basis

$$|00\rangle = \begin{pmatrix} 1 \\ 0 \\ 0 \\ 0 \end{pmatrix}, |01\rangle = \begin{pmatrix} 0 \\ 1 \\ 0 \\ 0 \end{pmatrix}, |10\rangle = \begin{pmatrix} 0 \\ 0 \\ 1 \\ 0 \end{pmatrix}, |11\rangle = \begin{pmatrix} 0 \\ 0 \\ 0 \\ 1 \end{pmatrix}. \quad (7.41)$$

A register of three qubits represents 2^3 different states represented in a Hilbert space H_8.

$$|xyz\rangle = |x\rangle \otimes |y\rangle \otimes |z\rangle =$$

$$\omega_0 \cdot |00\rangle + \omega_1 \cdot |001\rangle + \omega_2 \cdot |010\rangle + \omega_3 \cdot |011\rangle +$$

$$+\omega_4 \cdot |100\rangle + \omega_5 \cdot |001\rangle + \omega_6 \cdot |110\rangle + \omega_7 \cdot |111\rangle. \quad (7.42)$$

A quantum register of length m represents m qubits in a Hilbert space of dimension $n = 2^m$. A state in a n-dimensional Hilbert space H_n is defined by an orthonormal basis

$$|x_1\rangle, |x_1\rangle, \cdots |x_n\rangle$$

and is represented as a unit-length vector

$$\omega_1 \cdot |x_1\rangle + \omega_2 \cdot |x_2\rangle + \cdots + \omega_n \cdot |x_n\rangle$$

that determines the probability of distribution of the states. Each dimension correspond to a possible combination. The state is in a basis state $|x_i\rangle$ with a probability $|\omega_i|^2$.

The compund system of the Hilbert space H_n and a w-dimensional Hilbert space H_w defined by a orthonormal basis $|y_1\rangle, |y_1\rangle. \cdots |y_w\rangle$ is defined by the tensor product

$$H_{n \cdot w} = H_n \otimes H_w \tag{7.43}$$

According to this definition we can apply an operator on two qubits as

$$W \cdot (\omega_0 \cdot |0\rangle + \omega_1 \cdot |1\rangle) \otimes W \cdot (\omega_0 \cdot |0\rangle + \omega_1 \cdot |1\rangle) =$$

$$\left(W \cdot \begin{pmatrix} \omega_0 \\ \omega_1 \end{pmatrix} \right) \otimes \left(W \cdot \begin{pmatrix} \omega_0 \\ \omega_1 \end{pmatrix} \right) \tag{7.44}$$

$$(W \otimes W) \cdot (\omega_0 \cdot |0\rangle + \omega_1 \cdot |1\rangle) \otimes (\omega_0 \cdot |0\rangle + \omega_1 \cdot |1\rangle) = (W \otimes W) \cdot \begin{pmatrix} \omega_0 \\ \omega_1 \\ \omega_2 \\ \omega_3 \end{pmatrix} \tag{7.45}$$

it follows

$$\left(W \cdot \begin{pmatrix} \omega_0 \\ \omega_1 \end{pmatrix} \right) \otimes \left(W \cdot \begin{pmatrix} \omega_0 \\ \omega_1 \end{pmatrix} \right) = (W \otimes W) \cdot \begin{pmatrix} \omega_0 \\ \omega_1 \\ \omega_2 \\ \omega_3 \end{pmatrix}. \tag{7.46}$$

The tensor product between matrix is defined as

$$A \otimes B = \begin{pmatrix} a_{11} \cdot B & a_{12} \cdot B \\ a_{21} \cdot B & a_{22} \cdot B \end{pmatrix} = \begin{pmatrix} a_{11} \cdot b_{11} & a_{11} \cdot b_{12} & a_{12} \cdot b_{11} & a_{12} \cdot b_{12} \\ a_{11} \cdot b_{21} & a_{11} \cdot b_{22} & a_{12} \cdot b_{21} & a_{12} \cdot b_{22} \\ a_{21} \cdot b_{11} & a_{21} \cdot b_{12} & a_{22} \cdot b_{11} & a_{22} \cdot b_{12} \\ a_{21} \cdot b_{21} & a_{21} \cdot b_{22} & a_{22} \cdot b_{21} & a_{22} \cdot b_{22} \end{pmatrix}.$$

For example $W \otimes W$ is

$$W \otimes W = \frac{1}{\sqrt{2}} \cdot \begin{pmatrix} 1 & 1 \\ 1 & -1 \end{pmatrix} \otimes \frac{1}{\sqrt{2}} \cdot \begin{pmatrix} 1 & 1 \\ 1 & -1 \end{pmatrix} = \frac{1}{2} \cdot \begin{pmatrix} 1 & 1 & 1 & 1 \\ 1 & -1 & 1 & -1 \\ 1 & 1 & -1 & -1 \\ 1 & -1 & -1 & 1 \end{pmatrix}.$$

7.6   Von Neumann Entropy

A state $|x\rangle$ ($\|x\| = 1$) in a Hilbert space H_n can be represented by the corresponding density matrix $P = |x\rangle\langle x|$ with,

$$
|x\rangle\langle x| = \begin{pmatrix} x_1 \\ x_2 \\ \vdots \\ x_n \end{pmatrix} \cdot (x_1^*, x_2^*, \cdots, x_n^*) = \begin{pmatrix} |x_1|^2 & x_1 \cdot x_2^* & \cdots & x_1 \cdot x_n^* \\ x_2 \cdot x_1^* & |x_2|^2 & \cdots & x_2 \cdot x_n^* \\ \vdots & & \vdots & \ddots & \vdots \\ x_n \cdot x_1^* & x_1 \cdot x_n^* & \cdots & |x_n|^2 \end{pmatrix} \quad (7.47)
$$

A density matrix P has following properties

- P is a Hermitian matrix with $P^* = P$.
- P represents a self-adjoint operator P.
- P has a spectral representation.
- P is a projection with $P = P^2$, because $|x\rangle\langle x| = \||x\rangle\langle x|\|^2$.
- P is a linear combination of one-dimensional projections.
- The trace of P, $Tr(P) = 1$ with $Tr(P) = \sum_{i=1}^{n} |x_i|^2$.

For the density matrix P, the von Neumann entropy is defined as

$$
E(P) = -Tr(P \cdot \log P), \quad (7.48)
$$

with a logarithm of matrix $Q = \log P$, where Q is a matrix with $P = e^Q$. With the spectral decomposition of the self-adjoint operator P the von Neumann entropy can be easily computed without using logarithm of a matrix,

$$
P = \lambda_1 \cdot |x_1\rangle\langle x_1| + \lambda_2 \cdot |x_2\rangle\langle x_2| + \cdots + \lambda_n \cdot |x_n\rangle\langle x_n|
$$

with

$$
E(P) = -\sum_{i=1}^{n} (\lambda_i \cdot \log \lambda_i) \quad (7.49)
$$

and

$$
1 = \sum_{i=1}^{n} \lambda_i.
$$

The spectral representation of a state $|x\rangle$ in n-dimensional Hilbert space H_n is unique . It is defined by the orthonormal eigenvectors of the density matrix $P = |x\rangle\langle x|$. The representation of a state $|x\rangle$ by a vector of complex amplitudes depends on the orthonormal basis. For the orthonormal basis $|x_1\rangle = \mathbf{e}_1, |x_2\rangle = \mathbf{e}_2, \cdots, |x_n\rangle = \mathbf{e}_n$

$$
|x\rangle = \omega_1 \cdot |x_1\rangle| + \omega_2 \cdot |x_2\rangle + \cdots + \omega_n \cdot |x_n\rangle
$$

we can assume that

$$E(P) = -\sum_{i=1}^{n}(|\omega_i|^2 \cdot \log|\omega_i|^2). \tag{7.50}$$

States equal to a basis are called pure states. A pure state corresponds to a one-dimensional projection in a spectral representation with one eiganvalue $\lambda_i = 1$. Otherwise the states are called superposition. The von Neumann entropy of a pure state is zero, $0 = 1 \cdot \log 1$. The von Neumann entropy of a superposition measures the distribution of the probabilities represented by the eigenvalues. It describes the departure of the state from a pure state with a maximal value when all eigenvalues are equal.

$$E(P) = -\sum_{i=1}^{n}\lambda_i \cdot \log\lambda_i = -\sum_{i=1}^{n}\frac{1}{n} \cdot \log\frac{1}{n} = \log n \tag{7.51}$$

We represent a state by a sequence of m qubits by a $n = 2^m$ dimensional vector in H_n Hilbert space. In this case the maximal value of the von Neumann entropy is

$$E(P) = \log n = \log 2^m = \log 2 \cdot \log_2 2^m = \log 2 \cdot m. \tag{7.52}$$

The von Neumann entropy measure the information in nepit (nat). If the von Neumann entropy is measured in bits, yes no questions, its maximal value is just the number of present qubits.

Before the measurement of a state $|x\rangle$ we are uncertain about the outcome. We measure the uncertainty by the entropy. After the measure the state is pure, the von Neumann entropy is zero, $0 = 1 \cdot \log 1$. The measurement is a random process described by distributions of probabilities represented by the eigenvalues λ_i.

7.7 Measurement

After a unitary information processing starting form a initial basis state the result of the algorithm is determined by the measurement. The measurement corresponds to the collapse of the state vector, a projection into a basis state. The projection is not reversible and it is not consistent with the unitary time evolution. For a state represented by a unit-length vector

$$\omega_1 \cdot |x_1\rangle + \omega_2 \cdot |x_2\rangle + \cdots + \omega_n \cdot |x_n\rangle$$

in a n-dimensional Hilbert space $|x_k\rangle$ is observed. After the measurement (observation) the state is in a pure state

$$1 \cdot |x_k\rangle.$$

7.7.1   *Observables*

The measurement is preformed by an observable. A Hilbert space H_n can be represented as a collection of orthogonal subspaces

$$H_n = E_1 \oplus E_2 \oplus \ldots \oplus E_f \qquad (7.53)$$

with $f \leq n$. A state $|x\rangle$ can be represented with $|x_i\rangle \in E_i$ as

$$\omega_1 \cdot |x_1\rangle + \omega_2 \cdot |x_2\rangle + \cdots + \omega_f \cdot |x_f\rangle.$$

For one dimensional subspaces

$$H_n = E_1 \oplus E_2 \oplus \ldots \oplus E_n$$

the value $|x_k\rangle$ is observed with a probability $\|\omega_k \cdot |x_k\rangle\|^2 = |\omega_k|^2$.

Another description is through a projection into a subspace. A subspace defines a projection P_{E_k}. Because a projection is self-adjoint $P_{E_k} = P_{E_k}^*$ and $P_{E_k} = P_{E_k}^2$ the probability of observing $|x_k\rangle$ is

$$\langle x|P_{E_k} \cdot x\rangle = \langle x|P_{E_k}^2 \cdot x\rangle = \langle P_{E_k} \cdot x|P_{E_k} \cdot x\rangle = \|\omega_k \cdot |x_k\rangle\|^2 = |\omega_k|^2 \quad (7.54)$$

and the resulting value is

$$\frac{1}{\sqrt{\langle x|P_{E_k} \cdot x\rangle}} \cdot P_{E_k} \cdot |x\rangle = 1 \cdot |x_k\rangle.$$

Finally a state can be represented by the corresponding density matrix P with a corresponding spectral decomposition. The projection in the orthogonal subspace E_k is described by the projection matrix $|x_k\rangle\langle x_k|$ and the corresponding probability is λ_k. We can represent this probability as

$$\langle x|x_k\rangle\langle x_k|x\rangle = \lambda_k$$

and the resulting value of the projection is

$$\frac{1}{\sqrt{\langle x|x_k\rangle\langle x_k|x\rangle}}|x_k\rangle\langle x_k| \cdot |x\rangle = 1 \cdot |x_k\rangle.$$

All three different descriptions represent the same fact through different formalisms. An observation corresponds to a non-reversible projection onto one or several basis states.

7.7.2 Measuring a compound system

The state of the system is projected to the subspace that corresponds to the observed state and the vector representing the state is renormalized to the unit length. An observable describes a subspace of some dimensions with a special case of one dimension. A part of the system can be observed by a projection in a subspace with a dimension higher one. The compound system of n-dimensional Hilbert space $|x\rangle \in H_n$ and a w-dimensional Hilbert space $|y\rangle \in H_w$ defined by a orthonormal basis $|xy\rangle \in H_{n \cdot w}$. A state of the system is represented as

$$|xy\rangle = \sum_{i=1}^{n} \sum_{j=1}^{w} \omega_{ij} |x_i\rangle |y_j\rangle. \tag{7.55}$$

For example

$$|xy\rangle = \sum_{i=1}^{2} \sum_{j=1}^{2} \omega_{ij} |x_i\rangle |y_j\rangle =$$

$$= \omega_{11} \cdot |x_1\rangle |y_1\rangle + \omega_{12} \cdot |x_1\rangle |y_2\rangle + \omega_{21} \cdot |x_2\rangle |y_1\rangle + \omega_{22} \cdot |x_2\rangle |y_2\rangle.$$

For simplicity we use the following notation for a qubit register

$$|xy\rangle = \omega_0 \cdot |00\rangle + \omega_1 \cdot |01\rangle + \omega_2 \cdot |10\rangle + \omega_3 \cdot |11\rangle$$

The probability of observing x_k is $\sum_{j=1}^{w} |\omega_{kj}|^2$. If we observe x_k, the system after the observation is projected into

$$|xy\rangle = \frac{1}{\sqrt{\sum_{j=1}^{w} |\omega_{kj}|^2}} \sum_{j=1}^{w} \omega_{kj} |x_k\rangle |y_j\rangle.$$

Suppose the two qubits are in the following state

$$\sqrt{0.25} \cdot |00\rangle + \sqrt{0.25} \cdot |01\rangle + \sqrt{0.25} \cdot |10\rangle + \sqrt{0.25} \cdot |11\rangle = \begin{pmatrix} \frac{1}{2} \\ \frac{1}{2} \\ \frac{1}{2} \\ \frac{1}{2} \end{pmatrix}.$$

The observed first qubit is $|0\rangle$. The probability of the observation is

$$|\omega_{00}|^2 + |\omega_{01}|^2 = |\omega_0|^2 + |\omega_1|^2 = |\sqrt{0.25}|^2 + |\sqrt{0.25}|^2 = 0.25 + 0.25 = 0.5$$

the system after the observation is projected into

$$\frac{\sqrt{0.25} \cdot |00\rangle + \sqrt{0.25} \cdot |01\rangle}{\sqrt{0.5}} = \sqrt{0.5} \cdot |00\rangle + \sqrt{0.5} \cdot |01\rangle = \begin{pmatrix} \sqrt{\frac{1}{2}} \\ \sqrt{\frac{1}{2}} \\ 0 \\ 0 \end{pmatrix}.$$

7.7.3   *Heisenberg's uncertainty principle**

The commutator between two operators A and B is defined as

$$[A, B] := A \cdot B - B \cdot A \qquad (7.56)$$

so

$$[A, B] = 0 \Longleftrightarrow A \cdot B = B \cdot A. \qquad (7.57)$$

The anti-commutator between two operators A and B is defined as

$$\{A, B\} := A \cdot B + B \cdot A \qquad (7.58)$$

it follows that

$$A \cdot B = \frac{[A, B] + \{A, B\}}{2}. \qquad (7.59)$$

The expected value of observable M in state x is

$$\langle M \rangle = \langle x | M \cdot x \rangle \qquad (7.60)$$

and the standard deviation of observed values is

$$\Delta(M) = \sqrt{\langle (M - \langle M \rangle)^2 \rangle} = \sqrt{\langle M^2 \rangle - \langle M \rangle^2}. \qquad (7.61)$$

What happens if we try to measure two observable G and K?

A and B are Hermitian, $A^* = A, B^* = B$ and $|x\rangle$ is a quantum state. If

$$\langle x | A \cdot B \cdot x \rangle = a + ib \qquad (7.62)$$

then

$$\langle x | [A, B] \cdot x \rangle = 2 \cdot ib \qquad (7.63)$$

and

$$\langle x | \{A, B\} \cdot x \rangle = 2 \cdot a \qquad (7.64)$$

It follows that

$$|\langle x | [A, B] \cdot x \rangle|^2 + |\langle x | \{A, B\} \cdot x \rangle|^2 = 4 \cdot |\langle x | A \cdot B \cdot x \rangle|^2. \qquad (7.65)$$

Because by the Cauchy-Schwarz inequality

$$|\langle x | A \cdot B \cdot x \rangle|^2 \leq \langle x | A^2 \cdot x \rangle |\langle x | B^2 \cdot x \rangle| \qquad (7.66)$$

$$|\langle x | [A, B] \cdot x \rangle|^2 + |\langle x | \{A, B\} \cdot x \rangle|^2 \leq 4 \cdot \langle x | A^2 \cdot x \rangle |\langle x | B^2 \cdot x \rangle| \qquad (7.67)$$

and

$$|\langle x | [A, B] \cdot x \rangle|^2 + \leq 4 \cdot \langle x | A^2 \cdot x \rangle |\langle x | B^2 \cdot x \rangle| \qquad (7.68)$$

With

$$A = G - \langle G \rangle, \quad B = K - \langle K \rangle$$

we obtain the Heisenberg's uncertainty principle

$$\Delta(G)\Delta(K) \geq \frac{|\langle x | [G, K] \cdot x \rangle|}{2}. \qquad (7.69)$$

Example Suppose we have a large number of quantum systems in the state $|x\rangle$. If we measure the observable G on some and the observable K on others, then the standard deviation $\Delta(G)$ and $\Delta(K)$ will satisfy the Equation 7.69. For example the observable G is [Nielsen and Chuang (2000)]

$$G = \begin{pmatrix} 0 & 1 \\ 1 & 0 \end{pmatrix} \tag{7.70}$$

and

$$K = \begin{pmatrix} 0 & -i \\ i & 0 \end{pmatrix} \tag{7.71}$$

with

$$[G, K] = \begin{pmatrix} 0 & 1 \\ 1 & 0 \end{pmatrix} \cdot \begin{pmatrix} 0 & -i \\ i & 0 \end{pmatrix} - \begin{pmatrix} 0 & -i \\ i & 0 \end{pmatrix} \cdot \begin{pmatrix} 0 & 1 \\ 1 & 0 \end{pmatrix}$$

$$[G, K] = \begin{pmatrix} 2i & 0 \\ 0 & -2i \end{pmatrix}$$

then

$$\Delta(G)\Delta(K) \geq \frac{\left| \langle 0| \begin{pmatrix} 2i & 0 \\ 0 & -2i \end{pmatrix} \cdot 0\rangle \right|}{2} = 1 \tag{7.72}$$

$\Delta(G)$ and $\Delta(K)$ must be grater than 0.

Time-frequency information of a signal The uncertainty principle was originally applied to the momentum and location of moving particles. The uncertainty principle can also be applied to the classical time-frequency information of a signal. It is not possible to know the exact time-frequency representation of a signal. In short-time Fourier transform (STFT), the signal is divided into small segments. In each segment, the Fourier transform determines the frequency representation of the signal. The size of the window defines the time representation of the signal. The uncertainty principle of STFT is related to the width of the window function that is used.

- Narrow window: good time resolution, poor frequency resolution.
- Wide window: good frequency resolution, poor time resolution.

In classical physics, a possible solution exists. This solution is the multi resolution analysis of the signal, as described by the wavelet transform. The analysis is "repeated" several times. Each time, a different size (scale) of the window is used.

7.8   Randomness

Randomness can be defined by numbers in a sequence [Williams and Clearwatter (1997)]. A random number alone does not exist. A sequence of random numbers must correspond to some distribution, and there should be no correlation among the numbers in the sequence. For example, the following sequence, which represents the toss of a fair coin $0, 1$, is not random,

$$0, 1, 0, 1, 0, 1, 0, 1, 0, 1, 0, 1, 0, 1, 0, 1, 0, 1$$

because a correlation between 0 and 1 is present. Classical physics is deterministic. Because of that, no randomness exists in its context. Some facts could appear to be random. However, this arrangement is only the case because some essential information is missing.

7.8.1   *Deterministic chaos*

A sequence could look random even though it is generated by a simple nonlinear deterministic equation. Such behavior is called deterministic chaos. The logistic map is defined by a dynamical nonlinear difference equation

$$x_{t+1} = r \cdot x_t \cdot (1 - x_t) \tag{7.73}$$

with with some constant r. The rule generates a sequence

$$x_0, x, x_2, x_3, x_4, \cdots$$

that depending on the value r.

For $x_0 = 0.1$ and $r = 3.2$ the equation converges to a period (see Figure 7.1). However, for values that are approximately in $[3.5699, 4]$, the sequence does not converge to any pattern. A minimal change of x_0 leads to a different sequence (see the values $x_0 = 0.1$ and $r = 3.98$ represented in Figure 7.2 and the values $x_0 = 0.101$ and $r = 3.98$ in Figure 7.3).

There is no randomness in classical physics and in the resulting equations that describe it, in spite of the fact that a behavior can be generated that is highly unpredictable due to our lack of information. For example, in the logistic equation, exact knowledge of the initial condition is required.

7.8.2   *Kolmogorov complexity*

Kolmogorov complexity is defined as the shortest program that can produce its output. It is a measure of the amount of innate randomness of a

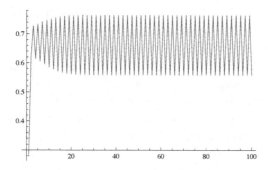

Fig. 7.1   For $x_0 = 0.1$ and $r = 3.2$ the logistic map converges to a period.

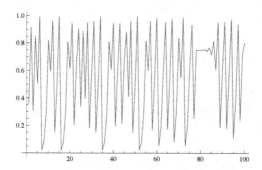

Fig. 7.2   For $x_0 = 0.1$ and $r = 3.98$ the logistic map behaves chaotically, it appears random.

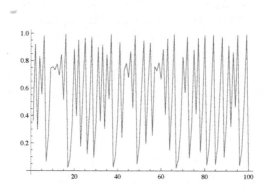

Fig. 7.3   The logistic map is sensitive to the initial condition. For $x_0 = 0.101$ and $r = 3.98$ it behaves diferentlys as the sequence with initial condition or $x_0 = 0.1$.

sequence. In the case of deterministic chaos, the randomness is low. It can be described by a very short program, such as in the case of the logistic map, by an equation together with the values of x_0 and r. Randomness is defined by the Kolmogorov complexity. The larger the shortest program that generates the sequence is, the more random it is. However, we cannot determine whether a sequence can be represented by a short program. The problem is related to the halting problem [Gardner (1979)]. We cannot generate a truly random sequence using a Turing machine.

7.8.3 *Humans and random numbers*

Randomness could be nature's way to avoid complexity. A decision could be chosen randomly, where no knowledge is present and planning is not possible. How well can people generate random sequences? It was indicated in one experiment that humans cannot generate true binary random sequences. Hagelbarger asked subjects to create a binary random sequence, and the sequence was analyzed for correlations by a computer program. The program attempted to predict the next symbol in the sequence and achieved a $55 - 60$ percent accuracy. For a random sequence, the accuracy should be approximately 50 percent [Shannon (1953)].

7.8.4 *Randomness in quantum physics*

Quantum physics is the only source of true randomness. Randomness can be generated by a quantum computing device that simulates a quantum coin. A quantum coin is defined by the unitary matrix

$$W = \frac{1}{\sqrt{2}} \cdot \begin{pmatrix} 1 & 1 \\ 1 & -1 \end{pmatrix}$$

and by the mapping

$$W \cdot |0\rangle = \frac{1}{\sqrt{2}} \cdot |0\rangle + \frac{1}{\sqrt{2}} \cdot |1\rangle \tag{7.74}$$

or

$$W \cdot |1\rangle = \frac{1}{\sqrt{2}} \cdot |0\rangle - \frac{1}{\sqrt{2}} \cdot |1\rangle. \tag{7.75}$$

The corresponding operator is indicated by the following unitary matrix,

$$W = \begin{pmatrix} \frac{1}{\sqrt{2}} & \frac{1}{\sqrt{2}} \\ \frac{1}{\sqrt{2}} & -\frac{1}{\sqrt{2}} \end{pmatrix} = \frac{1}{\sqrt{2}} \cdot \begin{pmatrix} 1 & 1 \\ 1 & -1 \end{pmatrix}. \tag{7.76}$$

After the mapping, a measurement is preformed. The probability of observing 0 or 1 is $\left|\frac{1}{\sqrt{2}}\right|^2 = \frac{1}{2}$. True randomness is present during the measurement; it is an effect of the measurement represented by the collapse. The collapse itself is not explained by quantum theory. Using a quantum coin, we can generate a true random binary sequence. It is easy to combine the results from a quantum coin to generate a random integer in the range 0 to 2^{n-1}. Later, we will see how to generate a true random dice using QFT.

Chapter 8

Computation with Qubits

8.1 Computation with one Qubit

A unitary operator on a qubit is called an unary quantum gate. It is described by a unitary matrix of the dimension 2×2. For the qubit with the basis

$$|0\rangle = \begin{pmatrix} 1 \\ 0 \end{pmatrix}, |1\rangle = \begin{pmatrix} 0 \\ 1 \end{pmatrix}$$

the quantum not gate $M_\neg$ does the not operation on a qubit

$$M_\neg|0\rangle = |1\rangle, M_\neg|1\rangle = |0\rangle$$

and is represented by the unitary matrix

$$M_\neg = \begin{pmatrix} 0 & 1 \\ 1 & 0 \end{pmatrix}. \tag{8.1}$$

The not operation can be written using $XOR = \oplus$ for $x \in \mathbf{B}^1$

$$M_\neg|x\rangle = |x \oplus 1\rangle$$

$$M_\neg|0\rangle = |0 \oplus 1\rangle = |0\rangle, \quad M_\neg|1\rangle = |1 \oplus 1\rangle = |1\rangle.$$

The square root of the not gate $M_\neg = \sqrt{M_\neg} \cdot \sqrt{M_\neg}$ is represented by the unitary matrix

$$\sqrt{M_\neg} = \begin{pmatrix} \frac{1+i}{2} & \frac{1-i}{2} \\ \frac{1-i}{2} & \frac{1+i}{2} \end{pmatrix} \tag{8.2}$$

with

$$\begin{pmatrix} \frac{1+i}{2} & \frac{1-i}{2} \\ \frac{1-i}{2} & \frac{1+i}{2} \end{pmatrix} \cdot \begin{pmatrix} \frac{1+i}{2} & \frac{1-i}{2} \\ \frac{1-i}{2} & \frac{1+i}{2} \end{pmatrix} = \begin{pmatrix} 0 & 1 \\ 1 & 0 \end{pmatrix} \tag{8.3}$$

and it is unitary because

$$\begin{pmatrix} \frac{1+i}{2} & \frac{1-i}{2} \\ \frac{1-i}{2} & \frac{1+i}{2} \end{pmatrix} \cdot \begin{pmatrix} \frac{1-i}{2} & \frac{1+i}{2} \\ \frac{1+i}{2} & \frac{1-i}{2} \end{pmatrix} = \begin{pmatrix} 1 & 0 \\ 0 & 1 \end{pmatrix} \tag{8.4}$$

with

$$M_\neg |0\rangle = \frac{1+i}{2} \cdot |0\rangle + \frac{1-i}{2} \cdot |1\rangle$$

and

$$M_\neg |1\rangle = \frac{1-i}{2} \cdot |0\rangle + \frac{1+i}{2} \cdot |1\rangle.$$

The probability of measuring $|0\rangle$ and $|1\rangle$ is 0.5, because

$$\left| \frac{1-i}{2} \right|^2 = \left| \frac{1+i}{2} \right|^2 = \frac{1}{2}.$$

$-\sqrt{M_\neg}$ has the same behavior with

$$M_\neg = -\sqrt{M_\neg} \cdot -\sqrt{M_\neg}.$$

The identity gate preforms no operation on a qubit, it is defined as the identity matrix

$$I_1 = \begin{pmatrix} 1 & 0 \\ 0 & 1 \end{pmatrix}. \tag{8.5}$$

The square root of the identity matrix is the identity I matrix is I and $-I$

$$-I_1 = \begin{pmatrix} -1 & 0 \\ 0 & -1 \end{pmatrix}. \tag{8.6}$$

$-I_1$ changes the sign of the amplitude but not the probabilities. The introduced unitary matrix W maps a pure state in a superposition.

$$|0\rangle \to \frac{1}{\sqrt{2}} \cdot |0\rangle + \frac{1}{\sqrt{2}} \cdot |1\rangle$$

$$|1\rangle \to \frac{1}{\sqrt{2}} \cdot |0\rangle - \frac{1}{\sqrt{2}} \cdot |1\rangle$$

The probability of measuring $|0\rangle$ and $|1\rangle$ is 0.5. The matrix W is called Walsh, Hadarmad or Hamarad Walsh, matrix.

8.2 Computation with m Qubit

The register of m qubits is represented as a direct product of m qubits. It defines $n = 2^m$ dimensional Hilbert space H_n with an orthonprmal basis $|x_1\rangle, |x_1\rangle, \cdots |x_n\rangle$. For example four qubits define a 16 dimensional Hilbert space H_{16} with the basis

$$|0000\rangle = \begin{pmatrix} 1 \\ 0 \\ 0 \\ 0 \\ 0 \\ 0 \\ 0 \\ 0 \\ 0 \\ 0 \\ 0 \\ 0 \\ 0 \\ 0 \\ 0 \\ 0 \end{pmatrix}, |0001\rangle = \begin{pmatrix} 0 \\ 1 \\ 0 \\ 0 \\ 0 \\ 0 \\ 0 \\ 0 \\ 0 \\ 0 \\ 0 \\ 0 \\ 0 \\ 0 \\ 0 \\ 0 \end{pmatrix}, |0010\rangle = \begin{pmatrix} 0 \\ 0 \\ 1 \\ 0 \\ 0 \\ 0 \\ 0 \\ 0 \\ 0 \\ 0 \\ 0 \\ 0 \\ 0 \\ 0 \\ 0 \\ 0 \end{pmatrix}, \cdots, |1111\rangle = \begin{pmatrix} 0 \\ 0 \\ 0 \\ 0 \\ 0 \\ 0 \\ 0 \\ 0 \\ 0 \\ 0 \\ 0 \\ 0 \\ 0 \\ 0 \\ 0 \\ 1 \end{pmatrix}.$$

$$(8.7)$$

It is difficult to simulate more than few of tens bits on an ordinary computer because the dimension of the Hilbert space grows exponentially in relation to the number of represented qubits. For example sixteen qubits are represented by a 65536 dimensional Hilbert space H_{65536}.

The Hadarmad matrix W on one qubit has the dimension 2×2 is also called a Hadamard gate and is indicated as W_1. A Hadarmad operator for m qubits W_m is represented by a $2^m \times 2^m$ dimensional matrix built by a direct product of m W_1 matrices. The complexity of the operator W_m corresponds to m Hadamard gates W_1.

$$W_m = \bigotimes^m W_1 = W_1 \otimes W_1 \cdots \otimes W_1 \qquad (8.8)$$

The Hadamard matrix is also called the Hadamard transform and can be defined recursively with $W_0 = 1$ and

$$W_m = \frac{1}{\sqrt{2}} \cdot \begin{pmatrix} W_{m-1} & W_{m-1} \\ W_{m-1} & -W_{m-1} \end{pmatrix} \qquad (8.9)$$

with W_3

$$W_3 = W_1 \otimes W_1 \otimes W_1$$

$$W_3 = \frac{1}{\sqrt{2}} \cdot \begin{pmatrix} W_2 & W_2 \\ W_2 & -W_2 \end{pmatrix} = \frac{1}{\sqrt{2^3}} \cdot \begin{pmatrix} 1 & 1 & 1 & 1 & 1 & 1 & 1 & 1 \\ 1 & -1 & 1 & -1 & 1 & -1 & 1 & -1 \\ 1 & 1 & -1 & -1 & 1 & 1 & -1 & -1 \\ 1 & -1 & -1 & 1 & 1 & -1 & -1 & 1 \\ 1 & 1 & 1 & 1 & -1 & -1 & -1 & -1 \\ 1 & -1 & 1 & -1 & -1 & -1 & -1 & 1 \\ 1 & 1 & -1 & -1 & -1 & -1 & 1 & 1 \\ 1 & -1 & -1 & 1 & -1 & 1 & 1 & -1 \end{pmatrix}.$$

The Hadamard operator W_m maps m qubits $|z\rangle$ representing a pure state in a Hilbert space H_{2^m} with $z \in B^m$

$$W_m|z\rangle = \frac{1}{\sqrt{2^m}} \sum_{x \in B^m} (-1)^{\langle z|x \rangle} \cdot |x\rangle \qquad (8.10)$$

with a scalar product ($\langle z|x \rangle$) over the binary field with two elements corresponding to the bits 0 and 1. The multiplication of two bits is equal to the *AND* operation with

$$0 \cdot 0 = 0 \wedge 0 = 0, \quad 0 \cdot 1 = 0 \wedge 1 = 0, \quad 1 \cdot 0 = 1 \wedge 0 = 0, \quad 1 \cdot 1 = 1 \wedge 1 = 1$$

and the addition is equal to the *XOR* operation $\oplus$

$$0 + 0 = 0 \oplus 0 = 0, \quad 0 + 1 = 0 \oplus 1 = 1,$$

$$1 + 0 = 1 \oplus 0 = 1, \quad 1 + 1 = 1 \oplus 1 = 0.$$

For the state zero represented by m qubits

$$|0\rangle^{\otimes m} = |0\rangle|0\rangle|0\rangle \cdots |0\rangle = \begin{pmatrix} 1 \\ 0 \\ \vdots \\ 0 \\ 0 \end{pmatrix}$$

the Hadamard operator W_m maps a pure state into a superposition of all possible states with no negative sign,

$$W_m|0\rangle^{\otimes m} = \frac{1}{\sqrt{2^m}} \sum_{x \in B^m} |x\rangle. \qquad (8.11)$$

For example

$$W_3|0\rangle^{\otimes^3} = W_3|000\rangle = \frac{1}{\sqrt{2^3}} \sum_{x \in B^3} |x\rangle$$

$$W_3|000\rangle =$$

$$= \frac{1}{\sqrt{2^3}} \left(|000\rangle + |001\rangle + |000\rangle + |010\rangle + |011\rangle + |100\rangle + |101\rangle + |111\rangle \right).$$

It can be expressed as

$$W_3|000\rangle = W_1|0\rangle \otimes W_1|0\rangle \otimes W_1|0\rangle = \left(\frac{|0\rangle + |1\rangle}{\sqrt{2}} \right) \cdot \left(\frac{|0\rangle + |1\rangle}{\sqrt{2}} \right) \cdot \left(\frac{|0\rangle + |1\rangle}{\sqrt{2}} \right)$$

and

$$W_3 \cdot W_3|000\rangle = |000\rangle.$$

This is because $W_m = W_m^*$ so that $I_m = W_m \cdot W_m$. The pure states $|11\rangle$ is maped into

$$W_2|11\rangle = W_1|1\rangle \otimes W_1|1\rangle = \left(\frac{|0\rangle - |1\rangle}{\sqrt{2}} \right) \cdot \left(\frac{|0\rangle - |1\rangle}{\sqrt{2}} \right)$$

$$W_2|11\rangle = \frac{1}{2} \cdot \left(|00\rangle - |01\rangle - |10\rangle + |11\rangle \right).$$

A Walsh matrix is a square matrix of the dimension power of two. It has the property that the scalar product of any two different rows or columns is zero. The vectors that represent the matrix are orthogonal. In Hadamard transform the vectors that represent the matrix are orthonormal. We indicate the matrix by W_m for m qubits (because of Walsh), not to be confused with the Hilbert space H_n of the dimension n with the relation $n = 2^m$.

8.3 Matrix Representation of Serial and Parallel Operations

A serial computation corresponds to a multiplication of matrices that represent the gates. The multiplication of matrices is usually not commutative, for example $W_1 \cdot M_\neg \neq M_\neg W_1$

$$\begin{pmatrix} \frac{1}{\sqrt{2}} & \frac{1}{\sqrt{2}} \\ \frac{1}{\sqrt{2}} & -\frac{1}{\sqrt{2}} \end{pmatrix} \cdot \begin{pmatrix} 0 & 1 \\ 1 & 0 \end{pmatrix} \neq \begin{pmatrix} 0 & 1 \\ 1 & 0 \end{pmatrix} \cdot \begin{pmatrix} \frac{1}{\sqrt{2}} & \frac{1}{\sqrt{2}} \\ \frac{1}{\sqrt{2}} & -\frac{1}{\sqrt{2}} \end{pmatrix}$$

$$\begin{pmatrix} \frac{1}{\sqrt{2}} & \frac{1}{\sqrt{2}} \\ -\frac{1}{\sqrt{2}} & \frac{1}{\sqrt{2}} \end{pmatrix} \neq \begin{pmatrix} \frac{1}{\sqrt{2}} & -\frac{1}{\sqrt{2}} \\ \frac{1}{\sqrt{2}} & \frac{1}{\sqrt{2}} \end{pmatrix}$$

it means

$$W_1 \cdot M_\neg \cdot |0\rangle = W_1 \cdot |1\rangle = \frac{|0\rangle - |1\rangle}{\sqrt{2}}$$

and

$$M_\neg \cdot W_1 \cdot |0\rangle = M_\neg \cdot \left(\frac{|0\rangle + |1\rangle}{\sqrt{2}} \right) =$$

$$= \frac{M_\neg \cdot |0\rangle + M_\neg \cdot |1\rangle}{\sqrt{2}} = \frac{|1\rangle + |0\rangle}{\sqrt{2}} = \frac{|0\rangle + |1\rangle}{\sqrt{2}}$$

it follows

$$M_\neg \cdot W_1 \cdot |0\rangle = W_1 \cdot |0\rangle.$$

Only the multiplication with the identity matrix and the inverse matrix are commutative operations. Parallel operations correspond to the direct product, also called the tensor product or Kronecker product when dealing with matrices. For example with

$$M_\neg \otimes I_1 \otimes W_1 \cdot |000\rangle = (M_\neg \cdot |0\rangle) \otimes (I_1 \cdot |0\rangle) \otimes (W_1 \cdot |0\rangle) =$$

$$|10\rangle \cdot \frac{|0\rangle + |1\rangle}{\sqrt{2}} = \frac{|100\rangle + |101\rangle}{\sqrt{2}}$$

in vector representation as

$$\left(\begin{pmatrix} 0 & 1 \\ 1 & 0 \end{pmatrix} \cdot \begin{pmatrix} 1 \\ 0 \end{pmatrix} \right) \otimes \left(\begin{pmatrix} 1 & 0 \\ 0 & 1 \end{pmatrix} \cdot \begin{pmatrix} 1 \\ 0 \end{pmatrix} \right) \otimes \left(\begin{pmatrix} \frac{1}{\sqrt{2}} & \frac{1}{\sqrt{2}} \\ \frac{1}{\sqrt{2}} & -\frac{1}{\sqrt{2}} \end{pmatrix} \cdot \begin{pmatrix} 1 \\ 0 \end{pmatrix} \right) =$$

$$\begin{pmatrix} 0 & 0 & 0 & 0 & \frac{1}{\sqrt{2}} & \frac{1}{\sqrt{2}} & 0 & 0 \\ 0 & 0 & 0 & 0 & \frac{1}{\sqrt{2}} & -\frac{1}{\sqrt{2}} & 0 & 0 \\ 0 & 0 & 0 & 0 & 0 & 0 & \frac{1}{\sqrt{2}} & \frac{1}{\sqrt{2}} \\ 0 & 0 & 0 & 0 & 0 & 0 & \frac{1}{\sqrt{2}} & -\frac{1}{\sqrt{2}} \\ \frac{1}{\sqrt{2}} & \frac{1}{\sqrt{2}} & 0 & 0 & 0 & 0 & 0 & 0 \\ \frac{1}{\sqrt{2}} & -\frac{1}{\sqrt{2}} & 0 & 0 & 0 & 0 & 0 & 0 \\ 0 & 0 & \frac{1}{\sqrt{2}} & \frac{1}{\sqrt{2}} & 0 & 0 & 0 & 0 \\ 0 & 0 & \frac{1}{\sqrt{2}} & -\frac{1}{\sqrt{2}} & 0 & 0 & 0 & 0 \end{pmatrix} \cdot \begin{pmatrix} 1 \\ 0 \\ 0 \\ 0 \\ 0 \\ 0 \\ 0 \\ 0 \end{pmatrix} = \begin{pmatrix} 0 \\ 0 \\ 0 \\ 0 \\ \frac{1}{\sqrt{2}} \\ \frac{1}{\sqrt{2}} \\ 0 \\ 0 \end{pmatrix}.$$

Matrices representing quantum operators can be decomposed, for example

$$W_4 = W_2 \otimes W_2 = W_1 \otimes W_1 \otimes W_1 \otimes W_1.$$

There are however matrices representing quantum operators that can be not decomposed with some serious consequences.

8.4 Entanglement

The following operator M_{CNOT} s unitary and defends an injective mapping on two qubits that is reversible

$$M_{CNOT}|00\rangle = |00\rangle, \quad M_{CNOT}|01\rangle = |01\rangle,$$

$$M_{CNOT}|10\rangle = |11\rangle, \quad M_{CNOT}|11\rangle = |10\rangle.$$

The operator M_{CNOT} is called a controlled not gate. The first qubit counting from the left is not changed. The second qubit is only flipped in the case that the first qubit is 1. In this case a NOT operation on the second qubit is executed. The control not gate can as well perform the fan-out operation. For this operation the second qubit has to be zero. In this case the value of the first qubit is copied into the second one. The M_{CNOT} can be represented by a matrix

$$M_{CNOT} = \begin{pmatrix} 1 & 0 & 0 & 0 \\ 0 & 1 & 0 & 0 \\ 0 & 0 & 0 & 1 \\ 0 & 0 & 1 & 0 \end{pmatrix}. \tag{8.12}$$

M_{CNOT} cannot be expressed as a tensor product of 2×2 matrices. Suppose we start with the state $|00\rangle$ and map the first qubit bit into the superposition using the Hadamard gate

$$W_1 \otimes I \cdot |00\rangle = (W_1 \cdot |0\rangle) \otimes |0\rangle = \frac{|0\rangle + |1\rangle}{\sqrt{2}} \otimes |0\rangle = \frac{|00\rangle + |10\rangle}{\sqrt{2}}.$$

To this state represented by the two qubit we apply M_{CNOT} gate

$$M_{CNOT} \cdot \left(\frac{|00\rangle + |10\rangle}{\sqrt{2}} \right) = \frac{M_{CNOT} \cdot |00\rangle + M_{CNOT} \cdot |10\rangle}{\sqrt{2}} = \frac{|00\rangle + |11\rangle}{\sqrt{2}}.$$

A register of two qubit is decomposable if it can be represented as a direct product of two qubits. For example the state

$$\frac{|00\rangle + |01\rangle + |10\rangle + |11\rangle}{2} = \left(\frac{|0\rangle + |1\rangle}{\sqrt{2}} \right) \otimes \left(\frac{|0\rangle + |1\rangle}{\sqrt{2}} \right)$$

is decomposable. In vector notation it is represented as

$$\begin{pmatrix} \frac{1}{2} \\ \frac{1}{2} \\ \frac{1}{2} \\ \frac{1}{2} \end{pmatrix} = \begin{pmatrix} \frac{1}{\sqrt{2}} \\ \frac{1}{\sqrt{2}} \end{pmatrix} \otimes \begin{pmatrix} \frac{1}{\sqrt{2}} \\ \frac{1}{\sqrt{2}} \end{pmatrix}.$$

However the state of two qubits

$$\frac{|00\rangle + |11\rangle}{\sqrt{2}} \qquad (8.13)$$

is not decomposable. We preform a proof by contradiction. From the assumption that the state is decomposable follows a contradiction,

$$\frac{|00\rangle + |11\rangle}{\sqrt{2}} = (a_o \cdot |0\rangle + a_1|1\rangle) \otimes (b_o \cdot |0\rangle + b_1|1\rangle) = \qquad (8.14)$$

$$= a_0 \cdot b_0 \cdot |00\rangle + a_0 \cdot b_1 \cdot |01\rangle + a_1 \cdot b_0 \cdot |10\rangle + a_1 \cdot b_1 \cdot |11\rangle$$

$$\rightarrow \quad a_0 \cdot b_0 = \frac{1}{\sqrt{2}}, \quad a_0 \cdot b_1 = 0, \quad a_1 \cdot b_0 = 0, \quad a_1 \cdot b_1 = \frac{1}{\sqrt{2}}$$

that is a contradiction.

A state that is not decomposable is called entangled. If two qubits are entangled in a state $\frac{|00\rangle + |11\rangle}{\sqrt{2}}$, then observing one of them will result in either $|0\rangle$ or $|1\rangle$ with probability $\frac{1}{2}$. However, it is not possible to observe a different value on the other, non-observed qubit. Both qubits behave as one unit and are called an *ebit*. There are four known *ebits*:

$$\frac{|00\rangle + |11\rangle}{\sqrt{2}}, \quad \frac{|00\rangle - |11\rangle}{\sqrt{2}}, \quad \frac{|01\rangle + |10\rangle}{\sqrt{2}}, \quad \frac{|01\rangle - |10\rangle}{\sqrt{2}}. \qquad (8.15)$$

Once either qubit of an ebit is measured, the states of both particles become definite. Experiments have shown that this correlation can remain even if the qubits are separated over a distance of several kilometers. Quantum collapse during measurement is a non-local force. A non-local interaction is not limited by the speed of light, and its strength is not mediated with distance. This arrangement conflicts with Einstein's Theory of Special Relativity, which states that nothing can travel faster than light. The conflict is resolved by the fact that one cannot use an ebit to send any information. If two qubits of an ebit are separated over a distance in two places, A and B, and there are no other means of communication, then measuring the qubit on place A determines the outcome on place B, but at place B, the outcome is unknown. Measuring at place B is a random process without the knowledge of the results of place A. More than two qubits can be entangled. The GHZ (Greenberger–Horne–Zeilinger) state is entangled over M qubits with $M > 2$

$$\frac{|0\rangle^{\otimes M} + |1\rangle^{\otimes M}}{\sqrt{2}}. \qquad (8.16)$$

For $M = 3$

$$\frac{|000\rangle + |111\rangle}{\sqrt{2}}.$$

The entanglement can arise during a computation that uses quantum gates due to the nature of the M_{CNOT} gate. During a computation, a part of the system can be observed by a projection, and the vector that represents the state is renormalized to the unit length. However, if an entanglement is present, then the observed part determines the rest of the state. In contrast to the conventional register, several qubits in a quantum register can form an entity, such as an ebit. Extra care must be taken when a part of the system is measured. A register is used to indicate if the computation is terminated, $|1\rangle$ for terminated and $|0\rangle$ for not terminated. If we measure $|1\rangle$, then we are done. If we measure $|0\rangle$, then we must start all of the computation from the beginning due to entanglement. There is no entanglement between two qubits of a state if

$$\sum_i \omega_i \cdot |x_i\rangle|y_i\rangle = \left(\sum_i \omega_i \cdot |x_i\rangle\right) \otimes |y_i\rangle$$

that is only valid if $|y_i\rangle = |y_j\rangle$ for all i and j. The states

$$\sum_i \omega_i \cdot |x_i\rangle|y_i\rangle, \qquad \sum_i \omega_i \cdot |x_i\rangle$$

behave differently.

8.5   Quantum Boolean Circuits

A reversible circuit that is composed of m bits corresponds to a unitary mapping that represents a permutation on m bits, defining an injective mapping $\mathbf{B}^m \to \mathbf{B}^m$. A unitary permutation matrix can represent this unitary mapping. A more elegant method is to map the reversible circuit into the quantum Boolean gates. Such a mapping allows us to determine the complexity of the circuit by the number of gates. The following quantum gates are Boolean quantum gates: the identity gate I, the NOT gate and the control not gate M_{CNOT}. The control not gate performs the essential fan-out operation. What is missing are the AND and OR operations. These operations can be represented by the universal reversible Toffoli gate (see chapter "Reversible Algorithms"). A reversible Toffoli gate is a unitary mapping. It defines a quantum gate on three qubits and can be represented by a unitary matrix M in Hilbert space H_8

$$M = \begin{pmatrix} I_1 & 0 & 0 & 0 \\ 0 & I_1 & 0 & 0 \\ 0 & 0 & I_1 & 0 \\ 0 & 0 & 0 & M_\neg \end{pmatrix} = \begin{pmatrix} 1 & 0 & 0 & 0 & 0 & 0 & 0 & 0 \\ 0 & 1 & 0 & 0 & 0 & 0 & 0 & 0 \\ 0 & 0 & 1 & 0 & 0 & 0 & 0 & 0 \\ 0 & 0 & 0 & 1 & 0 & 0 & 0 & 0 \\ 0 & 0 & 0 & 0 & 1 & 0 & 0 & 0 \\ 0 & 0 & 0 & 0 & 0 & 1 & 0 & 0 \\ 0 & 0 & 0 & 0 & 0 & 0 & 0 & 1 \\ 0 & 0 & 0 & 0 & 0 & 0 & 1 & 0 \end{pmatrix}. \tag{8.17}$$

The unitary matrix M can be decomposed into several ways using non Boolean quantum gates. However each decomposition involves the M_{CNOT}, indicating that an entanglement may arise when applying a quantum Toffoli gate. With the basis of three qubits of the Hilbert space H_8

$$|000\rangle = \begin{pmatrix} 1 \\ 0 \\ 0 \\ 0 \\ 0 \\ 0 \\ 0 \\ 0 \end{pmatrix}, |001\rangle = \begin{pmatrix} 0 \\ 1 \\ 0 \\ 0 \\ 0 \\ 0 \\ 0 \\ 0 \end{pmatrix}, |010\rangle = \begin{pmatrix} 0 \\ 0 \\ 1 \\ 0 \\ 0 \\ 0 \\ 0 \\ 0 \end{pmatrix}, |011\rangle = \begin{pmatrix} 0 \\ 0 \\ 0 \\ 1 \\ 0 \\ 0 \\ 0 \\ 0 \end{pmatrix},$$

$$|100\rangle = \begin{pmatrix} 0 \\ 0 \\ 0 \\ 0 \\ 1 \\ 0 \\ 0 \\ 0 \end{pmatrix}, |101\rangle = \begin{pmatrix} 0 \\ 0 \\ 0 \\ 0 \\ 0 \\ 1 \\ 0 \\ 0 \end{pmatrix}, |110\rangle = \begin{pmatrix} 0 \\ 0 \\ 0 \\ 0 \\ 0 \\ 0 \\ 1 \\ 0 \end{pmatrix}, |111\rangle = \begin{pmatrix} 0 \\ 0 \\ 0 \\ 0 \\ 0 \\ 0 \\ 0 \\ 1 \end{pmatrix}$$

the mapping of the reversible $T(x_1, x_2, x_3) = (x_1, x_2, (x_1 \wedge x_2) \oplus x_3)$ corresponds to the unitary mapping

$$M \cdot |xyz\rangle = M \cdot |x\rangle|y\rangle|z\rangle = |x\rangle|y\rangle|(x \wedge y) \oplus z\rangle. \tag{8.18}$$

For the AND operation, the ancilla bit z is set to 0

$$M \cdot |x\rangle|y\rangle|0\rangle = |x\rangle|y\rangle|(x \wedge y)\rangle. \tag{8.19}$$

The four bit conjunction $x \wedge y \wedge z \wedge v$ requires three quantum Toffoli gates and three additional qubits that are zero. The input:

$$|x\rangle|y\rangle|0\rangle|z\rangle|0\rangle|v\rangle|0\rangle.$$

First quantum Toffoli gate

$$(M \cdot |x\rangle|y\rangle|0\rangle) \otimes (I_4 \cdot |z\rangle|0\rangle|v\rangle|0\rangle) = |x\rangle|y\rangle|x \wedge y\rangle|z\rangle|0\rangle|v\rangle|0\rangle.$$

Second quantum Toffoli gate

$$(I_2 \cdot |x\rangle|y\rangle) \otimes (M \cdot |x \wedge y\rangle|z\rangle|0) \otimes (I_2 \cdot |v\rangle|0\rangle) =$$
$$= |x\rangle|y\rangle|x \wedge y\rangle|z\rangle|x \wedge y \wedge z\rangle|v\rangle|0\rangle.$$

Third quantum Toffoli gate

$$(I_4 \cdot |x\rangle|y\rangle|x \wedge y\rangle|z\rangle) \otimes (M \cdot |x \wedge y \wedge z\rangle|v\rangle|0\rangle) =$$
$$= |x\rangle|y\rangle|x \wedge y\rangle|z\rangle|x \wedge y \wedge z\rangle|v\rangle|x \wedge y \wedge z \wedge v\rangle.$$

The circuit corresponds to the following unitary mapping

$$((I_4 \otimes M)(I_2 \otimes M \otimes I_2) \cdot (M \otimes I_4)) \cdot |xy0z0v0\rangle$$

with the result

$$|x\rangle|y\rangle|x \wedge y\rangle|z\rangle|x \wedge y \wedge z\rangle|v\rangle|x \wedge y \wedge z \wedge v\rangle.$$

The third and the fifth qubit are usually not required for further computation because the result is represented in the output qubit seven. However they are entangled with the output qubit. It is not possible to reset them to zero. Instead they are un-computed. Because $M^{-1} = M$ we recompute the first and the second quantum Toffoli gate after determining the result. The steps are reversed, it follows

$$((I_2 \otimes M \otimes I_2) \cdot (M \otimes I_4) \cdot (I_4 \otimes M)(I_2 \otimes M \otimes I_2) \cdot (M \otimes I_4)) \cdot |xy0z0v0\rangle$$
$$= |x\rangle|y\rangle|0\rangle|z\rangle|0\rangle|v\rangle|x \wedge y \wedge z \wedge v\rangle = |xy0z0v(x \wedge y \wedge z \wedge v)\rangle.$$

The OR operation is represented by the unitary mapping according to the De Morgan's laws

$$((I_2 \otimes M_{NOT}) \cdot M \cdot (M_{NOT} \otimes M_{NOT} \otimes I_1)) \cdot |xy0\rangle = xy(x \vee y)\rangle.$$

For each quantum Boolean AND, OR operation a naïve implementation requires an ancilla bit. These bits can be reused for further computation only by reversing the preceding steps. The complexity of the circuit corresponds to the number of used quantum gates. A quantum circuit represents a permutation in Hilbert space and is not an algorithmic device. The computation does not alter the distribution of the amplitudes; the von Neumann entropy remains unchanged during the execution of the quantum Boolean gates. The probability of measuring certain states is the same before and after the computation; by itself, it does not offer any advantage over the classical computation.

8.6   Deutsch Algorithm

The Hadamard gate changes the von Neumann entropy before and after
the computation; it performs an operation that goes beyond the Boolean
truth operations. It maps a state with zero von Neumann entropy to a
superposition with maximal entropy. The Deutsch algorithm [Deutsch and
Jozsa (1992)] exploits the superposition of qubits generated by Hadamard
gates and is more powerful than any classical algorithm. It determines if
an unknown function $f : \mathbf{B}^1 \to \mathbf{B}^1 : f(x) = y$ of one bit is constant or
not by calling the function one time. A classical algorithm requires two
calls. A constant function on one bit is either $f(x) = 1$ or $f(x) = 0$. A non
constant function is either the identity function $f(0) = 0$ and $f(1) = 1$ or
the flip function $f(0) = 1$ and $f(1) = 0$. The condition of the function being
constant $f(0) = f(1)$ implies that the XOR operation $\oplus$ is $f(0) \oplus f(1) = 0$
is zero. On the other hand if the function is not constant $f(0) \neq f(1)$
implies that the XOR operation $\oplus$ is $f(0) \oplus f(1) = 1$ is one. We can define
a unitary operator U_f that acts on the two qubits

$$U_f \cdot |xy\rangle = |x\rangle |f(x) \oplus y\rangle.$$

U_f can be implemented by a quantum Boolean circuit including C_{NOT} gate.
There are four different cases, for $f(x) = 0$ with the identity mapping

$$i) \quad U_f|00\rangle = |0\rangle|0 \oplus 0\rangle = |00\rangle, \quad U_f|01\rangle = |01\rangle,$$
$$U_f|10\rangle = |10\rangle, \quad U_f|11\rangle = |11\rangle$$

for $f(x) = 1$ with the permutation of all elements.

$$ii) \quad U_f|00\rangle = |0\rangle|1 \oplus 0\rangle = |01\rangle, \quad U_f|01\rangle = |00\rangle,$$
$$U_f|10\rangle = |11\rangle, \quad U_f|11\rangle = |10\rangle$$

and for a non-constant function, $f(x) = x$ corresponds to a permutation of
two elements.

$$iii) \quad U_f|00\rangle = |0\rangle|0 \oplus 0\rangle = |00\rangle, \quad U_f|01\rangle = |01\rangle,$$
$$U_f|10\rangle = |11\rangle, \quad U_f|11\rangle = |10\rangle$$

and $f(x) = \neg x$ with a permutation of two elements as well

$$vi) \quad U_f|00\rangle = |0\rangle|1 \oplus 0\rangle = |01\rangle, \quad U_f|01\rangle = |00\rangle,$$
$$U_f|10\rangle = |10\rangle, \quad U_f|11\rangle = |11\rangle.$$

There are two classes:

- No permutation $i)$ or permutation of all elements $ii)$ indicates that the
  function is constant.
- Permutation of two elements $iii)$, $iv)$ indicates that the function is non
  constant.

The Algorithm to determine if $f(x)$ is constant or not is composed of four steps. In the first step of the algorithm we build a superposition of two qubits

$$W2 \cdot |01\rangle = W_1 \cdot |0\rangle \otimes W_1 \cdot |1\rangle = \left(\frac{|0\rangle + |1\rangle}{\sqrt{2}} \right) \otimes \left(\frac{|0\rangle - |1\rangle}{\sqrt{2}} \right) =$$

$$W2 \cdot |01\rangle = \frac{1}{2} \cdot (|00\rangle - |01\rangle + |10\rangle - |11\rangle).$$

In the second step we apply the U_f, gate.

$$U_f \cdot W2 \cdot |01\rangle = U_f \left(\frac{1}{2} \cdot (|00\rangle - |01\rangle + |10\rangle - |11\rangle) \right) =$$

$$= \frac{1}{2} \cdot (U_f \cdot |00\rangle - U_f \cdot |01\rangle + U_f \cdot |10\rangle - U_f \cdot |11\rangle).$$

There are four possible outcomes. For constant function

$$i) \quad = \frac{1}{2} \cdot (|00\rangle - |01\rangle + |10\rangle - |11\rangle) = \left(\frac{|0\rangle + |1\rangle}{\sqrt{2}} \right) \otimes \left(\frac{|0\rangle - |1\rangle}{\sqrt{2}} \right),$$

$$ii) \quad = \frac{1}{2} \cdot (|01\rangle - |00\rangle + |11\rangle - |10\rangle) = \frac{1}{2} \cdot (-|00\rangle + |01\rangle - |10\rangle + |11\rangle)$$

$$= \left(\frac{-|0\rangle - |1\rangle}{\sqrt{2}} \right) \otimes \left(\frac{|0\rangle - |1\rangle}{\sqrt{2}} \right) = - \left(\frac{|0\rangle + |1\rangle}{\sqrt{2}} \right) \otimes \left(\frac{|0\rangle - |1\rangle}{\sqrt{2}} \right),$$

and for non-constant function

$$iii) \quad = \frac{1}{2} \cdot (|00\rangle - |01\rangle + |11\rangle - |10\rangle) = \frac{1}{2} \cdot (|00\rangle - |01\rangle |10\rangle + |11\rangle)$$

$$= \left(\frac{|0\rangle - |1\rangle}{\sqrt{2}} \right) \otimes \left(\frac{|0\rangle - |1\rangle}{\sqrt{2}} \right),$$

$$iv) \quad = \frac{1}{2} \cdot (|01\rangle - |00\rangle + |10\rangle - |11\rangle) = \frac{1}{2} \cdot (-|00\rangle + |01\rangle + |10\rangle - |11\rangle)$$

$$\left(\frac{-|0\rangle + |1\rangle}{\sqrt{2}} \right) \otimes \left(\frac{|0\rangle - |1\rangle}{\sqrt{2}} \right) = - \left(\frac{|0\rangle - |1\rangle}{\sqrt{2}} \right) \otimes \left(\frac{|0\rangle - |1\rangle}{\sqrt{2}} \right).$$

In the third step a Hadamard gate is applied to the first qubit

$$(W_1 \otimes I_1) \cdot U_f \cdot W2 \cdot |01\rangle. \tag{8.20}$$

There are four possible outcomes,

$$i) \quad |0\rangle \otimes \left(\frac{|0\rangle - |1\rangle}{\sqrt{2}} \right),$$

$$ii) \quad -|0\rangle \otimes \left(\frac{|0\rangle - |1\rangle}{\sqrt{2}} \right),$$

$$iii) \quad |1\rangle \otimes \left(\frac{|0\rangle - |1\rangle}{\sqrt{2}} \right),$$

$$vi) \quad -|1\rangle \otimes \left(\frac{|0\rangle - |1\rangle}{\sqrt{2}} \right).$$

In the fourth step the first qubit (that is in the pure state) is measured. It is $|0\rangle$ if the function is constant, otherwise $|1\rangle$.

Even the Deutsch algorithm is more powerful than any classical algorithm, it determines a unknown function of one bit by calling it only one time, it needs three serial steps before a measurement can take place. In the next section we generalize the working principle of the algorithm even to a more powerful algorithm.

8.7 Deutsch Jozsa Algorithm

It determines if a unknown function $f : \mathbf{B}^m \rightarrow \mathbf{B}^1 : f(x) = y$ of m bit is constant or a balanced function. In constant function of m bits for all possible $n = 2^m$ inputs the output is either 0 or 1 [Deutsch and Jozsa (1992)]. In a balanced function half of the $n = 2^m$ input values output 0 the other half output 1. A set of the input values x of the size 2^m is mapped into two subsets called 0 and 1 each of the size $2^m/2 = 2^{m-1}$. Such a two subsets could be the subset of even and odd numbers. A classical algorithm has to call the function $2^{m-1} + 1$ times in the worst case, since in the worst case the output is 2^{m-1} times 0. If in the next call it is 0 then the function is constant, otherwise it is guaranteed to be balanced. The Deutsch Jozsa algorithm needs three serial steps before a measurement can take place. We define a unitary operator U_f that acts on the $m + 1$ qubits with $x \in B^m$ and $y \in B^1$

$$U_f \cdot |x\rangle |y\rangle = |x\rangle |f(x) \oplus y\rangle.$$

The Algorithm   to determine if $f(x)$ is constant or balanced is composed of four steps. In the first step of the algorithm we build a superposition of $m + 1$ qubits

$$W_{m+1} \cdot |0^{\otimes m}\rangle |1\rangle = W_m \cdot |0^{\otimes n}\rangle \otimes W_1 \cdot |1\rangle = \frac{1}{\sqrt{2^n}} \sum_{x \in B^m} |x\rangle \otimes \left(\frac{|0\rangle - |1\rangle}{\sqrt{2}} \right).$$

The first m qubits represent a superposition over all possible states with a positive amplitude, in the last qubit one amplitude of the two possible states is negative. In the second step we apply the U_f, operator,

$$U_f \cdot W_{m+1} \cdot |0^{\otimes m}\rangle |1\rangle = U_f \cdot \left(\frac{1}{\sqrt{2^m}} \sum_{x \in B^m} |x\rangle \otimes \left(\frac{|0\rangle - |1\rangle}{\sqrt{2}} \right) \right)$$

$$= U_f \cdot \left(\frac{1}{\sqrt{2^{m+1}}} \sum_{x \in B^m} |x\rangle \otimes (|0\rangle - |1\rangle) \right)$$

$$= \frac{1}{\sqrt{2^{m+1}}} \cdot U_f \cdot \left(\sum_{x \in B^m} (|x\rangle |0\rangle - |x\rangle |1\rangle) \right)$$

$$= \frac{1}{\sqrt{2^{n+1}}} \cdot \sum_{x \in B^m} U_f \cdot (|x\rangle |0\rangle - |x\rangle |1\rangle)$$

$$= \frac{1}{\sqrt{2^{m+1}}} \cdot \sum_{x \in B^m} (U_f \cdot |x\rangle |0\rangle - U_f \cdot |x\rangle |1\rangle)$$

$$= \frac{1}{\sqrt{2^{m+1}}} \cdot \sum_{x \in B^m} U_f \cdot |x\rangle |0\rangle - \frac{1}{\sqrt{2^{m+1}}} \cdot \sum_{x \in B^m} U_f \cdot |x\rangle |1\rangle$$

$$= \frac{1}{\sqrt{2^{m+1}}} \cdot \sum_{x \in B^m} |x\rangle |f(x) \oplus 0\rangle - \frac{1}{\sqrt{2^{m+1}}} \cdot \sum_{x \in B^m} |x\rangle |f(x) \oplus 1\rangle.$$

There are three possible outcomes. For constant function

$$i) \quad \frac{1}{\sqrt{2^{m+1}}} \cdot \sum_{x \in B^m} |x\rangle |0 \oplus 0\rangle - \frac{1}{\sqrt{2^{m+1}}} \cdot \sum_{x \in B^m} |x\rangle |0 \oplus 1\rangle =$$

$$= \frac{1}{\sqrt{2^m}} \sum_{x \in B^m} |x\rangle \otimes \left(\frac{|0\rangle - |1\rangle}{\sqrt{2}} \right),$$

$$ii) \quad \frac{1}{\sqrt{2^{m+1}}} \cdot \sum_{x \in B^m} |x\rangle |1 \oplus 0\rangle - \frac{1}{\sqrt{2^{m+1}}} \cdot \sum_{x \in B^m} |x\rangle |1 \oplus 1\rangle =$$

$$= -\frac{1}{\sqrt{2^m}} \sum_{x \in B^m} |x\rangle \otimes \left(\frac{|0\rangle - |1\rangle}{\sqrt{2}} \right),$$

and for non-constant function

$$iii) \quad \frac{1}{\sqrt{2^{n+1}}} \cdot \Big(\sum_{f(x)=0} |x\rangle|0 \oplus 0\rangle - \sum_{f(x)=0} |x\rangle|0 \oplus 1\rangle +$$

$$+ \sum_{f(x)=1} |x\rangle|1 \oplus 0\rangle - \sum_{f(x)=1} |x\rangle|1 \oplus 1\rangle \Big) =$$

$$= \frac{1}{\sqrt{2^n}} \cdot \left(\sum_{f(x)=0} |x\rangle - \sum_{f(x)=1} |x\rangle \right) \oplus \left(\frac{|0\rangle - |1\rangle}{\sqrt{2}} \right) =$$

$$= \frac{1}{\sqrt{2^n}} \sum_{x \in B^m} (-1)^{f(x)} \cdot |x\rangle \otimes \left(\frac{|0\rangle - |1\rangle}{\sqrt{2}} \right).$$

The result $i)$, $ii)$ can be as well represented by $iii)$. The representation

$$\frac{1}{\sqrt{2^m}} \sum_{x \in B^m} (-1)^{f(x)} \cdot |x\rangle \otimes \left(\frac{|0\rangle - |1\rangle}{\sqrt{2}} \right) \tag{8.21}$$

is one of the most used notations in quantum computation. The value of the function $f(x)$ is encoded by $(-1)^{f(x)}$, the sign of the amplitude. The last qubit $\left(\frac{|0\rangle - |1\rangle}{\sqrt{2}} \right)$ is called auxiliary, or target bit and is ignored, so the Equation 8.21 is written as

$$\frac{1}{\sqrt{2^m}} \sum_{x \in B^m} (-1)^{f(x)} \cdot |x\rangle. \tag{8.22}$$

In the third step a Hadamard gate is applied to the first n qubits, the target qubit is ignored

$$(W_m \otimes I_1) \cdot U_f \cdot W_{m+1} \cdot |0^{\otimes n}\rangle|1\rangle \tag{8.23}$$

there are four possible outcomes,

$$i) \quad |0^{\otimes n}\rangle \otimes \left(\frac{|0\rangle - |1\rangle}{\sqrt{2}} \right)$$

$$ii) \quad -|0^{\otimes n}\rangle \otimes \left(\frac{|0\rangle - |1\rangle}{\sqrt{2}} \right)$$

$$iii) \quad W_m \cdot \frac{1}{\sqrt{2^m}} \sum_{x \in B^m} (-1)^{f(x)} \cdot |x\rangle \otimes I_1 \cdot \left(\frac{|0\rangle - |1\rangle}{\sqrt{2}} \right) =$$

$$= W_m \cdot \left(\frac{1}{\sqrt{2^m}} \sum_{x \in B^n} (-1)^{\langle z|x \rangle} \cdot |x\rangle \right) \otimes \left(\frac{|0\rangle - |1\rangle}{\sqrt{2}} \right) = |z\rangle \otimes \left(\frac{|0\rangle - |1\rangle}{\sqrt{2}} \right)$$

$$vi) \ W_m \cdot \frac{1}{\sqrt{2^m}} \sum_{x \in B^m} (-1)^{f(x)} \cdot |x\rangle \otimes I_1 \cdot \left(\frac{|0\rangle - |1\rangle}{\sqrt{2}} \right) =$$

$$= W_m \cdot \left(\frac{-1}{\sqrt{2^m}} \sum_{x \in B^n} (-1)^{\langle z|x\rangle} \cdot |x\rangle \right) \otimes \left(\frac{|0\rangle - |1\rangle}{\sqrt{2}} \right) = -|z\rangle \otimes \left(\frac{|0\rangle - |1\rangle}{\sqrt{2}} \right).$$

The results i), ii), iii) and iv) can be represented as

$$\frac{1}{2^m} \sum_{z \in B^m} \sum_{x \in B^m} (-1)^{f(x)} \cdot |z\rangle \otimes \left(\frac{|0\rangle - |1\rangle}{\sqrt{2}} \right). \tag{8.24}$$

In the fourth step the first m qubits are measured. They are $|0^{\otimes m}\rangle$ if the function is constant, for a balanced function $|z\rangle \neq |0^{\otimes m}\rangle$. The algorithm determines as well the shape of the function $f(x)$. The shape is represented by the z row or column of the W_m matrix, in which either 1 represents the value zero of the function and -1 the value one or visa versa. Before the measurement this information is represented by the minus sign of the amplitude. The first n qubits are either $|z\rangle$ or $-|z\rangle$. After the measurement the m qubits are $|z\rangle$, the information about of the amplitude is lost, $|0^{\otimes m}\rangle$ is either the constant function $f(x) = 0$ or $f(x) = 1$. The Deutsch Jozsa algorithm is build on three serial steps. It maps a state with zero von Neumann entropy to a superposition with maximal entropy, does the computation on this superposition and maps the result into a state with zero entropy. It provides three most important principles of quantum computation:

- The function $f(x)$ is represented by a quantum Boolean circuit.
- The properties of the function $f(x)$ are determined using the superposition principle and a generalized class of Fourier transform (The Hadamard transform).
- The values of the function $f(x)$ are encoded by $(-1)^{f(x)}$, the sign of the amplitude.

This principles are the basis for the two most revolutionary quantum algorithms, Shor's algorithm and Grover's algorithm. Before their introduction, some limitations of quantum computation are highlighted.

8.8 Amplitude Distribution

The register of m qubits is represented as a direct product of m qubits. It defines $n = 2^m$ dimensional Hilbert space H_n with an orthonormal basis

$|x_1\rangle, |x_1\rangle \cdots |x_n\rangle$ and a state is represented as a unit-length vector

$$|x\rangle = \omega_1 \cdot |x_1\rangle + \omega_2 \cdot |x_2\rangle + \cdots + \omega_n \cdot |x_n\rangle.$$

After the measurement, observation the state $|x\rangle$ is projected into a pure state

$$1 \cdot |x_k\rangle.$$

All the information about the amplitude distribution $\omega_1, \cdots, \omega_n$ of $|x\rangle$ is lost. Could we save this inform by coping the unit-length vector $|x\rangle$ to another state? Could we clone a state?

8.8.1   *Cloning*

To preform this task we define a copy machine. We chose one orthonormal basis state of the orthonormal basis, for example $|x_1\rangle$ and define a unitary copy operator that copies an state $|x\rangle \in H_n$ as

$$U_{copy}(|x\rangle, |x_1\rangle) = |x\rangle|x\rangle. \tag{8.25}$$

Does U_{copy} exist? For pure states U_{copy} is defined. It can be realized for example by M_{CNOT} with $|x_1\rangle = |0\rangle$ and $|x_2\rangle = |1\rangle$,

$$U_{copy}(|x_1\rangle, |x_1\rangle) = |x_1\rangle|x_1\rangle, \quad U_{copy}(|x_2\rangle, |x_1\rangle) = |x_2\rangle|x_2\rangle.$$

If the state is in a superposition

$$|x\rangle = \frac{|x_1\rangle + |x_2\rangle}{\sqrt{2}}$$

it implies that

$$U_{copy}(|x\rangle, |x_1\rangle) = |x\rangle|x\rangle = \left(\frac{|x_1\rangle + |x_2\rangle}{\sqrt{2}} \right) \otimes \left(\frac{|x_1\rangle + |x_2\rangle}{\sqrt{2}} \right) =$$

$$\frac{1}{2} \cdot (|x_1\rangle|x_1\rangle + |x_1\rangle|x_2\rangle + |x_2\rangle|x_1\rangle + |x_2\rangle|x_2\rangle).$$

Because of the linearity of U_{copy} it follows,

$$U_{copy}(|x\rangle, |x_1\rangle) = U_{copy}\left(\frac{|x_1\rangle + |x_2\rangle}{\sqrt{2}}, |x_1\rangle \right) =$$

$$U_{copy}(|x\rangle, |x_1\rangle) = U_{copy}\left(\frac{|x_1\rangle|x_1\rangle + |x_2\rangle|x_1\rangle}{\sqrt{2}} \right) =$$

$$\frac{U_{copy}(|x_1\rangle|x_1\rangle) + U_{copy}(|x_2\rangle|x_1\rangle)}{\sqrt{2}} = \frac{1}{\sqrt{2}} \cdot (|x_1\rangle|x_1\rangle + |x_2\rangle|x_2\rangle)$$

it leads to a contradiction. An operation that would produce a copy of an arbitrary quantum state is not possible, we cannot copy an unknown amplitude distribution of a state. For example we cannot copy an unknown qubit $\alpha \cdot |0\rangle + \beta \cdot |1\rangle$. The amplitude distribution is specified by the values of α and β. However we can copy the basis, $\alpha \cdot |0\rangle + \beta \cdot |1\rangle$ into the basis $\alpha \cdot |00\rangle + \beta \cdot |11\rangle$. The operator copy base U_{copy*}

$$U_{copy*}(\alpha \cdot |x_1\rangle + \beta \cdot |x_2\rangle, |x_1\rangle)$$

$$= U_{copy*}(\alpha \cdot |x_1 x_1\rangle + \beta \cdot |x_2 x_1\rangle) = \alpha \cdot |x_1 x_1\rangle + \beta \cdot |x_2 x_2\rangle \qquad (8.26)$$

exist, it can be realized by M_{CNOT}. U_{copy*} does not change the entropy of the register, U_{copy} would change it.

8.8.2 Teleportation

It is possible to teleport a qubit from one location to another using an *ebit* [Bennett *et al.* (1993)]. The two qubits in an *ebit* behave as one unit, even if the qubits are separated. This nonlocal interaction is not limited by speed of light, not mediated by the distance. The qubit is transferred from one point to another without traversing the physical space. Suppose we have two qubits that are entangled in a state $\frac{|00\rangle + |11\rangle}{\sqrt{2}}$. We separate the two qubits of the *ebit* over a distance on two places A and B.

$$\frac{|0_A\rangle|0_B\rangle + |1_A\rangle|1_B\rangle}{\sqrt{2}}. \qquad (8.27)$$

In the first step of the teleportation of the qubit $\alpha \cdot |0_A\rangle + \beta \cdot |1_A\rangle$ from the place A to the place B we interact with the corresponding *ebit*

$$(\alpha \cdot |0_A\rangle + \beta \cdot |1_A\rangle) \otimes \left(\frac{|0_A\rangle|0_B\rangle + |1_A\rangle|1_B\rangle}{\sqrt{2}} \right) \qquad (8.28)$$

$$\frac{\alpha \cdot (|0_A\rangle|0_A\rangle|0_B\rangle + |0_A\rangle|1_A\rangle|1_B\rangle) + \beta \cdot (|1_A\rangle|0_A\rangle|0_B\rangle + |1_A\rangle|1_A\rangle|1_B\rangle)}{\sqrt{2}}.$$
$$(8.29)$$

After the interaction there are two qubits on the location A and on the location B. In the second step we apply the M_{CNOT} quantum gate to the first two qubits at the location A and on the location B we do noting

$$(M_{CNOT} \otimes I_1) \cdot \frac{1}{\sqrt{2}} \cdot (\alpha \cdot (|0_A\rangle|0_A\rangle|0_B\rangle + |0_A\rangle|1_A\rangle|1_B\rangle) +$$

$$\beta \cdot (|1_A\rangle|0_A\rangle|0_B\rangle + |1_A\rangle|1_A\rangle|1_B\rangle)) =$$

$$\frac{\alpha \cdot (|0_A\rangle|0_A\rangle|0_B\rangle + |0_A\rangle|1_A\rangle|1_B\rangle) + \beta \cdot (|1_A\rangle|1_A\rangle|0_B\rangle + |1_A\rangle|0_A\rangle|1_B\rangle)}{\sqrt{2}}.$$

(8.30)

This can be rewritten as

$$\frac{\alpha \cdot |0_A\rangle \otimes (|0_A\rangle|0_B\rangle + |1_A\rangle|1_B\rangle) + \beta \cdot |1_A\rangle \otimes (|1_A\rangle|0_B\rangle + |0_A\rangle|1_B\rangle)}{\sqrt{2}}.$$

(8.31)

In the third step we apply the W_1 quantum gate to the first qubit at the location A and on the location B we do noting.

$$(W_1 \otimes I_2) \cdot \frac{1}{\sqrt{2}} \cdot (\alpha \cdot |0_A\rangle \otimes (|0_A\rangle|0_B\rangle + |1_A\rangle|1_B\rangle)) +$$

$$\beta \cdot |1_A\rangle \otimes (|1_A\rangle|0_B\rangle + |0_A\rangle|1_B\rangle))) =$$

$$\frac{1}{2} \cdot (\alpha \cdot (|0_A\rangle + 1_A\rangle) \otimes (|0_A\rangle|0_B\rangle + |1_A\rangle|1_B\rangle)) +$$

$$+\beta \cdot (|0_A\rangle - 1_A\rangle) \otimes (|1_A\rangle|0_B\rangle + |0_A\rangle|1_B\rangle))) =$$

$$\frac{1}{2} \cdot (\alpha \cdot |0_A\rangle 0_A\rangle|0_B\rangle + \alpha \cdot |0_A|1_A\rangle|1_B\rangle +$$

$$\alpha \cdot |1_A\rangle 0_A\rangle|0_B\rangle + \alpha \cdot |1_A|1_A\rangle|1_B\rangle +$$

$$\beta \cdot |0_A\rangle|1_A\rangle|0_B\rangle + \beta \cdot |0_A\rangle 0_A\rangle|1_B\rangle - \beta \cdot |0_A\rangle 1_A\rangle|0_B\rangle - \beta \cdot |0_A\rangle|0_A\rangle|1_B\rangle)$$

after rewriting the equation we get the following representation

$$\frac{1}{2} \cdot (|0_A\rangle|0_A\rangle \otimes (\alpha \cdot |0_B\rangle + \beta \cdot |1_B\rangle) + |0_A\rangle|1_A\rangle \otimes (\alpha \cdot |1_B\rangle + \beta \cdot |0_B\rangle) +$$

$$|1_A\rangle|0_A\rangle \otimes (\alpha \cdot |0_B\rangle - \beta \cdot |1_B\rangle) + |1_A\rangle|1_A\rangle \otimes (\alpha \cdot |1_B\rangle - \beta \cdot |0_B\rangle)).$$

In the fourth step a measurement of the first two qubits at the place A is done. There are four possible results; each of them has an equal probability of being measured.

$|00\rangle$ is measured the state collapses at place B to

$$\alpha \cdot |0\rangle + \beta \cdot |1\rangle$$

at place B no correction is nesseascary, the qubit described by its amplitude distribution was teleported.

$|01\rangle$ is measured the state collapses at place B to

$$\alpha \cdot |1\rangle + \beta \cdot |0\rangle$$

at place B a correction is necessary to reconstruct the teleported qubit. M_{NOT} gate is applied.

$$M_{NOT} \cdot (\alpha \cdot |1\rangle + \beta \cdot |0\rangle) = \alpha \cdot |0\rangle + \beta \cdot |1\rangle$$

$|10\rangle$ is measured the state collapses at place B to

$$\alpha \cdot |0\rangle - \beta \cdot |1\rangle$$

at place B a correction is necessary to reconstruct the teleported qubit. Z gate is applied.

$$Z = \begin{pmatrix} 1 & 0 \\ 0 & -1 \end{pmatrix} \tag{8.32}$$

$$Z \cdot (\alpha \cdot |0\rangle - \beta \cdot |1\rangle) = \alpha \cdot |0\rangle + \beta \cdot |1\rangle$$

$|11\rangle$ is measured the state collapses at place B to

$$\alpha \cdot |1\rangle - \beta \cdot |0\rangle$$

at place B a correction is necessary to reconstruct the teleported qubit. M_{NOT} gate and then the Z gate is applied.

$$Z \cdot M_{NOT} \cdot (\alpha \cdot |1\rangle - \beta \cdot |0\rangle) = \alpha \cdot |0\rangle + \beta \cdot |1\rangle.$$

This transformation is also called the Y gate

$$Y = Z \cdot M_{NOT} = \begin{pmatrix} 1 & 0 \\ 0 & -1 \end{pmatrix} \cdot \begin{pmatrix} 0 & 1 \\ 1 & 0 \end{pmatrix} = \begin{pmatrix} 0 & 1 \\ -1 & 0 \end{pmatrix}. \tag{8.33}$$

For the teleportation of qubits classical communication is required. To indicate how to reconstruct one qubit two bits have to be send over a classical channel, since one teleported qubit can take four different superpositions. It follows that an *ebit* cannot be used to send or teleport information, additionally a classical channel is required.

8.9 Geometric Operations

A unitary operator performs a rotation or a reflection of a state represented by a unit length vector in a Hilbert space. States may be equivalent if they differ only by the relative amplitudes, different states when measured are always equal.

Equivalent states   Two equivalent states represent the same state when a measurement is preformed, but they can have behave differently during the unitary evolution. Two states $|x\rangle$ and $|y\rangle$ are equivalent $|x\rangle \equiv |y\rangle$ if

$$|x\rangle = e^{i \cdot \theta} \cdot |y\rangle \qquad (8.34)$$

with

$$e^{i \cdot \theta} = \cos \theta + i \cdot \sin \theta. \qquad (8.35)$$

For example $|0\rangle$ and $-|0\rangle$ are two equivalent states

$$|0\rangle \equiv -|0\rangle \Leftrightarrow |0\rangle = -e^{i \cdot \pi} \cdot |0\rangle \qquad (8.36)$$

for $\theta = \pi$

$$e^{i \cdot \pi} = \cos \pi + i \cdot \sin \pi = -1.$$

Other examples are

$$|0\rangle \equiv i \cdot |0\rangle \Leftrightarrow |0\rangle = i \cdot e^{i \cdot -\pi/2} \cdot |0\rangle \qquad (8.37)$$

for $\theta = -\pi/2$

$$e^{i \cdot -\pi/2} = \cos -\pi/2 + i \cdot \sin -\pi/2 = -i$$

and

$$|0\rangle \equiv \frac{|0\rangle + i \cdot |0\rangle}{\sqrt{2}} \Leftrightarrow |0\rangle = \frac{1 + i}{\sqrt{2}} \cdot e^{i \cdot \pi/4} \cdot |0\rangle \qquad (8.38)$$

for $\theta = -\pi/4$

$$e^{i \cdot (-\pi/4)} = \cos(-\pi/4) + i \cdot \sin(-\pi/4) = \frac{1 - i}{\sqrt{2}}$$

$$\frac{1 - i}{\sqrt{2}} \cdot \frac{1 + i}{\sqrt{2}} = \frac{2}{2} = 1.$$

However the following two state is not equal nor not equivalent

$$\frac{|0\rangle + |1\rangle}{\sqrt{2}} \neq \frac{|0\rangle - |1\rangle}{\sqrt{2}}.$$

They are the reflection of each other.

Reflection An example of a reflection operator is the Z operator

$$Z = \begin{pmatrix} 1 & 0 \\ 0 & -1 \end{pmatrix}.$$

It preforms a reflection on the basis defined by $|0\rangle$. The Z gate is a special case of the phase gate

$$P = \begin{pmatrix} 1 & 0 \\ 0 & e^{i \cdot \theta} \end{pmatrix} \tag{8.39}$$

with $\theta = \pi$. A phase gate alters the relative amplitudes but represents the same state value when a measurement is preformed and can be used together with the M_{NOT} gate

$$\begin{pmatrix} e^{i \cdot \theta} & 0 \\ 0 & e^{i \cdot \theta} \end{pmatrix} = \begin{pmatrix} 1 & 0 \\ 0 & e^{i \cdot \theta} \end{pmatrix} \cdot \begin{pmatrix} 0 & 1 \\ 1 & 0 \end{pmatrix} \cdot \begin{pmatrix} 1 & 0 \\ 0 & e^{-i \cdot \theta} \end{pmatrix}. \tag{8.40}$$

Rotation A rotation by an angle α is represented by the unitary operator R

$$R = \begin{pmatrix} \cos\alpha & -\sin\alpha \\ \sin\alpha & \cos\alpha \end{pmatrix}. \tag{8.41}$$

It can be shown that a unitary transformation is a rotation of $n = 2^m$ Hilbert space [Rieffel and Polak (2011)].

Changing the basis In data analysis the Karhunen-Loève transformation rotates the coordinate system in such a way that the covariance matrix is diagonal, means each dimension is uncorrelated. In quantum computation a unitary transformation is equivalent to a change of the basis.

Closure relation For a basis an orthonormal basis

$$|x_1\rangle, |x_1\rangle, \cdots |x_n\rangle$$

the identity operator is represented as

$$\sum_{i=1}^{n} |x_i\rangle\langle x_i|. \tag{8.42}$$

With the inner product

$$\langle x|x_i\rangle = \omega_i$$

an state $|x\rangle$ can be represented as

$$|x\rangle = I \cdot |x\rangle = \left(\sum_{i=1}^{n} |x_i\rangle\langle x_i| \right) |x\rangle = \sum_{i=1}^{n} |x_i\rangle\langle x_i|x\rangle = \sum_{i=1}^{n} \omega_i \cdot |x_i\rangle. \tag{8.43}$$

An operator A can be represented using the closure relation as

$$A = I \cdot A \cdot I = \left(\sum_{i=1}^{n} |x_i\rangle\langle x_i| \right) \cdot A \cdot \left(\sum_{j=1}^{n} |x_j\rangle\langle x_j| \right) = \sum_{i,j} \langle x_i|A \cdot |x_j\rangle \cdot |x_i\rangle\langle x_j|$$

(8.44)

with $a_{ij} = \langle x_i|A \cdot |x_j\rangle$ being the number of the operator matrix A at row i and column j for the base $|x_1\rangle, |x_1\rangle. \cdots |x_n\rangle$. For a different orthonormal basis

$$|y_1\rangle, |y_1\rangle. \cdots |y_n\rangle$$

the operator A is represented as $a'_{ij} = \langle y_i|A \cdot |y_j\rangle$

$$A' = \begin{pmatrix} \langle y_1|A \cdot |y_1\rangle & \langle y_1|A \cdot |y_2\rangle & \cdots & \langle y_1|A \cdot |y_n\rangle \\ \langle y_2|A \cdot |y_1\rangle & \langle y_2|A \cdot |y_2\rangle & \cdots & \langle y_2|A \cdot |y_n\rangle \\ \vdots & \vdots & \ddots & \vdots \\ \langle y_n|A \cdot |y_1\rangle & \langle y_n|A \cdot |y_2\rangle & \cdots & \langle y_n|A \cdot |y_n\rangle \end{pmatrix}.$$

(8.45)

The change of the basis $|x_i\rangle$ to $y_i\rangle$ is represented by the operator U

$$U = \begin{pmatrix} \langle y_1|x_1\rangle & \langle y_1|x_2\rangle & \cdots & \langle y_1|x_n\rangle \\ \langle y_2|x_1\rangle & \langle y_2|x_2\rangle & \cdots & \langle y_2|x_n\rangle \\ \vdots & \vdots & \ddots & \vdots \\ \langle y_n|x_1\rangle & \langle y_n|x_2\rangle & \cdots & \langle y_n|x_n\rangle \end{pmatrix}.$$

(8.46)

A vector $|x\rangle$ is changed to the basis $|y_i\rangle$ by the basis change

$$|x'\rangle = U \cdot |x\rangle$$

(8.47)

$|x'\rangle$ is the same vector as $|x\rangle$ represented in the basis $|y_i\rangle$. This method is also called the *unitary transformation*. If we apply an operator A to $|x\rangle$ and represent the result in the basis $|y_i\rangle$ we do the following operation

$$|z\rangle = U \cdot A \cdot |x\rangle = U \cdot A \cdot U^* \cdot U \cdot |x\rangle.$$

(8.48)

The operator A is represented in the new basis as

$$A' = U \cdot A \cdot U^*.$$

(8.49)

In the following example in H_2 we change from the basis

$$|0\rangle = \begin{pmatrix} 1 \\ 0 \end{pmatrix}, \quad |1\rangle = \begin{pmatrix} 0 \\ 1 \end{pmatrix}$$

to the the Hadarmad basis

$$|+\rangle = \begin{pmatrix} \frac{1}{\sqrt{2}} \\ \frac{1}{\sqrt{2}} \end{pmatrix}, \quad |-\rangle = \begin{pmatrix} \frac{1}{\sqrt{2}} \\ \frac{-1}{\sqrt{2}} \end{pmatrix}.$$

The change of the basis $|0\rangle, |1\rangle$ to $|+\rangle, |-\rangle$ is represented by the operator U

$$U = \begin{pmatrix} \langle+|0\rangle & \langle+|1\rangle \\ \langle-|0\rangle & \langle-|1\rangle \end{pmatrix} = \begin{pmatrix} \frac{1}{\sqrt{2}} & \frac{1}{\sqrt{2}} \\ \frac{1}{\sqrt{2}} & \frac{-1}{\sqrt{2}} \end{pmatrix} = W_1. \tag{8.50}$$

The M_{NOT} gate

$$M_{NOT} = \begin{pmatrix} 0 & 1 \\ 1 & 0 \end{pmatrix}$$

is represented in the basis $|+\rangle, |-\rangle$ as

$$M'_{NOT} = U \cdot M_{NOT} \cdot U^* = \begin{pmatrix} \frac{1}{\sqrt{2}} & \frac{1}{\sqrt{2}} \\ \frac{1}{\sqrt{2}} & \frac{-1}{\sqrt{2}} \end{pmatrix} \cdot \begin{pmatrix} 0 & 1 \\ 1 & 0 \end{pmatrix} \cdot \begin{pmatrix} \frac{1}{\sqrt{2}} & \frac{1}{\sqrt{2}} \\ \frac{1}{\sqrt{2}} & \frac{-1}{\sqrt{2}} \end{pmatrix} = \begin{pmatrix} 1 & 0 \\ 0 & -1 \end{pmatrix}. \tag{8.51}$$

A base change corresponds to the unitary transformation.

In quantum physics there are two models:

- The Heisenberg picture, the state vectors are time-independent, the basis change in time.
- The Schrödinger picture, the states evolve in time, the basis does not change in time.

Both approaches are similar and depend on observer. Either he is inside the coordinate system or outside. Either the sun is rotating around the earth, or the earth is rotating around the sun. In quantum computation the Schrödinge picture is used.

Chapter 9

Periodicity

9.1 Fourier Transform

A way to solve a problem is to transform it into some other problem, for which a solution is known. Transformations are applied to signals to obtain further information from the signal that is not readily available in the raw signal. One such transformation is the Fourier transform. Many signals are represented in the time domain, and some additional information is present in the frequency content. A Fourier transform maps the signal from the time domain to the frequency domain. The frequency is the number of occurrences of a repeating event per unit time. The period is the duration of one cycle of an event, and the period is the reciprocal of the frequency f. For example, if we count 40 events in two seconds, then the frequency is

$$\frac{40}{2\ s} = \frac{20}{1\ s} = 20\ \frac{1}{s} = 20\ hertz$$

then the period is

$$T = p = \frac{1}{20}s.$$

A repeated event can be a rotation, oscillation, or a periodic wave. For periodic waves, one period corresponds to the time in which a full cycle of a wave passes. A cycle is represented by the wavelength. The velocity v of the wave is represented by the wavelength λ divided by the period p. Because the frequency f is the inverse of the period, we can represent the velocity as

$$v = \frac{\lambda}{p} = \lambda \cdot f \tag{9.1}$$

and the frequency as

$$f = \frac{1}{T} = \frac{1}{p} = \frac{v}{\lambda}. \tag{9.2}$$

145

If something changes rapidly, then we say that it has a high frequency. If it does not change rapidly, i.e., it changes smoothly, we say that it has a low frequency. The Fourier transform changes a signal from the time domain $x(t) \in \mathbf{C}$ to the frequency domain $X(f) \in \mathbf{C}$. The representation of the signal $x(t)$ in the frequency domain $X(f)$ is the frequency spectrum. This representation has the amplitude or phase plotted versus the frequency. In a wave, the amplitude describes the magnitude of change and the phase of the fraction of the wave cycle that has elapsed relative to the origin. The complex number $X(f)$ conveys both the amplitude and phase of the frequency f. The absolute value $|X(f)|$ represents the amplitude of the frequency f. The phase is represented by the argument of $X(f)$, $arg(X(f))$. For a complex number

$$z = x + i \cdot y = |z| \cdot e^{i \cdot \theta} \tag{9.3}$$

θ is the phase

$$\theta = arg(z) = tan^{-1}\left(\frac{y}{x}\right) \tag{9.4}$$

and

$$|z| = \sqrt{x^2 + y^2} \tag{9.5}$$

phase is an angle (radians), and that negative phase corresponds to positive time delay of the wave. For example if we shift the cosines function by the angle θ

$$\cos(x) \rightarrow \cos(x - \theta)$$

the phase of the cosines wave is shifted. It follows as well that

$$\sin(x) = \cos(x - \pi/2). \tag{9.6}$$

The Fourier transform of $x(t)$ is

$$X(f) = \int_{-\infty}^{\infty} x(t) \cdot e^{-2 \cdot \pi \cdot i \cdot t \cdot f} dt \tag{9.7}$$

t stands for time and f for frequency. The signal $x(t)$ is multiplied with an exponential term at some certain frequency f, and then integrated over all times. The frequency spectrum of a real valued signal is always symmetric, since the symmetric part is exactly a mirror image of the first part the second part is usually not shown. The inverse Fourier transform of $X(f)$ is

$$x(t) = \int_{-\infty}^{\infty} X(f) \cdot e^{2 \cdot \pi \cdot i \cdot t \cdot f} df. \tag{9.8}$$

9.2 Discrete Fourier Transform

The discrete Fourier transforms discrete time-based or space-based data into the frequency sequency-based data. Given a seqience α

$$\alpha_t : [1, 2, \cdots, n] \to C. \tag{9.9}$$

The discrete Fourier transform produces a sequence ω:

$$\omega_f : [1, 2, \cdots, n] \to C. \tag{9.10}$$

The discrete Fourier transform of $\alpha(t)$ is

$$\omega_f = \frac{1}{\sqrt{n}} \cdot \sum_{t=1}^{n} \alpha_t \cdot e^{-2 \cdot \pi \cdot i \cdot (t-1) \cdot \frac{(f-1)}{n}} \tag{9.11}$$

its wave frequency is $\frac{(f-1)}{n}$ events per sample. The inverse discrete Fourier transform of ω_f is

$$\alpha_t = \frac{1}{\sqrt{n}} \cdot \sum_{f=1}^{n} \omega_f \cdot e^{2 \cdot \pi \cdot i \cdot (t-1) \cdot \frac{(f-1)}{n}}. \tag{9.12}$$

Discrete Fourier transform (DFT) can be seen as a linear transform F talking the column vector α to a column vector ω

$$\omega = F \cdot \alpha \tag{9.13}$$

$$\begin{pmatrix} \omega_1 \\ \omega_2 \\ \vdots \\ \omega_n \end{pmatrix} = F \cdot \alpha =$$

$$= \frac{1}{\sqrt{n}} \cdot \begin{pmatrix} e^{-2 \cdot \pi \cdot i \cdot (0) \cdot \frac{(0)}{n}} & e^{-2 \cdot \pi \cdot i \cdot (0) \cdot \frac{(1)}{n}} & \cdots & e^{-2 \cdot \pi \cdot i \cdot (0) \cdot \frac{(n-1)}{n}} \\ e^{-2 \cdot \pi \cdot i \cdot (1) \cdot \frac{(0)}{n}} & e^{-2 \cdot \pi \cdot i \cdot (1) \cdot \frac{(1)}{n}} & \cdots & e^{-2 \cdot \pi \cdot i \cdot (1) \cdot \frac{(n-1)}{n}} \\ \vdots & \vdots & \ddots & \vdots \\ e^{-2 \cdot \pi \cdot i \cdot (n-1) \cdot \frac{(0)}{n}} & e^{-2 \cdot \pi \cdot i \cdot (n-1) \cdot \frac{(1)}{n}} & \cdots & e^{-2 \cdot \pi \cdot i \cdot (n) \cdot \frac{(n-1)}{n}} \end{pmatrix} \cdot \begin{pmatrix} \alpha_1 \\ \alpha_2 \\ \vdots \\ \alpha_n \end{pmatrix} \tag{9.14}$$

and the inverse discrete Fourier transform (IDFT) can be seen as a linear transform IF talking the column vector ω to a column vector α

$$\alpha = IF \cdot \omega \tag{9.15}$$

$$
\begin{pmatrix} \alpha_1 \\ \alpha_2 \\ \vdots \\ \alpha_n \end{pmatrix} = \frac{1}{\sqrt{n}} \cdot \begin{pmatrix} e^{2 \cdot \pi \cdot i \cdot (0) \cdot \frac{(0)}{n}} & e^{2 \cdot \pi \cdot i \cdot (0) \cdot \frac{(1)}{n}} & \cdots & e^{2 \cdot \pi \cdot i \cdot (0) \cdot \frac{(n-1)}{n}} \\ e^{2 \cdot \pi \cdot i \cdot (1) \cdot \frac{(0)}{n}} & e^{2 \cdot \pi \cdot i \cdot (1) \cdot \frac{(1)}{n}} & \cdots & e^{2 \cdot \pi \cdot i \cdot (1) \cdot \frac{(n-1)}{n}} \\ \vdots & \vdots & \ddots & \vdots \\ e^{2 \cdot \pi \cdot i \cdot (n-1) \cdot \frac{(0)}{n}} & e^{2 \cdot \pi \cdot i \cdot (n-1) \cdot \frac{(1)}{n}} & \cdots & e^{2 \cdot \pi \cdot i \cdot (n) \cdot \frac{(n-1)}{n}} \end{pmatrix} \cdot \begin{pmatrix} \omega_1 \\ \omega_2 \\ \vdots \\ \omega_n \end{pmatrix}.
$$
$$(9.16)$$

The the matrix F can be represented as a Vandermonde matrix using the nth root of unity. An nth root of unity is a complex number ζ satisfying the equation

$$\zeta^n = 1 \tag{9.17}$$

with $n = 1, 2, 3, \cdots, n - 1$ being a a positive integer, for example

$$\zeta_n = e^{-2 \cdot \pi \cdot i \cdot \frac{1}{n}} = \cos\left(2 \cdot \pi \cdot \frac{1}{n}\right) - i \cdot \sin\left(2 \cdot \pi \cdot \frac{1}{n}\right) \tag{9.18}$$

with exponential of the complex number

$$e^{i \cdot x} = \cos(x) + i \cdot \sin(x) \tag{9.19}$$

and

$$e^{-i \cdot x} = \cos(x) - i \cdot \sin(x). \tag{9.20}$$

With $\zeta_n = e^{-2 \cdot \pi \cdot i \cdot \frac{1}{n}}$ the matrix F can be represented as

$$
F = \frac{1}{\sqrt{n}} \cdot \begin{pmatrix} \zeta_n^{(0) \cdot (0)} & \zeta_n^{(0) \cdot (1)} & \cdots & \zeta_n^{(0) \cdot (n-1)} \\ \zeta_n^{(1) \cdot (0)} & \zeta_n^{(1) \cdot (1)} & \cdots & \zeta_n^{(1) \cdot (n-1)} \\ \vdots & \vdots & \ddots & \vdots \\ \zeta_n^{(n-1) \cdot (0)} & \zeta_n^{(n-1) \cdot (1)} & \cdots & \zeta_n^{(n-1) \cdot (n-1)} \end{pmatrix}. \tag{9.21}
$$

A Vandermonde matrix V is a matrix with the terms of a geometric progression in each row

$$
V = \begin{pmatrix} 1 & \gamma_1 & \gamma_1^2 & \gamma_1^3 & \cdots & \gamma_1^{(n-1)} \\ 1 & \gamma_2 & \gamma_2^2 & \gamma_2^3 & \cdots & \gamma_2^{(n-1)} \\ 1 & \gamma_3 & \gamma_3^2 & \gamma_3^3 & \cdots & \gamma_3^{(n-1)} \\ \vdots & \vdots & \ddots & \vdots & \vdots & \vdots \\ 1 & \gamma_n & \gamma_n^2 & \gamma_n^3 & \cdots & \gamma_n^{(n-1)} \end{pmatrix}. \tag{9.22}
$$

F is a Vandermonde matrix, it can be represented as

$$
F = \frac{1}{\sqrt{n}} \cdot \begin{pmatrix} 1 & 1 & 1 & 1 & \cdots & 1 \\ 1 & \zeta_n & \zeta_n^2 & \zeta_n^3 & \cdots & \zeta_n^{(n-1)} \\ 1 & \zeta_n^2 & \zeta_n^4 & \zeta_n^6 & \cdots & \zeta_n^{2 \cdot (n-1)} \\ 1 & \zeta_n^3 & \zeta_n^6 & \zeta_n^9 & \cdots & \zeta_n^{3 \cdot (n-1)} \\ \vdots & \vdots & \ddots & \vdots & \ddots & \vdots \\ 1 & \zeta_n^{(n-1)} & \zeta_n^{2 \cdot (n-1)} & \zeta_n^{3 \cdot (n-1)} & \cdots & \zeta_n^{(n-1) \cdot (n-1)} \end{pmatrix}. \tag{9.23}
$$

The matrix F, also called DFT matrix is unitary

$$F^{-1} = F^* = IF. \qquad (9.24)$$

Because F is unitary it implies that the length of a vector is preserved as stated in Parseval's theorem

$$\|\omega\| = \|F \cdot \alpha\| = \|\alpha\|. \qquad (9.25)$$

9.2.1 Example

We generates a list with $256 = 2^8$ elements containing a periodic signal α_t with Gaussian random noise from the interval $[-0.5, 0.5]$.

$$\alpha_t = sin\left(\frac{50 \cdot t \cdot 2 \cdot \cdot \pi}{256}\right) + noise.$$

The represented data looks random (see Figure 9.1).

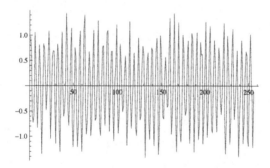

Fig. 9.1 A periodic signal α_t with with Gaussian random noise.

The discrete Fourier transform ω_f of the real valued signal α_t is symmetric. It shows a strong peak at $50+1$ and a symmetric peak at $256-50+1$ representing the frequency component of the signal α_t (see Figure 9.2). The zero frequency term represents the DC average and appears at position 1 instead at the position 0.

A filter that reduces Gaussian noise based on DFT removes frequencies with low amplitude of ω_f and performs inverse discrete Fourier transform.

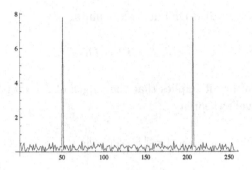

Fig. 9.2   The discrete Fourier transform ω_f . It shows a strong peak at $50 + 1$ and a symmetric peak at $256 - 50 + 1$ representing the frequency component of the signal α_t. The zero frequency term represents the DC average and appears at position 1 instead at the position 0.

9.3   Quantum Fourier Transform

For $n = 2^m$ F performs a Quantum Fourier Transform (QFT) on a state $|x\rangle$ of m qubits in a n-dimensional Hilbert space H_n

$$|x\rangle = \alpha_1 \cdot |x_1\rangle + \alpha_2 \cdot |x_2\rangle + \cdots + \alpha_n \cdot |x_n\rangle.$$

The QFT is defined as

$$|y\rangle = F_m \cdot |x\rangle \qquad (9.26)$$

with

$$|y\rangle = \omega_1 \cdot |x_1\rangle + \omega_2 \cdot |x_2\rangle + \cdots + \omega_n \cdot |x_n\rangle$$

and inverse QFT is defined as

$$|x\rangle = IF_m \cdot |y\rangle = F_m^* \cdot |y\rangle. \qquad (9.27)$$

For one qubit $m = 1$, $n = 2$

$$\zeta_2 = e^{-2\cdot\pi\cdot i\cdot\frac{1}{2}} = e^{-\pi\cdot i} = e^{\pi\cdot i} = -1$$

and the QFT F_1 is

$$F_1 = \frac{1}{\sqrt{2}} \cdot \begin{pmatrix} 1 & 1 \\ 1 & \zeta_2 \end{pmatrix} = \frac{1}{\sqrt{2}} \cdot \begin{pmatrix} 1 & 1 \\ 1 & -1 \end{pmatrix} = W_1. \qquad (9.28)$$

F_1 is just a Hadamard transform W_1 of one qubit in Hilbert space H_2. A Hadamard transform of m qubits in Hilbert space H_n with $n = 2^m$ is equivalent to a multidimensional two size discrete Fourier transforms F_1

$$W_m = \bigotimes^m W_1 = \bigotimes^m F_1 = F_1 \otimes F_1 \cdots \otimes F_1. \qquad (9.29)$$

For two qubits $m = 2$, $n = 4$

$$\zeta_4 = e^{-2\cdot\pi\cdot i\cdot\frac{1}{4}} = e^{-\pi\cdot i\cdot\frac{1}{2}} = -i$$

and the QFT F_2 is

$$F_2 = \frac{1}{\sqrt{4}} \cdot \begin{pmatrix} 1 & 1 & 1 & 1 \\ 1 & \zeta_4 & \zeta_4^2 & \zeta_4^3 \\ 1 & \zeta_4^2 & \zeta_4^4 & \zeta_4^6 \\ 1 & \zeta_4^3 & \zeta_4^6 & \zeta_4^9 \end{pmatrix} = \frac{1}{2} \cdot \begin{pmatrix} 1 & 1 & 1 & 1 \\ 1 & -i & -1 & i \\ 1 & -1 & 1 & -1 \\ 1 & i & -1 & -i \end{pmatrix} \tag{9.30}$$

and the inverse QFT IF_2 is

$$IF_2 = F_2^* = \frac{1}{2} \cdot \begin{pmatrix} 1 & 1 & 1 & 1 \\ 1 & i & -1 & -i \\ 1 & -1 & 1 & -1 \\ 1 & -i & -1 & i \end{pmatrix}. \tag{9.31}$$

For three qubits $m = 3$, $n = 8$

$$\zeta_8 = e^{-2\cdot\pi\cdot i\cdot\frac{1}{8}} = e^{-\pi\cdot i\cdot\frac{1}{4}} = \frac{1-i}{\sqrt{2}}$$

$$F_3 = \frac{1}{\sqrt{8}} \cdot \begin{pmatrix} 1 & 1 & 1 & 1 & 1 & 1 & 1 & 1 \\ 1 & \zeta_8^1 & \zeta_8^2 & \zeta_8^3 & \zeta_8^4 & \zeta_8^5 & \zeta_8^6 & \zeta_8^7 \\ 1 & \zeta_8^2 & \zeta_8^4 & \zeta_8^6 & \zeta_8^8 & \zeta_8^{10} & \zeta_8^{12} & \zeta_8^{14} \\ 1 & \zeta_8^3 & \zeta_8^6 & \zeta_8^9 & \zeta_8^{12} & \zeta_8^{15} & \zeta_8^{18} & \zeta_8^{21} \\ 1 & \zeta_8^4 & \zeta_8^8 & \zeta_8^{12} & \zeta_8^{16} & \zeta_8^{20} & \zeta_8^{24} & \zeta_8^{28} \\ 1 & \zeta_8^5 & \zeta_8^{10} & \zeta_8^{15} & \zeta_8^{20} & \zeta_8^{25} & \zeta_8^{30} & \zeta_8^{35} \\ 1 & \zeta_8^6 & \zeta_8^{12} & \zeta_8^{18} & \zeta_8^{24} & \zeta_8^{30} & \zeta_8^{36} & \zeta_8^{42} \\ 1 & \zeta_8^7 & \zeta_8^{14} & \zeta_8^{21} & \zeta_8^{28} & \zeta_8^{35} & \zeta_8^{42} & \zeta_8^{49} \end{pmatrix} \tag{9.32}$$

$$F_3 = \frac{1}{\sqrt{8}} \cdot \begin{pmatrix} 1 & 1 & 1 & 1 & 1 & 1 & 1 & 1 \\ 1 & e^{-\pi\cdot i\cdot\frac{1}{4}} & -i & e^{-\pi\cdot i\cdot\frac{3}{4}} & -1 & e^{\pi\cdot i\cdot\frac{3}{4}} & i & e^{\pi\cdot i\cdot\frac{1}{4}} \\ 1 & -i & -1 & i & 1 & -i & -1 & i \\ 1 & e^{-\pi\cdot i\cdot\frac{3}{4}} & i & e^{-\pi\cdot i\cdot\frac{1}{4}} & -1 & e^{\pi\cdot i\cdot\frac{1}{4}} & i & e^{\pi\cdot i\cdot\frac{3}{4}} \\ 1 & -1 & 1 & -1 & 1 & -1 & 1 & -1 \\ 1 & e^{\pi\cdot i\cdot\frac{3}{4}} & -i & e^{\pi\cdot i\cdot\frac{1}{4}} & -1 & e^{-\pi\cdot i\cdot\frac{1}{4}} & i & e^{-\pi\cdot i\cdot\frac{3}{4}} \\ 1 & i & -1 & -i & 1 & i & -1 & -i \\ 1 & e^{\pi\cdot i\cdot\frac{1}{4}} & i & e^{\pi\cdot i\cdot\frac{3}{4}} & -1 & e^{-\pi\cdot i\cdot\frac{3}{4}} & -i & e^{-\pi\cdot i\cdot\frac{1}{4}} \end{pmatrix}. \tag{9.33}$$

The first row of F_3 is the DC average of the amplitude of the input state when measured, the following rows represent the AC (difference) of the input state amplitudes. The QFT operation on the state $|x\rangle$ is

$$
\begin{pmatrix} \omega_1 \\ \omega_2 \\ \omega_3 \\ \omega_4 \\ \omega_5 \\ \omega_6 \\ \omega_7 \\ \omega_8 \end{pmatrix} = \frac{1}{\sqrt{8}} \cdot \begin{pmatrix}
1 & 1 & 1 & 1 & 1 & 1 & 1 & 1 \\
1 & \frac{1-i}{\sqrt{2}} & -i & \frac{-1-i}{\sqrt{2}} & -1 & \frac{-1+i}{\sqrt{2}} & i & \frac{1+i}{\sqrt{2}} \\
1 & -i & -1 & i & 1 & -i & -1 & i \\
1 & \frac{-1-i}{\sqrt{2}} & -i & \frac{1-i}{\sqrt{2}} & -1 & \frac{1+i}{\sqrt{2}} & i & \frac{-1+i}{\sqrt{2}} \\
1 & -1 & 1 & -1 & 1 & -1 & 1 & -1 \\
1 & \frac{-1+i}{\sqrt{2}} & -i & \frac{1+i}{\sqrt{2}} & -1 & \frac{1-i}{\sqrt{2}} & i & \frac{-1-i}{\sqrt{2}} \\
1 & i & -1 & -i & 1 & i & -1 & -i \\
1 & \frac{1+i}{\sqrt{2}} & -i & \frac{-1+i}{\sqrt{2}} & -1 & \frac{-1-i}{\sqrt{2}} & i & \frac{1-i}{\sqrt{2}}
\end{pmatrix} \cdot \begin{pmatrix} \alpha_1 \\ \alpha_2 \\ \alpha_3 \\ \alpha_4 \\ \alpha_5 \\ \alpha_6 \\ \alpha_7 \\ \alpha_8 \end{pmatrix} \quad (9.34)
$$

F_3 can be represented as a sum of a real and imaginary matrix.

$$
F3 = \frac{1}{\sqrt{8}} \cdot \begin{pmatrix}
1 & 1 & 1 & 1 & 1 & 1 & 1 & 1 \\
1 & \frac{1}{\sqrt{2}} & 0 & \frac{-1}{\sqrt{2}} & -1 & \frac{-1}{\sqrt{2}} & 0 & \frac{1}{\sqrt{2}} \\
1 & 0 & -1 & 0 & 1 & 0 & -1 & 0 \\
1 & \frac{-1}{\sqrt{2}} & 0 & \frac{1}{\sqrt{2}} & -1 & \frac{1}{\sqrt{2}} & 0 & \frac{-1}{\sqrt{2}} \\
1 & -1 & 1 & -1 & 1 & -1 & 1 & -1 \\
1 & \frac{-1}{\sqrt{2}} & 0 & \frac{1}{\sqrt{2}} & -1 & \frac{1}{\sqrt{2}} & 0 & \frac{-1}{\sqrt{2}} \\
1 & 0 & -1 & 0 & 1 & 0 & -1 & 0 \\
1 & \frac{1}{\sqrt{2}} & 0 & \frac{-1}{\sqrt{2}} & -1 & \frac{-1}{\sqrt{2}} & 0 & \frac{1}{\sqrt{2}}
\end{pmatrix} + \quad (9.35)
$$

$$
+ \frac{1}{\sqrt{8}} \cdot \begin{pmatrix}
0 & 0 & 0 & 0 & 0 & 0 & 0 & 0 \\
0 & \frac{-i}{\sqrt{2}} & -i & \frac{-i}{\sqrt{2}} & 0 & \frac{i}{\sqrt{2}} & i & \frac{i}{\sqrt{2}} \\
0 & -i & 0 & i & 0 & -i & 0 & i \\
0 & \frac{-i}{\sqrt{2}} & -i & \frac{-i}{\sqrt{2}} & 0 & \frac{i}{\sqrt{2}} & i & \frac{-i}{\sqrt{2}} \\
0 & 0 & 0 & 0 & 0 & 0 & 0 & 0 \\
0 & \frac{i}{\sqrt{2}} & -i & \frac{i}{\sqrt{2}} & 0 & \frac{-i}{\sqrt{2}} & i & \frac{-i}{\sqrt{2}} \\
0 & i & 0 & -i & 0 & i & 0 & -i \\
0 & \frac{i}{\sqrt{2}} & -i & \frac{i}{\sqrt{2}} & 0 & \frac{-i}{\sqrt{2}} & i & \frac{-i}{\sqrt{2}}
\end{pmatrix}. \quad (9.36)
$$

The first row measures the DC, the second row fractional frequency of the amplitude of the input state of $1/8$, the third of $1/4 = 2/8$, the fourth of $3/8$, the fifth of $1/2 = 4/8$, the sixth of $5/8$, the seventh of $3/4 = 6/8$ and the eighth of $7/8$ or equivalently the fractional frequency of $-1/8$. The resulting frequency of the amplitude vector ω of the state $|y\rangle$ for a real valued amplitude vector α of the state $|x\rangle$ is symmetric, $\omega_2 = \omega_6$, $\omega_3 = \omega_7$ and $\omega_4 = \omega_8$.

9.4 FFT

The Hadamard transform H_m is composed of multidimensional two size discrete Fourier transforms F_1, it is a subset of DFT [Cormen *et al.* (2001)]. DFT F_m is related to the Hadamard transform but cannot be decomposed as a tensor product of 2×2 matrices. Any operator can be represented by single qubit gates together with M_{CNOT} gates, however their number can grow exponential in the number if qubits [Rieffel and Polak (2011)]. An efficient decomposition is represented by the fast Fourier transform (FFT). Carl Friedrich Gauss invented the FFT algorithm around 1805. However because the corresponding article was written in Latin it did not gain any popularity. FFT was several times rediscovered and it was made popular by J. W. Cooley and J. W. Tukey in 1965 [Cormen *et al.* (2001)]. The original algorithm is limited to the DFT matrix of the size $2^m \times 2^m$, power of two. Variants of the algorithm for the case in which the size of the matrix is not power of two exist. The original algorithm decomposes F_m recursively.

$$F_{m+1} = \frac{1}{\sqrt{2}} \cdot \begin{pmatrix} I_m & D_m \\ I_m & -D_m \end{pmatrix} \cdot \begin{pmatrix} F_m & 0 \\ 0 & F_m \end{pmatrix} \cdot R_{m+1} \qquad (9.37)$$

with the permutation matrix R_m given that $n = 2^m$

$$R_m = \begin{pmatrix} r_{11} & \cdots & r_{1n} \\ \vdots & \ddots & \vdots \\ r_{n1} & \cdots & r_{nn} \end{pmatrix} \qquad (9.38)$$

with

$$r_{ab} = \begin{cases} 1 & if \quad 2 \cdot a - 1 = b \\ 1 & if \quad 2 \cdot a - n = b \\ 0 & else \end{cases} \qquad (9.39)$$

and the diagonal matrix with $n \cdot 2 = 2^{m+1}$

$$D_m = \begin{pmatrix} \zeta_{n \cdot 2}^0 & 0 & \cdots & 0 \\ 0 & \zeta_{n \cdot 2}^1 & \cdots & 0 \\ \vdots & \vdots & \ddots & \vdots \\ 0 & 0 & \cdots & \zeta_{n \cdot 2}^{n-1} \end{pmatrix} . \qquad (9.40)$$

For example F_2 is decomposed with

$$D_1, \zeta_4 = e^{-2 \cdot \pi \cdot i \cdot \frac{1}{4}} \to D_1 = \begin{pmatrix} e^{-\cdot \pi \cdot i \cdot \frac{0}{2}} & 0 \\ 0 & e^{-\cdot \pi \cdot i \cdot \frac{1}{2}} \end{pmatrix} = \begin{pmatrix} 1 & 0 \\ 0 & -i \end{pmatrix} \qquad (9.41)$$

and

$$R_2 = \begin{pmatrix} 1 & 0 & 0 & 0 \\ 0 & 0 & 1 & 0 \\ 0 & 1 & 0 & 0 \\ 0 & 0 & 0 & 1 \end{pmatrix} \qquad (9.42)$$

it follows

$$F_2 = \frac{1}{\sqrt{2}} \cdot \begin{pmatrix} 1 & 0 & 1 & 0 \\ 0 & 1 & 0 & -i \\ 1 & 0 & -1 & 0 \\ 0 & 1 & 0 & i \end{pmatrix} \cdot \frac{1}{\sqrt{2}} \cdot \begin{pmatrix} 1 & 1 & 0 & 0 \\ 1 & -1 & 0 & 0 \\ 0 & 0 & 1 & 1 \\ 0 & 0 & 1 & -1 \end{pmatrix} \cdot \begin{pmatrix} 1 & 0 & 0 & 0 \\ 0 & 0 & 1 & 0 \\ 0 & 1 & 0 & 0 \\ 0 & 0 & 0 & 1 \end{pmatrix} \qquad (9.43)$$

$$F_2 = \frac{1}{2} \cdot \begin{pmatrix} 1 & 1 & 1 & 1 \\ 1 & -i & -1 & i \\ 1 & -1 & 1 & -1 \\ 1 & i & -1 & -i \end{pmatrix}. \qquad (9.44)$$

The complexity of the FFT algorithm that decomposes F_m recursively is $O(n \cdot m)$.

9.5 QFT Decomposition

The Hadamard transform W_m can be decomposed into a tensor product of m 2×2 matrices representing W_1

$$W_m = \bigotimes^m W_1 = W_1 \otimes W_1 \cdots \otimes W_1$$

so that the quantum complexity is $O(m)$ [Rieffel and Polak (2011)]. F_m cannot be decomposed as a tensor product of 2×2 matrices. Using the decomposition of the FFT algorithm and decomposing the corresponding matrices by the tensor product a quantum complexity of $O(m^2) = O(m \cdot m)$ can be achieved. The decomposition performs m steps. In each step is represented by a product of three unitary matrices. They can be decomposed at the step k into k tensor products. It follows

$$m + (m-1) + (m-2) + \cdots + 1 = \frac{m \cdot (m-1)}{2} = O(m^2). \qquad (9.45)$$

The permutation matrix R_m is unitary and can be decomposed into a tensor product of m swap operators S preforming a swap operation on one qubit states $|x\rangle$ and $|y\rangle$,

$$S|xy\rangle = |yx\rangle \qquad (9.46)$$

with

$$S|00\rangle = |00\rangle, \quad S|01\rangle = |10\rangle, \quad S|10\rangle = |01\rangle, \quad S|11\rangle = |11\rangle$$

and the matrix representation

$$S = \begin{pmatrix} 1 & 0 & 0 & 0 \\ 0 & 0 & 1 & 0 \\ 0 & 1 & 0 & 0 \\ 0 & 0 & 0 & 1 \end{pmatrix}. \tag{9.47}$$

The following matrix can be recursively decomposed

$$\begin{pmatrix} F_m & 0 \\ 0 & F_m \end{pmatrix} = I_1 \otimes F_m \tag{9.48}$$

and

$$\frac{1}{\sqrt{2}} \cdot \begin{pmatrix} I_m & D_m \\ I_m & -D_m \end{pmatrix} = (W_1 \cdot |0\rangle\langle 0|\cdot) \otimes I_m + (W_1 \cdot |1\rangle\langle 1|\cdot) \otimes D_m \tag{9.49}$$

with

$$D_m = D_{m-1} \otimes \begin{pmatrix} 1 & 0 \\ 0 & \zeta_{n \cdot 2} \end{pmatrix}. \tag{9.50}$$

9.5.1   *QFT quantum circuit**

We can rewrite the recursive decomposition into a "kind" of tensor product using the binary representation of $|x\rangle, |y\rangle$. This representation is popular, however it not a real tensor decomposition. The QFT on a state $|x\rangle$ of m qubits in a n-dimensional Hilbert space $H_n = H_{2^m}$ can be represented as [Kaye *et al.* (2007)]

$$|y\rangle = F_m \cdot |x\rangle = \frac{1}{\sqrt{n}} \sum_{y \in B^m} e^{-2 \cdot \pi \cdot i \cdot \frac{y}{n} \cdot x} \cdot |y\rangle. \tag{9.51}$$

It is just the discrete Fourier transform of $\alpha(t)$ in the bra-ket notation

$$\omega_f = \frac{1}{\sqrt{n}} \cdot \sum_{t=1}^{n} \alpha_t \cdot e^{-2 \cdot \pi \cdot i \cdot \frac{(f-1)}{n} \cdot (t-1)}.$$

The binary representation of x of m bits is given by

$$x = x_m \cdot 2^{m-1} + x_{m-1} \cdot 2^{m-2} + \cdots + x_2 \cdot 2^1 + x_1 \cdot 2^0 \tag{9.52}$$

and of y by

$$y = y_m \cdot 2^{m-1} + y_{m-1} \cdot 2^{m-2} + \cdots + y_2 \cdot 2^1 + y_1 \cdot 2^0. \tag{9.53}$$

We can represent the multiplication of

$$e^{\frac{-2\cdot\pi\cdot i\cdot y\cdot x}{n}} = e^{\frac{-2\cdot\pi\cdot i\cdot y\cdot x}{2^m}}$$

$$= e^{\frac{-2\cdot\pi\cdot i\cdot(y_m\cdot 2^{m-1}+\cdots+1+y_1\cdot 2^0\cdot x)\cdot(x_m\cdot 2^{m-1}\cdots+x_2\cdot 2^1+x_1\cdot 2^0)}{2^m}} = \tag{9.54}$$

$$= e^{\frac{-2\cdot\pi\cdot i\cdot(y_m\cdot 2^{m-1}\cdot(x_m\cdot 2^{m-1}\cdots+x_2\cdot 2^1+x_1\cdot 2^0)+\cdots+y_1\cdot 2^0\cdot(x_m\cdot 2^{m-1}\cdots+x_2\cdot 2^1+x_1\cdot 2^0))}{2^m}}.$$

$$\tag{9.55}$$

Because

$$e^{-2\cdot\pi\cdot i\cdot(a+b+c)} = e^{(-2\cdot\pi\cdot i\cdot a)+(-2\cdot\pi\cdot i\cdot b)+(-2\cdot\pi\cdot i\cdot c)} =$$

$$= e^{(-2\cdot\pi\cdot i\cdot a)}\cdot e^{(-2\cdot\pi\cdot i\cdot b)}\cdot e^{(-2\cdot\pi\cdot i\cdot c)}$$

and $e^{-2\cdot\pi\cdot i}$ is a nth root of unity

$$e^{-2\cdot\pi\cdot i\cdot n} = 1, \quad n \in N_0 = \{0,1,2,3,\cdots\}.$$

we can ignore in

$$e^{\frac{-2\cdot\pi\cdot i\cdot(y_m\cdot 2^{m-1}\cdot(x_m\cdot 2^{m-1}\cdots+x_2\cdot 2^1+x_1\cdot 2^0)+\cdots+y_1\cdot 2^0\cdot(x_m\cdot 2^{m-1}\cdots+x_2\cdot 2^1+x_1\cdot 2^0))}{2^m}}$$

the terms divisible by $n = 2^m$. For example

$$e^{-2\cdot\pi\cdot i\cdot(1+\frac{1}{2}+2)} = e^{(-2\cdot\pi\cdot i\cdot 1)}\cdot e^{(-2\cdot\pi\cdot i\cdot\frac{1}{2})}\cdot e^{(-2\cdot\pi\cdot i\cdot 3)} = 1\cdot e^{(-2\cdot\pi\cdot i\cdot\frac{1}{2})}\cdot 1 = -1.$$

It follows that

$$e^{\frac{-2\cdot\pi\cdot i\cdot y\cdot x}{2^m}} =$$

$$= e^{-2\cdot\pi\cdot i\cdot\left(y_m\cdot\frac{x_1}{2^1}+y_{m-1}\cdot\left(\frac{x_2}{2^1}+\frac{x_1}{2^2}\right)+y_{m-2}\cdot\left(\frac{x_3}{2^1}+\frac{x_2}{2^2}+\frac{x_1}{2^3}\right)+\cdots+y_1\cdot\left(\frac{x_m}{2^1}+\frac{x_{m-1}}{2^2}+\cdots+\frac{x_1}{2^m}\right)\right)}$$

$$\tag{9.56}$$

using the binary fraction notation for binary numbers

$$e^{\frac{-2\cdot\pi\cdot i\cdot y\cdot x}{2^m}} =$$

$$= e^{-2\cdot\pi\cdot i\cdot(y_m\cdot 0.x_1+y_{m-1}\cdot 0.x_2 x_1+y_{m-2}\cdot 0.x_3 x_2 x_1+\cdots+y_1\cdot 0.x_m x_{m\ 1} x_{m-2}\cdots x_2 x_1)}$$

$$\tag{9.57}$$

binary fractions are represented as

$$0.x_m x_{m\ 1} x_{m-2}\cdots x_2 x_1 = \frac{x_m}{2^1} + \frac{x_{m-1}}{2^2} + \cdots + \frac{x_1}{2^m}.$$

So the QFT can be factored into the tensor product of m single-qubit operations,

$$|y\rangle = F_m\cdot|x\rangle = \frac{1}{\sqrt{n}}\sum_{y\in B^m} e^{-2\cdot\pi\cdot i\cdot\frac{y}{n}\cdot x}\cdot|y\rangle =$$

$$\frac{1}{\sqrt{n}} \cdot \left(\sum_{y_m \in \{0,1\}} e^{-2 \cdot \pi \cdot i \cdot y_m \cdot 0.x_1} \right) \cdot \left(\sum_{y_{m-1} \in \{0,1\}} e^{-2 \cdot \pi \cdot i \cdot y_{m-1} \cdot 0.x_2 x_1} \right) \cdots$$

$$\cdots \left(\sum_{y_1 \in \{0,1\}} e^{-2 \cdot \pi \cdot i \cdot y_1 \cdot 0.x_m \cdots x_2 x_1} \right) \tag{9.58}$$

$$= \frac{1}{\sqrt{n}} \cdot \left(|0\rangle + e^{-2 \cdot \pi \cdot i \cdot 0.x_1} \cdot |1\rangle \right) \otimes \left(|0\rangle + e^{-2 \cdot \pi \cdot i \cdot 0.x_2 x_1} \cdot |1\rangle \right) \otimes \cdots \otimes \tag{9.59}$$

$$\otimes \left(|0\rangle + e^{-2 \cdot \pi \cdot i \cdot 0.x_m \cdots x_2 x_1} \cdot |1\rangle \right).$$

The representation involeves the input in the tensor decomposition. For example the equivalent decomposition of the the Hadamard matrix would involve the input to determine the sign,

$$W_m = \frac{1}{\sqrt{n}} \cdot \left(|0\rangle + (-1)^{x_m} \cdot |1\rangle \right) \otimes \left(|0\rangle + (-1)^{x_{m-1}} \cdot |1\rangle \right) \otimes \cdots$$

$$\otimes \left(|0\rangle + (-1)^{x_1} \cdot |1\rangle \right)$$

if the corresponding input is zero the sign is positive, if it is one the sign is negative. The product of m single-qubit operations of the QFT allows us to define a quantum circuit. The circuit will use a controlled phase gate CR_k that performs following mapping on two qubits

$$CR_k|00\rangle = |00\rangle, \quad CR_k|01\rangle = |01\rangle,$$

$$CR_k|10\rangle = |10\rangle, \quad CR_k|11\rangle = e^{-2 \cdot \pi \cdot i/2^k} \cdot |11\rangle.$$

The general phase gate is

$$P = \begin{pmatrix} 1 & 0 \\ 0 & e^{i \cdot \theta} \end{pmatrix}.$$

The phase gate R_k is

$$R_k = \begin{pmatrix} 1 & 0 \\ 0 & e^{-2 \cdot \pi \cdot i/2^k} \end{pmatrix} \tag{9.60}$$

and the controlled phase gate CR_k is

$$CR_k = \begin{pmatrix} 1 & 0 & 0 & 0 \\ 0 & 1 & 0 & 0 \\ 0 & 0 & 1 & 0 \\ 0 & 0 & 0 & e^{-2 \cdot \pi \cdot i/2^k} \end{pmatrix}. \tag{9.61}$$

We demonstrate the definition of the quantum circuit on F_2

$$F_2 = \frac{1}{\sqrt{4}} \cdot \left(|0\rangle + e^{-2 \cdot \pi \cdot i \cdot 0.x_1} \cdot |1\rangle\right) \otimes \left(|0\rangle + e^{-2 \cdot \pi \cdot i \cdot 0.x_2 x_1} \cdot |1\rangle\right) \qquad (9.62)$$

on the input $|x_2 x_1\rangle$. We define the circuit recursively from the back. Because

$$e^{-2 \cdot \pi \cdot i \cdot 0.x_1} = e^{-2 \cdot \pi \cdot i \cdot \frac{x_1}{2}} = (-1)^{x_1}$$

it follows that

$$\frac{1}{\sqrt{2}} \cdot \left(|0\rangle + e^{-2 \cdot \pi \cdot i \cdot 0.x_1} \cdot |1\rangle\right) = \frac{1}{\sqrt{2}} \cdot \left(|0\rangle + (-1)^{x_1} \cdot |1\rangle\right)$$

can be represented by

$$(I_1 \otimes W_1) \cdot |x_2 x_1\rangle.$$

The "first" operation can be represented as

$$\frac{1}{\sqrt{2}} \cdot \left(|0\rangle + e^{-2 \cdot \pi \cdot i \cdot 0.x_2 x_1} \cdot |1\rangle\right) = \frac{1}{\sqrt{2}} \cdot \left(|0\rangle + e^{-2 \cdot \pi \cdot i \cdot \frac{x_2}{2^1}} \cdot e^{-2 \cdot \pi \cdot i \cdot \frac{x_1}{2^2}} \cdot |1\rangle\right)$$

and can be represented as

$$CR_1 \cdot (W_1 \otimes I_1) \cdot |x_2 x_1\rangle.$$

Together we get

$$(I_1 \otimes W_1) \cdot CR_2 \cdot (W_1 \otimes I_1) \cdot |x_2 x_1\rangle =$$

$$= \frac{1}{\sqrt{4}} \cdot \left(|0\rangle + e^{-2 \cdot \pi \cdot i \cdot 0.x_2 x_1} \cdot |1\rangle\right) \otimes \left(|0\rangle + e^{-2 \cdot \pi \cdot i \cdot 0.x_1} \cdot |1\rangle\right) \qquad (9.63)$$

The arrangement of the bits is is not correct. This is because the last qubit in the result uses the first input qubit and so on. To correct the order we have to apply swap gate S as defined for the FFT. The decomposition is given by

$$F_2 \cdot |x_2 x_1\rangle = S \cdot (I_1 \otimes W_1) \cdot CR_1 \cdot (W_1 \otimes I_1) \cdot |x_2 x_1\rangle. \qquad (9.64)$$

or in matrix notation

$$F_2 = \frac{1}{2} \cdot \begin{pmatrix} 1 & 1 & 1 & 1 \\ 1 & -i & -1 & i \\ 1 & -1 & 1 & -1 \\ 1 & i & -1 & -i \end{pmatrix} = \begin{pmatrix} 1 & 0 & 0 & 0 \\ 0 & 0 & 1 & 0 \\ 0 & 1 & 0 & 0 \\ 0 & 0 & 0 & 1 \end{pmatrix} \cdot \left(\begin{pmatrix} 1 & 0 \\ 0 & 1 \end{pmatrix} \otimes \frac{1}{\sqrt{2}} \cdot \begin{pmatrix} 1 & 1 \\ 1 & -1 \end{pmatrix} \right) \cdot$$

$$\cdot \begin{pmatrix} 1 & 0 & 0 & 0 \\ 0 & 1 & 0 & 0 \\ 0 & 0 & 1 & 0 \\ 0 & 0 & 0 & -i \end{pmatrix} \cdot \left(\frac{1}{\sqrt{2}} \cdot \begin{pmatrix} 1 & 1 \\ 1 & -1 \end{pmatrix} \otimes \begin{pmatrix} 1 & 0 \\ 0 & 1 \end{pmatrix} \right) \cdot$$

For F_3 we need to define phase gate on three qubits $|x_3 x_2 x_1\rangle$ and a swap operation of the first and last qubit. The swap operation is simply the swap of the value of x_1 with the value of x_2, of the value of x_2 with the value of x_3 and finally of the value of x_1 with the value of x_2,

$$(I_1 \otimes S) \cdot (S \otimes I_1) \cdot (I_1 \otimes S).$$

The phase gate on third qubit controlled by the second qubit is simply

$$CR_k \otimes I_1.$$

The phase gate on third qubit controlled by the first qubit is

$$(I_1 \otimes S) \cdot (CR_k \otimes I_1) \cdot (I_1 \otimes S)$$

$$F_3 = \frac{1}{\sqrt{8}} \cdot \left(|0\rangle + e^{-2 \cdot \pi \cdot i \cdot 0.x_1} \cdot |1\rangle\right) \otimes \left(|0\rangle + e^{-2 \cdot \pi \cdot i \cdot 0.x_2 x_1} \cdot |1\rangle\right) \otimes$$

$$\otimes \left(|0\rangle + e^{-2 \cdot \pi \cdot i \cdot 0.x_3 x_2 x_1} \cdot |1\rangle\right) \tag{9.65}$$

the decomposition is given by

$$[(I_1 \otimes S) \cdot (S \otimes I_1) \cdot (I_1 \otimes S)] \cdot [(I_2 \otimes W_1)] \cdot [(I_1 \otimes CR_1) \cdot (I_1 \otimes W_1 \otimes I_1)]$$

$$\cdot [(I_1 \otimes S) \cdot (CR_2 \otimes I_1) \cdot (I_1 \otimes S) \cdot (CR_1 \otimes I_1) \cdot (W_1 \otimes I_2)] \cdot |x_3 x_2 x_1\rangle.$$

The first term requires one Hadamard gate, the second one requires a Hadamard gate and a controlled phase gate. Each following term requires an additional controlled phase gate. Summing up

$$1 + 2 + 3 + \cdots (m-1) + m = \frac{m \cdot (m-1)}{2} = O(m^2).$$

9.6 QFT Properties

QFT is just a simple DFT represented by the DFT matrix. However one should take *care* of the fact that in quantum computing literature it is common that the QFT is defined as the inverse discrete Fourier transform (IDFT) and the inverse QFT as the DFT. QFT decomposition is motivated by FFT. The complexity of QFT is $O(m^2)$ that is exponentially less then $O(n \cdot m)$ of the classical FFT. The saving results from the possible tensor decomposition that can be computed in parallel. The main difference between DFT and QFT beside the time complexity is quite obvious. In QFT we cannot access the frequency domain of a signal represented by the amplitude distribution of the state $|y\rangle$. We can only gain some insight by repeated experiments, measurements. DFT can be defined for any dimension n, for example $n = 3$ or $n = 6$. With $n = 6$ we could define a quantum dice that cannot be represented by qubits. The basis of a 6 dimensional Hilbert space H_6 is

$$|I\rangle = \begin{pmatrix} 1 \\ 0 \\ 0 \\ 0 \\ 0 \\ 0 \end{pmatrix}, |II\rangle = \begin{pmatrix} 0 \\ 1 \\ 0 \\ 0 \\ 0 \\ 0 \end{pmatrix}, |III\rangle = \begin{pmatrix} 0 \\ 0 \\ 1 \\ 0 \\ 0 \\ 0 \end{pmatrix},$$

$$|IV\rangle = \begin{pmatrix} 0 \\ 0 \\ 0 \\ 1 \\ 0 \\ 0 \end{pmatrix}, |V\rangle = \begin{pmatrix} 1 \\ 0 \\ 0 \\ 0 \\ 1 \\ 0 \end{pmatrix}, |VI\rangle = \begin{pmatrix} 0 \\ 0 \\ 0 \\ 0 \\ 0 \\ 1 \end{pmatrix}. \tag{9.66}$$

The DFT for the basis in H_6 is F^6

$$\zeta_6 = e^{-2 \cdot \pi \cdot i \cdot \frac{1}{6}} = e^{-\pi \cdot i \cdot \frac{1}{3}} = \frac{1 - i \cdot \sqrt{3}}{2}$$

$$F^6 = \frac{1}{\sqrt{6}} \cdot \begin{pmatrix} 1 & 1 & 1 & 1 & 1 & 1 \\ 1 & \zeta_6^1 & \zeta_6^2 & \zeta_6^3 & \zeta_6^4 & \zeta_6^5 \\ 1 & \zeta_6^2 & \zeta_6^4 & \zeta_6^6 & \zeta_6^8 & \zeta_6^{10} \\ 1 & \zeta_6^3 & \zeta_6^6 & \zeta_6^9 & \zeta_6^{12} & \zeta_6^{15} \\ 1 & \zeta_6^4 & \zeta_6^8 & \zeta_6^{12} & \zeta_6^{16} & \zeta_6^{20} \\ 1 & \zeta_6^5 & \zeta_6^{10} & \zeta_6^{15} & \zeta_6^{20} & \zeta_6^{25} \end{pmatrix} \tag{9.67}$$

$$F^6 = \frac{1}{\sqrt{6}} \cdot \begin{pmatrix} 1 & 1 & 1 & 1 & 1 & 1 \\ 1 & \frac{1-i\cdot\sqrt{3}}{2} & \frac{-1-i\cdot\sqrt{3}}{2} & -1 & \frac{-1+i\cdot\sqrt{3}}{2} & \frac{1+i\cdot\sqrt{3}}{2} \\ 1 & \frac{-1-i\cdot\sqrt{3}}{2} & \frac{-1+i\cdot\sqrt{3}}{2} & 1 & \frac{-1-i\cdot\sqrt{3}}{2} & \frac{-1+i\cdot\sqrt{3}}{2} \\ 1 & -1 & 1 & -1 & 1 & -1 \\ 1 & \frac{-1+i\cdot\sqrt{3}}{2} & \frac{-1-i\cdot\sqrt{3}}{2} & 1 & \frac{-1+i\cdot\sqrt{3}}{2} & \frac{-1-i\cdot\sqrt{3}}{2} \\ 1 & \frac{1+i\cdot\sqrt{3}}{2} & \frac{-1+i\cdot\sqrt{3}}{2} & -1 & \frac{-1-i\cdot\sqrt{3}}{2} & \frac{1-i\cdot\sqrt{3}}{2} \end{pmatrix}. \tag{9.68}$$

We can use F^6 to map the dice from a pure state in a superposition of maximal entropy

$$F^6|I\rangle = \frac{1}{\sqrt{6}} \cdot |I\rangle + |\frac{1}{\sqrt{6}} \cdot II\rangle + \frac{1}{\sqrt{6}} \cdot |III\rangle + \frac{1}{\sqrt{6}} \cdot |IV\rangle + \frac{1}{\sqrt{6}} \cdot |V\rangle + \frac{1}{\sqrt{6}} \cdot |VI\rangle.$$

We can define a register of m quantum dices using the tensor product, and map a pure sate $|I\rangle$ in a superposition by

$$F_m^6 = \bigotimes{}^m F^6 = F^6 \otimes F^6 \cdots \otimes F^6. \qquad (9.69)$$

We can define quantum computation on any base B besides qubits, base $B = 2$. The qubit representation as the bit representation is the most popular one.

9.7 The QFT Period Algorithm

QFT and F_m is used equivalently as W_m in the Deutsch Jozsa algorithm to determine the properties of the function $f(x)$. In Deutsch Jozsa algorithm the function must be balanced or constant. In the algorithm based on QFT the function $f(x)$ must be periodic. The determined property is the period of the function $f(x)$. We cannot use QFT to determine if a function is periodic or not. The QFT algorithm is built on three serial steps. It maps a state with zero von Neumann entropy to a superposition with the maximal entropy, does the computation in this superposition and maps the result into a state with low entropy. It should be noted that the entropy is not zero and consequently the algorithm is probabilistic. The algorithms is build on three principles of quantum computation that are related to the Deutsch Jozsa algorithm,

- The function $f(x)$ is represented by a quantum Boolean circuit.
- The properties of the function $f(x)$ are determined using the superposition principle and QFT.
- The values of the function $f(x)$ are determined by measuring a compound system.

We represent the function $f(x)$ by a quantum Boolean circuit represented by a unitary operator U_f that acts on two registers of m qubits,

$$U_f \cdot |x\rangle|0^{\otimes m}\rangle = |x\rangle|f(x)\rangle$$

after the application of U_f the two registers are entangled. In the first step of the algorithm we build a superposition of m qubits

$$W_m \cdot |0^{\otimes m}\rangle|0^{\otimes m}\rangle = \frac{1}{\sqrt{2^m}} \sum_{x \in B^m} |x\rangle|0^{\otimes m}\rangle.$$

In the second step we apply the U_f operator

$$U_f \left(\frac{1}{\sqrt{2^m}} \sum_{x \in B^m} |x\rangle|0^{\otimes m}\rangle \right) =$$

$$= \frac{1}{\sqrt{2^m}} \sum_{x \in B^m} U_f \cdot |x\rangle|0^{\otimes m}\rangle = \frac{1}{\sqrt{2^m}} \sum_{x \in B^m} |x\rangle|f(x)\rangle.$$

In the third step we measure the second register of the compound system [Shor (1994)], [Shor (1995)]. The state of the system is projected to the subspace that corresponds to the observed state and the vector representing the state is renormalized to the unit length. Because the function $f(x)$ is periodic, the new amplitude distribution is normalized and has the same period as $f(x)$. Before the measurement the amplitude distribution is at a constant value $\frac{1}{\sqrt{2^m}}$, it corresponding to the maximum entropy. The measured value γ corresponds to all k x_i values for which the periodic function is $\gamma = f(x_i)$. The function $\alpha(x)$ after the measurement is defined as

$$\alpha(x) = \begin{cases} \frac{1}{\sqrt{k}} & if \quad \gamma = f(x) \\ 0 & else \end{cases}. \tag{9.70}$$

After the measurement the state is represented as

$$\sum_{x \in B^m} \alpha(x) \cdot |x\rangle|\gamma\rangle.$$

In the fourth step we apply QFT that computes the discrete Fourier transform. The discrete Fourier transform of $\alpha(x)$ is $\omega(x)$. F_m s a linear transform talking the column vector α to a column vector ω

$$F_m \cdot \sum_{x \in B^m} \alpha(x) \cdot |x\rangle|\gamma\rangle = \sum_{x \in B^m} \omega(x) \cdot |x\rangle|\gamma\rangle.$$

In the fifth step we measure the first register. The measurement gives us a value v that is close to a multiple value of $\frac{n}{period}$. There are three possible cases:

Period r happens to be power of 2, the discrete Fourier transform gives exact multiplies

$$v = t \cdot \frac{n}{r} = t \cdot \frac{2^m}{r}. \tag{9.71}$$

In this case we can estimate r by several experiments if necessary

$$\frac{v}{2^m} = \frac{t}{r} \tag{9.72}$$

where the lowest term of $\frac{v}{2^m}$ will yield a fraction $\frac{t}{r}$ whose denominator is the period r.

Period r is not power of 2, the discrete Fourier transform gives approximate multiples

$$v \approx t \cdot \frac{n}{r} = t \cdot \frac{2^m}{r}. \tag{9.73}$$

In this case we can estimate r by continued finite fraction expansion of $\frac{v}{2^m}$ resulting in a unique fraction $\frac{p}{q}$ with $r \approx q$. For unique fraction $\frac{p}{q}$ of $\frac{v}{2^m}$ with $q < M$

$$\left| \frac{v}{2^m} - \frac{p}{q} \right| < \frac{1}{M^2}. \tag{9.74}$$

The fraction can be obtained by the following algorithm:

$$a_0 = \left\lfloor \frac{v}{2^m} \right\rfloor, \quad \epsilon_0 = \frac{v}{2^m} - a_0, \quad p_0 = a_0, \quad q_0 = 1$$

$$a_1 = \left\lfloor \frac{1}{\epsilon_0} \right\rfloor, \quad \epsilon_1 = \frac{1}{\epsilon_0} - a_0, \quad p_1 = a_1 \cdot a_0 + 1, \quad q_1 = a_1$$

$$a_i = \left\lfloor \frac{1}{\epsilon_{i-1}} \right\rfloor, \quad \epsilon_i = \frac{1}{\epsilon_{i-1}} - a_i, \quad p_i = a_i \cdot p_{i-1} + p_{i-2}, \quad q_i = a_i \cdot q_{i-1} + q_{i-2}.$$

We stop the algorithm with the output $\frac{p_i}{q_i}$ with $r \approx q_i$ if

$$q_i < M \leq q_{i+1}.$$

$f(x)$ is a periodic block function, the measured value γ in a block function corresponds to all k x_i values for which the periodic function is $\gamma = f(x_i)$. The amplitude function $\alpha(x)$ after the measurement has less or equal number of zeros with

$$n - k \leq k.$$

The $\frac{1}{\sqrt{k}}$ dominates the amplitude distribution. After the DFT the DC average of the amplitude dominates the distribution. The measured value will be with high probability $v = 1$, we cannot estimate the period. It is important to remember that the first row of DFT matrix F_m is the DC average of the amplitude of the input state. However during data analysis using mathematical software care has to to be taken because many DFT plot functions omit the DC component.

9.8 Factorization

The application of QFT gained popularity by Shor's algorithm for factorization of numbers in polynomial time [Shor (1994)], [Shor (1995)]. The widely used RSA-public key cryptography scheme is secure. Its security corresponds to the difficulty in factoring large numbers on conventional computers. Shor's algorithm indicated how to do it on a quantum computer in polynomial time.

Number theory relates the period of a particular function to the factor of an integer. Given an integer number M to be factored, a function $f(x)_M$ is defined

$$f_M(x) = a^x \bmod M, \tag{9.75}$$

a is a randomly chosen coprime to M, means the greatest common divisor of a and M is 1. $f(x)_M$ is periodic. For a value a the period of a modulo M is r.

$$a^r = 1 \bmod M, \tag{9.76}$$

if r is an even number (r is dependent on a, if r is not even, chose different a), then

$$\left(a^{\frac{r}{2}}\right)^2 = 1 \bmod M \tag{9.77}$$

$$\left(a^{\frac{r}{2}}\right)^2 - 1 = 0 \bmod M \Rightarrow \left(a^{\frac{r}{2}}\right)^2 - 1^2 = 0 \bmod M$$

$$\left(a^{\frac{r}{2}} - 1\right) \cdot \left(a^{\frac{r}{2}} + 1\right) = 1 \bmod M. \tag{9.78}$$

The product $\left(a^{\frac{r}{2}} - 1\right) \cdot \left(a^{\frac{r}{2}} + 1\right)$ is some integer multiple of M, because if we divide it by M the reminder is zero. A common factor between them can be efficiently determined by the greatest common divisor (gcd) Euclidean algorithm.

$$gcd\left(\left(a^{\frac{r}{2}} - 1\right), M\right), \quad gcd\left(\left(a^{\frac{r}{2}} + 1\right), M\right).$$

9.8.1 Example

In this example we will factor the number $M = 15$. We chose $a = 13$.

$$f_{15}(x) = 13^x \bmod 15.$$

We apply the $U_{f_{15}}$ operator

$$U_{f_{15}}\left(\frac{1}{\sqrt{2^8}} \sum_{x \in B^8} |x\rangle|0^{\otimes 8}\rangle\right) = \frac{1}{16} \sum_{x \in B^8} |x\rangle|f(x)\rangle.$$

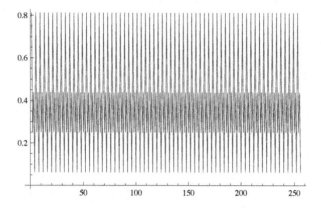

Fig. 9.3 The periodic signal $f_{15}(x) = 13^x \bmod 15$. It represents the superposition described by the amplitude of the second register.

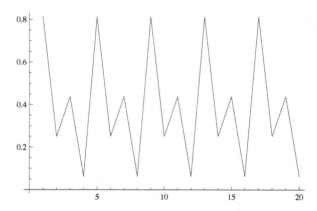

Fig. 9.4 The periodic signal $f_{15}(x) = 13^x \bmod 15$ in a higher resolution. We can recognize a period of four.

In Figure 9.3 and 9.4 a superposition is indicated that is described by the amplitude of the second register. We measure the second register of the compound system. In our experiment the function $\alpha(x)$ of the first register after the measurement is defined as

$$\alpha(x) = \begin{cases} \frac{1}{\sqrt{64}} & if \quad 0.25 = f(x) \\ 0 & else \end{cases}. \tag{9.79}$$

We indicate the periodic block function $\alpha(x)$ of the first register in Figure 9.5 and 9.6. We apply QFT that computes the discrete Fourier transform

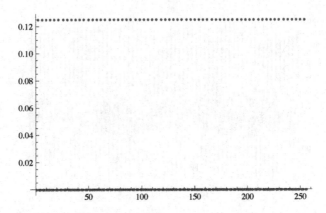

Fig. 9.5   The periodic block function $\alpha(x)$ of the first register.

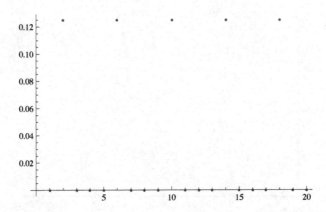

Fig. 9.6   The periodic block function $\alpha(x)$ of the first register in a higher resolution. We can recognize a period of four.

in the first register (see Figure 9.7 and 9.8). The measurement gives us a value v that is close to a multiple value of $\frac{n}{period}$. We measure the first register. The measurement gives us a value $64 + 1$ that is close to a multiple value of $\frac{256}{period}$. In our experiment the period r happens to be power of 2. The zero frequency term represents the DC average and appears at position 1 instead at the position 0, so $v = 64$. It follows for the period r

$$r = \frac{256}{v} = \frac{256}{64}.$$

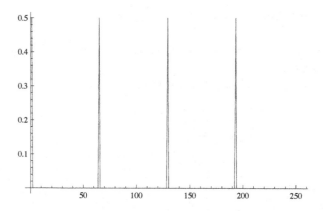

Fig. 9.7 DFT transform of the first register. It shows a strong peak at 1 and 64 + 1, 2 · 64 + 1 = 129 and 3 · 64 + 1 = 193.

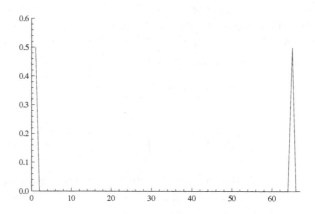

Fig. 9.8 DFT transform of the first register, higher resolution. The zero frequency term represents the DC average and appears at position 1 instead at the position 0.

A common factor between them can be efficiently determined by the greatest common divisor (*gcd*) Euclidean algorithm,

$$gcd\left(\left(13^{\frac{4}{2}}-1\right),15\right)=3, \quad gcd\left(\left(13^{\frac{4}{2}}+1\right),15\right)=5.$$

The factors of 15 are 3 and 5. The algorithm is probabilistic and it can fail. Suppose the measurement gives us the value 1, in this case we have to repeat the whole procedure.

9.9   Kitaev's Phase Estimation Algorithm*

Given a unitary operator U on m qubits with an eigenvector $|u\rangle$ with an unknown eigenvalue $e^{2\cdot\pi\cdot i\cdot\theta}$ we want to determine the phase θ [Kitaev (1996)], [Kaye *et al.* (2007)]. For a complex number

$$z = x + i \cdot y = |z| \cdot e^{i\cdot\theta}$$

θ is the phase. if we apply U to $|u\rangle$ we get

$$U \cdot |u\rangle = e^{2\cdot\pi\cdot i\cdot\theta} \cdot |u\rangle \tag{9.80}$$

if we apply U to $|u\rangle$ w times we get

$$U^w \cdot |u\rangle = U^{w-1} \cdot \left(e^{2\cdot\pi\cdot i\cdot\theta} \cdot |u\rangle\right) = \left(e^{2\cdot\pi\cdot i\cdot\theta}\right)^w \cdot |u\rangle = e^{2\cdot\pi\cdot i\cdot\theta\cdot w} \cdot |u\rangle. \tag{9.81}$$

However we will not gain any information, because $|u\rangle$ and $e^{2\cdot\pi\cdot i\cdot\theta\cdot w} \cdot |u\rangle$ are equivalent states, they represent the same state when a measurement is preformed. Instead of the unitary operator U^w we use the controlled U^w operator cU^w. If the control qubit is set then U^w is applied to the target qubits, otherwise not. The operator cU^w is unitary and defines an injective mapping on two qubits that is reversible

$$cU^w \cdot |0\rangle|u\rangle = |0\rangle|u\rangle, \quad cU^w \cdot |1\rangle|u\rangle = |1\rangle\left(e^{2\cdot\pi\cdot i\cdot\theta\cdot w} \cdot |u\rangle\right) = e^{2\cdot\pi\cdot i\cdot\theta\cdot w} \cdot |1\rangle|u\rangle.$$

So with $w = 2^j$

$$cU^{2^j} \cdot \left(\left(\frac{|0\rangle + |1\rangle}{\sqrt{2}}\right) \cdot |u\rangle\right) = \left(\frac{|0\rangle + e^{2\cdot\pi\cdot i\cdot\theta\cdot\cdot 2^j}|1\rangle}{\sqrt{2}}\right) \cdot |u\rangle.$$

The QFT is represented as a tensor product of m single-qubit operations. The inverse QFT can be factored into the tensor product of m single-qubit operations,

$$|y\rangle = IF_m \cdot |x\rangle = \frac{1}{\sqrt{n}} \sum_{y\in B^m} e^{2\cdot\pi\cdot i\cdot\frac{y}{n}\cdot x} \cdot |y\rangle =$$

$$= \frac{1}{\sqrt{n}} \cdot \left(|0\rangle + e^{2\cdot\pi\cdot i\cdot 0.x_1} \cdot |1\rangle\right) \otimes \left(|0\rangle + e^{2\cdot\pi\cdot i\cdot 0.x_2 x_1} \cdot |1\rangle\right) \otimes \cdots \otimes \tag{9.82}$$

$$\otimes \left(|0\rangle + e^{2\cdot\pi\cdot i\cdot 0.x_m\cdots x_2 x_1} \cdot |1\rangle\right).$$

If we set $\theta = 0.x_m \cdots x_2 x_1$ we can rewrite the equation as

$$|y\rangle = IF_m \cdot |x\rangle = \frac{1}{\sqrt{n}} \sum_{y\in B^m} e^{2\cdot\pi\cdot i\cdot y\cdot\theta} \cdot |y\rangle =$$

$$= \frac{1}{\sqrt{n}} \cdot \left(|0\rangle + e^{2 \cdot \pi \cdot i \cdot \left(\theta \cdot 2^{m-1}\right)} \cdot |1\rangle \right) \otimes \left(|0\rangle + e^{2 \cdot \pi \cdot i \cdot \left(\theta \cdot 2^{m-2}\right)} \cdot |1\rangle \right) \otimes \cdots \otimes$$

$$\otimes \left(|0\rangle + e^{2 \cdot \pi \cdot i \cdot \left(\theta \cdot 2^0\right)} \cdot |1\rangle \right). \tag{9.83}$$

For m control qubits we define $c_{j+1}U^{2^j}$ in the following way. For $j \in \{0, 1, 2, \cdots, m-1\}$ the control qubit $j+1$ of the m qubits is set then $c_{j+1}U^{2^j}$ is applied to the target $|u\rangle$, otherwise not. The initial state of the algorithm is

$$|0^{\otimes m}\rangle |u\rangle$$

with u being the eigenvector of U. In the first step of the algorithm we build a superposition of m control qubits

$$W_m \cdot |0^{\otimes m}\rangle |u\rangle = \frac{1}{\sqrt{2^m}} \sum_{x \in B^m} |x\rangle |u\rangle =$$

$$= \frac{1}{\sqrt{n}} \cdot (|0\rangle + |1\rangle) \otimes (|0\rangle + |1\rangle) \otimes \cdots \otimes (|0\rangle + |1\rangle) |u\rangle. \tag{9.84}$$

In the second step we apply m $c_{j+1}U^{2^j}$ operators to the target $|u\rangle$

$$\prod_{j=0}^{m-1} c_{j+1}U^{2^j} \cdot \left(\frac{1}{\sqrt{2^m}} \sum_{x \in B^m} |x\rangle |u\rangle \right) =$$

$$= IF_m \cdot |x\rangle |u\rangle = \frac{1}{\sqrt{n}} \sum_{y \in B^m} e^{2 \cdot \pi \cdot i \cdot y \cdot \theta} \cdot |y\rangle |u\rangle =$$

$$= \frac{1}{\sqrt{n}} \cdot \left(|0\rangle + e^{2 \cdot \pi \cdot i \cdot \left(\theta \cdot 2^{m-1}\right)} \cdot |1\rangle \right) \otimes \left(|0\rangle + e^{2 \cdot \pi \cdot i \cdot \left(\theta \cdot 2^{m-2}\right)} \cdot |1\rangle \right) \otimes \cdots \tag{9.85}$$

$$\otimes \left(|0\rangle + e^{2 \cdot \pi \cdot i \cdot \left(\theta \cdot 2^0\right)} \cdot |1\rangle \right) \cdot |u\rangle$$

In the third step we apply QFT to the m control qubtis

$$F_m \cdot \left(\frac{1}{\sqrt{n}} \sum_{y \in B^m} e^{2 \cdot \pi \cdot i \cdot y \cdot \theta} \cdot |y\rangle \right) \cdot |u\rangle =$$

$$= F_m \cdot \left(\frac{1}{\sqrt{n}} \sum_{y \in B^m} e^{2 \cdot \pi \cdot i \cdot \frac{y}{n} \cdot x} \cdot |y\rangle \right) \cdot |u\rangle = |x\rangle |u\rangle. \tag{9.86}$$

In the fourth step we measure the first register composed of m control qubtis and estimate θ

$$\theta = 0.x_m \cdots x_2 x_1 = \frac{x}{n} = \frac{x}{2^m}. \tag{9.87}$$

9.9.1   *Order finding*

It seem that with Kitaev's phase estimation algorithm we do not need to apply continued finite fraction expansion. But actually this is not the case. One big problem when using Kitaev's phase estimation algorithm is the determination of the eigenvector $|u\rangle$ of the unitary operator U. Usually this is non trivial and the computational costs are expensive. But for order finding (period estimation), there is an elegant way around the problem. For the unitary operator

$$U_a \cdot |x\rangle = |x \cdot a \bmod M\rangle, \quad x \leq M \tag{9.88}$$

a is a coprime of M. Because $a^r = 1 \bmod M$ is a rth root of unity, it follows

$$U_a^r \cdot |x\rangle = |x \cdot a \bmod M\rangle = |x\rangle$$

that U_a^r is a rth root of unity operation, and U_a has the following eigenvector

$$|u_t\rangle = \frac{1}{\sqrt{r}} \sum_{x=0}^{r-1} e^{-2 \cdot \pi \cdot i \cdot \frac{t}{r} \cdot x} \cdot |a^x \bmod M\rangle \tag{9.89}$$

in this case we can determine the eigenvalue

$$U_a \cdot |u_t\rangle = e^{2 \cdot \pi \cdot i \cdot \frac{t}{r}} \cdot |u_t\rangle. \tag{9.90}$$

With the Kitaev's phase estimation algorithm we could determine $\frac{t}{r}$ and $r \approx q$ as before. Without knowing r in advance we cannot determine $|u_t\rangle$. However we can use the following relation

$$|a^x \bmod M\rangle = 1 \Leftrightarrow x = 0 \bmod r$$

it follows

$$\frac{1}{\sqrt{r}} \sum_{t=0}^{r-1} |u_t\rangle = |1\rangle \tag{9.91}$$

with this relation we can use Kitaev's phase estimation. In the first step of the algorithm we build a superposition of m control qubits and with $|u\rangle = |1\rangle$

$$W_m \cdot |0^{\otimes m}\rangle |1\rangle = \frac{1}{\sqrt{2^m}} \sum_{x \in B^m} |x\rangle |u\rangle =$$

$$= \frac{1}{\sqrt{n}} \cdot (|0\rangle + |1\rangle) \otimes (|0\rangle + |1\rangle) \otimes \cdots \otimes (|0\rangle + |1\rangle) |1\rangle.$$

In the second step we apply m $c_{j+1} U^{2^j}$ operators to the target $|1\rangle = |u\rangle$. After applying QFT we get actually a superposition

$$\frac{1}{\sqrt{r}} \sum_{t=0}^{r-1} \left| \frac{t}{r} \right\rangle |u_t\rangle \tag{9.92}$$

after measuring the first register we can estimate $\frac{t}{r}$ and by continued finite fraction expansion $r \approx q$.

9.10 Unitary Transforms

Other unitary transforms beside DFT can be applied in quantum computation. Examples of such transforms are the Discrete Cosine Transform DCT and the Haar-Wavelet-Transform (HWT).

DCT corresponds to the sum of cosine functions oscillating at different frequencies with no imaginary number representation.

HWT The Haar transform analyzes the signal at different frequencies with different resolutions. The Haar-Wavelet-Transform (HWT) is represented by the unitary matrix (HW). For $n = 2^m$ HW_m performs a Quantum Haar-Wavelet-Transform on a state $|x\rangle$ of m qubits in a n-dimensional Hilbert space H_n.

$$HW_1 = W_1. \tag{9.93}$$

For three qubits HWT is,

$$HW_3 = \frac{1}{\sqrt{8}} \cdot \begin{pmatrix} 1 & 1 & 1 & 1 & 1 & 1 & 1 & 1 \\ 1 & 1 & 1 & 1 & -1 & -1 & -1 & -1 \\ \sqrt{2} & \sqrt{2} & -\sqrt{2} & -\sqrt{2} & 0 & 0 & 0 & 0 \\ 0 & 0 & 0 & 0 & \sqrt{2} & \sqrt{2} & -\sqrt{2} & -\sqrt{2} \\ 2 & -2 & 0 & 0 & 0 & 0 & 0 & 0 \\ 0 & 0 & 2 & -2 & 0 & 0 & 0 & 0 \\ 0 & 0 & 0 & 0 & 2 & -2 & 0 & 0 \\ 0 & 0 & 0 & 0 & 0 & 0 & 2 & -2 \end{pmatrix}. \tag{9.94}$$

Interestingly The introduced unitary matrix W maps a pure state $|000\rangle$ in a superposition,

$$HW_3 \cdot |000\rangle = \frac{1}{2 \cdot \sqrt{2}} \cdot |000\rangle + \frac{1}{2 \cdot \sqrt{2}} \cdot |001\rangle + \frac{1}{\sqrt{2}} \cdot |011\rangle \tag{9.95}$$

where the distribution of the amplitudes does not corresponds to the maximal entropy.

Chapter 10

Search

10.1 Search and Quantum Oracle

For a function $f(x)$

$$f_\xi(x) = \begin{cases} 1 & if \quad x = \xi \\ 0 & else \end{cases} \tag{10.1}$$

we want to find x for which $f(x) = 1$, $x = \xi$. The task is equivalent to a decision problem with a binary answer $1 = yes$ and $0 = no$ and the instance x. We can describe by the function $f(x)$ $NP - complete$ problems. A problem is $NP - complete$, if it is in NP and every other problem in NP can be reduced to it. For NP a deterministic algorithm verifies if an instance (ticket) leads to a "yes" answer in polynomial time. The verification of an instance (ticket) is in polynomial time P and can be represented by a uniformly polynomial circuit, a circuit with a polynomial number of gates. If $f(x)$ is $NP - complete$ a quantum circuit U_f with a polynomial number of quantum gates can verify for a given instance x_{ticket} if $f(x_{ticket}) = 1, x_{ticket} = \xi$ or $f(x_{ticket}) = 0$. The search for ξ is based on the three principles of quantum computation:

- The function $f(x)$ is represented by a quantum Boolean circuit U_f.
- The properties of the function $f(x)$ are determined using the superposition principle and a some kind of unitary transform.
- The values of the function $f(x)$ are encoded by $(-1)^{f(x)}$, the sign of the amplitude.

Often $f(x)$ is represented by an abstract black box function and not by a quantum circuit. In this case U_f is a quantum oracle. The U_f quantum oracle or quantum circuit is a unitary operator that acts on the $m+1$ qubits

173

with $x \in B^m$ and $y \in B^1$

$$U_f \cdot |x\rangle|y\rangle = |x\rangle|f(x) \oplus y\rangle.$$

The function $f(x)$, the solution is encoded by $(-1)^{f(x)}$, the sign of the amplitude. In correspondence with the Deutsch Jozsa algorithm we build a superposition of $m + 1$ qubits

$$W_{m+1} \cdot |0^{\otimes m}\rangle|1\rangle = W_m \cdot |0^{\otimes m}\rangle \otimes W_1 \cdot |1\rangle = \frac{1}{\sqrt{2^m}} \sum_{x \in B^m} |x\rangle \otimes \left(\frac{|0\rangle - |1\rangle}{\sqrt{2}} \right)$$

and we apply the U_f, operator,

$$U_f \cdot W_{m+1} \cdot |0^{\otimes n}\rangle|1\rangle =$$

$$= \frac{1}{\sqrt{2^{m+1}}} \cdot \sum_{x \in B^m} U_f \cdot |x\rangle|0\rangle - \frac{1}{\sqrt{2^{m+1}}} \cdot \sum_{x \in B^m} U_f \cdot |x\rangle|1\rangle$$

$$= \frac{1}{\sqrt{2^{m+1}}} \cdot \sum_{x \in B^m} |x\rangle|f(x) \oplus 0\rangle - \frac{1}{\sqrt{2^{m+1}}} \cdot \sum_{x \in B^m} |x\rangle|f(x) \oplus 1\rangle$$

$$= \frac{1}{\sqrt{2^{m+1}}} \cdot \left(\sum_{x \in B^m} |x\rangle|f(x) \oplus 0\rangle - \sum_{x \in B^m} |x\rangle|f(x) \oplus 1\rangle \right).$$

There are four possible cases:

$$U_f \cdot |x\rangle|0\rangle = |x\rangle|f(x) \oplus 0\rangle = |x\rangle|0\rangle,$$

$$U_f \cdot |x\rangle|1\rangle = |x\rangle|f(x) \oplus 1\rangle = |x\rangle|1\rangle,$$

$$U_f \cdot |\xi\rangle|0\rangle = |\xi\rangle|f(\xi) \oplus 0\rangle = |\xi\rangle|1\rangle,$$

$$U_f \cdot |\xi\rangle|1\rangle = |\xi\rangle|f(\xi) \oplus 1\rangle = |\xi\rangle|0\rangle.$$

It follows that

$$= \frac{1}{\sqrt{2^{m+1}}} \cdot \left(\sum_{x \neq \xi} |x\rangle|0\rangle + |\xi\rangle|1\rangle - \sum_{x \neq \xi} |x\rangle|1\rangle - |\xi\rangle|0\rangle \right)$$

$$= \frac{1}{\sqrt{2^{m+1}}} \cdot \left(\sum_{x \neq \xi} |x\rangle (|0\rangle - |1\rangle) + |\xi\rangle (|1\rangle - |0\rangle) \right)$$

$$= \frac{1}{\sqrt{n}} \sum_{x \in B^m} (-1)^{f(x)} \cdot |x\rangle \otimes \left(\frac{|0\rangle - |1\rangle}{\sqrt{2}} \right). \tag{10.2}$$

The value of the function $f(x)$ is encoded by $(-1)^{f(x)}$, in most cases again the auxiliary bit is ignored,

$$\frac{1}{\sqrt{2^m}} \sum_{x \in B^m} (-1)^{f(x)} \cdot |x\rangle = \frac{1}{\sqrt{n}} \sum_{x \in B^m} (-1)^{f(x)} \cdot |x\rangle. \tag{10.3}$$

For $m = 1$ we could use the Deutsch algorithm to decide if ξ exist, for $m = 2$ there exist the unitary operator described by the unitary matrix

$$S = \frac{1}{2} \cdot \begin{pmatrix} -1 & 1 & 1 & 1 \\ 1 & -1 & 1 & 1 \\ 1 & 1 & -1 & 1 \\ 1 & 1 & 1 & -1 \end{pmatrix} \tag{10.4}$$

with $I = S \cdot S^*$. We can determine $x = \xi$ by a simple approach. We apply the U_f operator and then the operator S,

$$(S \otimes I_1) \cdot U_f \cdot W_{2+1} \cdot |00\rangle|1\rangle = S \cdot \left(\frac{1}{\sqrt{4}} \sum_{x \in B^2} (-1)^{f(x)} \cdot |x\rangle \right) \otimes \left(\frac{|0\rangle - |1\rangle}{\sqrt{2}} \right) \tag{10.5}$$

$$(S \otimes I_1) \cdot U_f \cdot W_{2+1} \cdot |00\rangle|1\rangle = |\xi\rangle \otimes \left(\frac{|0\rangle - |1\rangle}{\sqrt{2}} \right) \tag{10.6}$$

and measure the first register and obtain $|\xi\rangle$ with probability 1. For example if $\xi = |10\rangle = 3$,

$$\frac{1}{2} \cdot \begin{pmatrix} -1 & 1 & 1 & 1 \\ 1 & -1 & 1 & 1 \\ 1 & 1 & -1 & 1 \\ 1 & 1 & 1 & -1 \end{pmatrix} \cdot \frac{1}{2} \cdot \begin{pmatrix} 1 \\ 1 \\ -1 \\ 1 \end{pmatrix} = \begin{pmatrix} 0 \\ 0 \\ 1 \\ 0 \end{pmatrix}. \tag{10.7}$$

Such a "spy" matrix S exist only for $m = 2$. Is it possible to get an exponential speed up for $m \gg 2$? To determine ξ for we would require only $O(m) = O(\log 2^m) = O(\log n)$ steps. This naïve hope can not be fulfilled.

10.2 Lower Bound $\Omega(\sqrt{n})$ for U_f-based Search*

If the operator U_f is represented by $O(m)$ gates, then we can get a speed up of maximum $O(\sqrt{n})$ steps, in fact $\Omega(\sqrt{n})$ is the lower bound. The proof for lower bound $\Omega(\sqrt{n})$ for U_f-based search is based on a sequence in a Hilbert space and the Euclidean norm properties of Hilbert space as well as the definition of the probabilities as normed squared amplitudes [Bennett *et al.* (1997)], [Boyer *et al.* (1998)]. Suppose we start with a state $|x\rangle$ of m qubits in a n-dimensional Hilbert space H_n

$$|x\rangle = \alpha_1 \cdot |x_1\rangle + \alpha_2 \cdot |x_2\rangle + \cdots + \alpha_n \cdot |x_n\rangle$$

and we are searching for one solution represented by the pure state $|\xi\rangle$ that corresponds to some basis of $|x\rangle$. We apply U_f which performs a phase shift to the amplitude of the corresponding basis, if $|x_i\rangle = |\xi\rangle$ then $-\alpha_i \cdot |x_i\rangle$. The Von Neumann Entropy is not changed by this operation. We will apply t times U_f and some arbitrary unitary operation A_t that would reduce the Von Neumann Entropy. The reduction is realized by changing the amplitude that indicates the solution together with the amplitudes of non solutions,

$$|x_t^\xi\rangle = A_t \cdot U_f \cdot A_{t-1} \cdot U_f \cdots \cdots A_1 \cdot U_f \cdot |x\rangle. \tag{10.8}$$

We will apply t times some arbitrary unitary operation A_t without indicating the solution by phase shift to the amplitude by U_f,

$$|x_t\rangle = A_t \cdot A_{t-1} \cdots \cdots A_1 \cdot |x\rangle. \tag{10.9}$$

We define a sequence a_t as the deviation after t steps between informed and uninformed evaluation of unitary operators on the a state $|x\rangle$

$$a_t = \| |x_t^\xi\rangle - |x_t\rangle \|^2 \tag{10.10}$$

with

$$\| |x_t\rangle \|^2 = \langle x_t | x_t \rangle.$$

The norm of difference between informed and uninformed evaluation is taken to the power of two, because the probabilities correspond to the normed amplitudes power two.

10.2.1 *Lower bound of a_t*

We suppose that an observation yields to the solution of the search with probability al least 0.5.

$$\| \langle \xi | x_t^\xi \rangle \|^2 \geq \frac{1}{2}. \tag{10.11}$$

We can rewrite a_t as

$$a_t = \| |x_t^\xi\rangle - |\xi\rangle + |\xi\rangle - |x_t\rangle \|^2 = \| \left(|x_t^\xi\rangle - |\xi\rangle \right) + (|\xi\rangle - |x_t\rangle) \|^2.$$

We define two sequences, the deviation after t steps between informed evaluation of unitary operators and the solution $|\xi\rangle$ with

$$a_t^+ = \| |x_t^\xi\rangle - |\xi\rangle \|^2$$

and the deviation after t steps between uninformed evaluation of unitary operators and the solution $|\xi\rangle$ with

$$a_t^- = \| \, |\xi\rangle - |x_t\rangle \|^2$$

Because of the inequality

$$\|\alpha + \beta\|^2 \geq \|\alpha\|^2 - 2 \cdot \|\alpha\| \cdot \|\beta\| + \|\beta\|^2$$

it follows that

$$a_t = \| \left(|x_t^\xi\rangle - |\xi\rangle \right) + (|\xi\rangle - |x_t\rangle) \|^2 \geq a_t^+ - 2 \cdot \sqrt{a_t^+} \cdot \sqrt{a_t^-} + a_t^-. \quad (10.12)$$

Using the two sequence we indicate a lower bound for a_t and $t \gg 1$

$$a_t \geq a_t^+ - 2 \cdot \sqrt{a_t^+} \cdot \sqrt{a_t^-} + a_t^- = \left(\sqrt{a_t^+} - \sqrt{a_t^-} \right)^2 \geq c. \quad (10.13)$$

With a_t^+ we indicate that in Hilbert space H_n a lower bound $c > 0$ exists

$$a_t^+ = \langle x_t^\xi | x_t^\xi \rangle - 2 \cdot \langle \xi | x_t^\xi \rangle + \langle \xi | \xi \rangle = 1 - 2 \cdot \langle \xi | x_t^\xi \rangle + 1. \quad (10.14)$$

The value of

$$2 \cdot \langle \xi | x_t^\xi \rangle$$

can be estimated. In the first step we notice that we can replace the state $\langle \xi |$ by an equivalent state

$$|\xi\rangle = e^{i \cdot \theta} \cdot |\xi\rangle.$$

Because of the Equation 10.11 for $t \gg 1$

$$2 \cdot \langle \xi | x_t^\xi \rangle = 2 \cdot |\langle \xi | x_t^\xi \rangle| \geq \frac{2}{\sqrt{2}} = \sqrt{2} \quad (10.15)$$

and

$$a_t^+ \leq 2 - \sqrt{2}. \quad (10.16)$$

For

$$a_t^- = \langle x_t | x_t \rangle - 2 \cdot \langle \xi | x_t \rangle + \langle \xi | \xi \rangle = 1 - 2 \cdot \langle \xi | x_t^\xi \rangle + 1 \quad (10.17)$$

with

$$2 \cdot \langle \xi | x_t \rangle = 2 \cdot |\langle \xi | x_t \rangle| \leq \frac{2}{\sqrt{n}} \quad (10.18)$$

it follows that

$$2 - \frac{2}{\sqrt{n}} \leq a_t^- \leq 2 \quad (10.19)$$

putting a_t+ and a_t^- together we get

$$a_t \geq \left(\sqrt{a_t^+} - \sqrt{a_t^-} \right)^2 \geq \left(\sqrt{2 - \sqrt{2}} - \sqrt{2} \right)^2 = c = 0.421002. \quad (10.20)$$

10.2.2   *Upper bound of a_t*

The deviation cannot grow faster as $O(t^2)$, this can be proven by induction. We prove that $4 \cdot \frac{t^2}{n} \geq a_t$. For $t = 0$

$$|x_0^\xi\rangle = |x\rangle$$

because no unitary operators were applied. The induction step is if $4 \cdot \frac{t^2}{n} \geq a_t$, then $4 \cdot \frac{(t+1)^2}{n} \geq a_{t+1}$ as well,

$$a_{t+1} = \|A_{t+1} \cdot U_f \cdot |x_t^\xi\rangle - A_{t+1} \cdot |x_t\rangle\|^2$$

$$a_{t+1} = \|A_{t+1} \cdot \left(U_f \cdot |x_t^\xi\rangle - |x_t\rangle\right)\|^2 \leq \||A_{t+1}\|^2 \cdot \|U_f \cdot |x_t^\xi\rangle - |x_t\rangle\|^2.$$

The norm for square matrices A in Hilbert space H_n is the Frobenius norm

$$\|A\|_F = \left(\sum_{i=1, j=1}^{n} |a_{ij}|\right)^{\frac{1}{2}} = \sqrt{tr(A \cdot A^*)} \qquad (10.21)$$

$\|A\|_2$ is also called the spectral norm. For unitary matrices A

$$\|A\|_F = \|A\|_2 = 1. \qquad (10.22)$$

Because the matrix A_{t+1} is unitary it follows that

$$a_{t+1} = \||A_{t+1} \cdot \left(U_f \cdot |x_t^\xi\rangle - |x_t\rangle\right)\|^2 = \|U_f \cdot |x_t^\xi\rangle - |x_t\rangle\|^2$$

$$a_{t+1} = \||U_f \cdot \left(|x_t^\xi\rangle - |x_t\rangle\right) + (U_f - I_m) \cdot |x_t\rangle\|^2.$$

Note that if a solution exist the amplitude of the corresponding basis of $|x_t\rangle$ that is equal to $|\xi\rangle$ is $\langle\xi|x_t\rangle$, then

$$(U_f - I_m) \cdot |x_t\rangle = U_f \cdot |x_t\rangle - |x_t\rangle = -2 \cdot \langle\xi|x_t\rangle \cdot |\xi\rangle$$

and

$$-2 \cdot \|\langle\xi|x_t\rangle \cdot |\xi\rangle\| = -2 \cdot |\langle\xi|x_t\rangle|$$

also

$$\|U_f \cdot \left(|x_t^\xi\rangle - |x_t\rangle\right)\|^2 = \||x_t^\xi\rangle - |x_t\rangle\|^2$$

because

$$\|\alpha + \beta\|^2 \leq \|\alpha\|^2 + 2 \cdot \|\alpha\| \cdot \|\beta\| + \|\beta\|^2$$

it follows

$$a_{t+1} = \|U_f \cdot \left(|x_t^\xi\rangle - |x_t\rangle \right) - 2 \cdot \langle \xi|x_t\rangle \cdot |\xi\rangle \|^2$$
$$a_{t+1} \leq \||x_t^\xi\rangle - |x_t\rangle\|^2 + 4 \cdot \||x_t^\xi\rangle - |x_t\rangle t\| \cdot |\langle\xi|x_t\rangle| + 4 \cdot |\langle\xi|x_t\rangle|^2$$
$$a_{t+1} \leq a_t + 4 \cdot \sqrt{a_t} \cdot |\langle\xi|x_t\rangle| + 4 \cdot |\langle\xi|x_t\rangle|^2 \qquad (10.23)$$

with

$$\langle\xi|x_t\rangle = |\langle\xi|x_t\rangle| \leq \frac{1}{\sqrt{n}} \qquad (10.24)$$

it follows that

$$a_{t+1} \leq 4 \cdot \frac{t^2}{n} + 4 \cdot \sqrt{4 \cdot \frac{t^2}{n}} \cdot \frac{1}{\sqrt{n}} + \frac{4}{n} = 4 \cdot \frac{t^2}{n} + 4 \cdot \sqrt{4 \cdot \frac{t^2}{n^2}} + \frac{4}{n} \qquad (10.25)$$

$$a_{t+1} \leq 4 \cdot \frac{t^2}{n} + 8 \cdot \frac{t}{n} + \frac{4}{n} = 4 \cdot \frac{(t+1)^2}{n} \qquad (10.26)$$

and the induction step t to $t + 1$ is concluded.

10.2.3 $\Omega(\sqrt{n})$

With the lower and upper bound of a_t we can estimate the lower bound of t. a_t grows quadratically,

$$4 \cdot \frac{t^2}{n} \geq a_t \geq c = 0.421002$$

it follows that

$$t \geq \sqrt{n \cdot \frac{c}{4}} = \sqrt{n} \cdot 0.324423. \qquad (10.27)$$

The speed up of $O(\sqrt{n})$ compared to $O(n)$ is due to the definition of the probabilities as normed squared amplitudes. If the operator U_f is represented by $O(m)$ gates, then we can get a speed up of maximum $O(\sqrt{n})$ steps, in fact $\Omega(\sqrt{n})$ is the lower bound [Bennett *et al.* (1997)], [Boyer *et al.* (1998)], [Zalka (1999)]. This is the case when $f(x)$ is a $NP - complete$ problem. It follows that for U_f-based search using a quantum computer $NP - complete$ problems remain $NP - complete$. Despite the fact the saving of $O(2^{\frac{m}{2}})$ compared to $O(2^m)$ is huge, $2^m \neq O(2^{\frac{m}{2}})$ means

$$\Theta(2^{\frac{m}{2}}) \neq \Theta(2^m). \qquad (10.28)$$

For $2^m \neq O(2^{\frac{m}{2}})$ we assume there exist a constant c, that for certain value $m_0 > 0$

$$0 \leq 2^m \leq c \cdot 2^{\frac{m}{2}} \quad \forall m \geq m_0.$$

However such a constant does not exist because from

$$2^m = 2^{\frac{m}{2}} \cdot 2^{\frac{m}{2}} \leq c \cdot 2^{\frac{m}{2}}$$

follows the simple contradiction

$$2^{\frac{m}{2}} \leq c.$$

10.3   Grover's Amplification

If the operator U_f is represented by $O(m)$ gates, then Grover's amplification algorithm implements exhaustive search in $O(\sqrt{n})$ steps in n-dimensional Hilbert space H_n [Grover (1996)], [Grover (1997)], [Grover (1998a)], [Grover (1998b)], [Grover (1996)], [Grover (1996)]. It is as good as any possible quantum algorithm for exhaustive search due to the lower bound $\Omega(\sqrt{n})$ [Aharonov (1999)]. The algorithm is based on the Householder reflection of state $|x\rangle$ of m qubits with $n = 2^m$ [Zalka (1999)].

10.3.1   *Householder reflection*

Beside rotation and permutation the Householder reflection is an important class of unitary transformations (some times also called the elementary reflector). The Householder reflection reflects one vector $|x\rangle \in H_n$ to its negative and leaves invariant the orthogonal complement of this vectors. It is described by the Householder matrix Q_x With $\||x\rangle\| = 1$ representing m qubits with $n = 2^m$

$$Q_x = I_m - 2 \cdot |x\rangle\langle x| \qquad (10.29)$$

Q_x is unitary,

$$Q_x \cdot Q_x^* = (I_m - 2 \cdot |x\rangle\langle x|) \cdot (I_m - 2 \cdot |x\rangle\langle x|)^*$$

$$Q_x \cdot Q_x^* = I_m - 2 \cdot |x\rangle\langle x| - 2 \cdot |x\rangle\langle x| + 4 \cdot |x\rangle\langle x| \cdot |x\rangle\langle x|$$

$$Q_x \cdot Q_x^* = I_m - 4 \cdot |x\rangle\langle x| + 4 \cdot \langle x|x\rangle \cdot |x\rangle\langle x| = I_m$$

$\langle x|x\rangle = 1$ because $\||x\rangle\| = 1$. With

$$P = |x\rangle\langle x|.$$

For example with

$$|x\rangle = \cos(\alpha) \cdot |x_1\rangle + \sin(\alpha) \cdot |x_2\rangle$$

we get

$$Q_x = \begin{pmatrix} 1 - 2 \cdot \cos^2 \cdot \alpha & -2 \cdot \cos\alpha \cdot \sin\alpha \\ -2 \cdot \cos\alpha \cdot \sin\alpha & 1 - 2 \cdot \sin^2\alpha \end{pmatrix} = \begin{pmatrix} -\cos 2 \cdot \alpha & -\sin 2 \cdot \alpha \\ -\sin 2 \cdot \alpha & \cos 2 \cdot \alpha \end{pmatrix}. \qquad (10.30)$$

It becomes clear with

$$Q_x \cdot |0\rangle = \begin{pmatrix} -\cos 2 \cdot \alpha \\ -\sin 2 \cdot \alpha \end{pmatrix}$$

and

$$Q_x \cdot |1\rangle = \begin{pmatrix} -\sin 2 \cdot \alpha \\ \cos 2 \cdot \alpha \end{pmatrix}$$

that Q_x is not a rotation by the angle $2 \cdot \alpha$

$$R_{2\alpha} = \begin{pmatrix} \cos 2 \cdot \alpha & -\sin 2 \cdot \alpha \\ \sin 2 \cdot \alpha & \cos 2 \cdot \alpha \end{pmatrix}.$$

It is a one dimensional reflection

$$S = \begin{pmatrix} -1 & 0 \\ 0 & 1 \end{pmatrix}$$

and a rotation by $R_{2\alpha}$

$$Q_x = R_{2\alpha} \cdot S.$$

10.3.2 Householder reflection and the mean value

Suppose P_m is generated by the normalized vector $|x\rangle$ indicating the direction of the bisecting line,

$$|x\rangle = \frac{1}{\sqrt{n}} \cdot |x_1\rangle + \frac{1}{\sqrt{n}} \cdot |x_2\rangle + \cdots + \frac{1}{\sqrt{n}} \cdot |x_n\rangle = \begin{pmatrix} \frac{1}{\sqrt{n}} \\ \vdots \\ \frac{1}{\sqrt{n}} \end{pmatrix} \qquad (10.31)$$

or in qubit notation (binary)

$$|x\rangle = \frac{1}{\sqrt{2^m}} \cdot \sum_{y \in B^m} |y\rangle \qquad (10.32)$$

then the projection matrix P_m is

$$P_m = |x\rangle\langle x| = \begin{pmatrix} \frac{1}{n} & \frac{1}{n} & \cdots & \frac{1}{n} \\ \frac{1}{n} & \frac{1}{n} & \cdots & \frac{1}{n} \\ \vdots & \vdots & \ddots & \vdots \\ \frac{1}{n} & \frac{1}{n} & \cdots & \frac{1}{n} \end{pmatrix} \qquad (10.33)$$

it computes for each dimension described by the fixed basis he mean value of all dimensions.

$$\begin{pmatrix} \frac{\sum_{i=1}^{n} x_i}{n} \\ \frac{\sum_{i=1}^{n} x_i}{n} \\ \vdots \\ \frac{\sum_{i=1}^{n} x_i}{n} \end{pmatrix} = \begin{pmatrix} \frac{1}{n} & \frac{1}{n} & \cdots & \frac{1}{n} \\ \frac{1}{n} & \frac{1}{n} & \cdots & \frac{1}{n} \\ \vdots & \vdots & \ddots & \vdots \\ \frac{1}{n} & \frac{1}{n} & \cdots & \frac{1}{n} \end{pmatrix} \cdot \begin{pmatrix} x_1 \\ x_2 \\ \vdots \\ x_n \end{pmatrix} \qquad (10.34)$$

we get

$$Q_x = I_m - 2 \cdot P_m. \tag{10.35}$$

For each dimension the Householder reflection in the direction of the bisecting line computes the following mapping,

$$x_i = x_i - 2 \cdot \frac{\sum_{i=1}^n x_i}{n}. \tag{10.36}$$

10.3.3 Amplification

Grover's amplification is based on $-Q_x$. It is a unitary operator with

$$G_m := -Q_x = -I_m + 2 \cdot P_m = 2 \cdot P_m - I_m \tag{10.37}$$

the mapping is defined as,

$$x_i = 2 \cdot \frac{\sum_{i=1}^n x_i}{n} - x_i. \tag{10.38}$$

Suppose only one amplitude of x_j is negative and the other one are positive. Then the corresponding amplitude grows with

$$x_j = 2 \cdot \frac{\sum_{i=1}^n x_j}{n} + x_i \tag{10.39}$$

the other x_i with $i \neq j$ diminish. With $j = 2$ we get

$$\begin{pmatrix} 2 \cdot \frac{\sum_{i=1}^n x_i}{n} - x_1 \\ 2 \cdot \frac{\sum_{i=1}^n x_i}{n} + x_2 \\ \vdots \\ 2 \cdot \frac{\sum_{i=1}^n x_i}{n} - x_n \end{pmatrix} = \begin{pmatrix} \frac{2}{n} - 1 & \frac{2}{n} & \cdots & \frac{2}{n} \\ \frac{2}{n} & \frac{2}{n} - 1 & \cdots & \frac{2}{n} \\ \vdots & \vdots & \ddots & \vdots \\ \frac{2}{n} & \frac{2}{n} & \cdots & \frac{2}{n} - 1 \end{pmatrix} \cdot \begin{pmatrix} x_1 \\ -x_2 \\ \vdots \\ x_n \end{pmatrix}. \tag{10.40}$$

Amplitude amplification is based on G_m and U_f. For a register of m qubits in a Hilbert space H_n we apply the U_f operator and then the operator G_m,

$$(G_m \otimes I_1) \cdot U_f \cdot W_{m+1} \cdot |0^{\oplus m}\rangle|1\rangle =$$

$$= G_m \cdot \left(\frac{1}{\sqrt{n}} \sum_{x \in B^m} (-1)^{f(x)} \cdot |x\rangle \right) \otimes \left(\frac{|0\rangle - |1\rangle}{\sqrt{2}} \right) \tag{10.41}$$

with G_m

$$G_m = \begin{pmatrix} \frac{2}{n} - 1 & \frac{2}{n} & \cdots & \frac{2}{n} \\ \frac{2}{n} & \frac{2}{n} - 1 & \cdots & \frac{2}{n} \\ \vdots & \vdots & \ddots & \vdots \\ \frac{2}{n} & \frac{2}{n} & \cdots & \frac{2}{n} - 1 \end{pmatrix} \tag{10.42}$$

note that for $m = 2$, G_2 is equal to the "spy" matrix S

$$G_2 = S = \frac{1}{2} \cdot \begin{pmatrix} -1 & 1 & 1 & 1 \\ 1 & -1 & 1 & 1 \\ 1 & 1 & -1 & 1 \\ 1 & 1 & 1 & -1 \end{pmatrix} \tag{10.43}$$

the resulting state is $|\tau\rangle$

$$(G_m \otimes I_1) \cdot U_f \cdot W_{m+1} \cdot |0^{\oplus m}\rangle |1\rangle = |\tau\rangle \otimes \left(\frac{|0\rangle - |1\rangle}{\sqrt{2}} \right). \tag{10.44}$$

The state $|\tau\rangle$ has an amplitude distribution with a lower entropy as the state with the maximum entropy $\log n$ represented by the maximal superposition

$$|y\rangle = \frac{1}{\sqrt{n}} \sum_{x \in B^m} (-1)^{f(x)} \cdot |x\rangle.$$

The new amplitude distribution is computed by

$$G_m \cdot |y\rangle = (2 \cdot P_m - I_m) \cdot |y\rangle.$$

First two times the average amplitude is computed. The amplitude values for non solution are $\frac{1}{\sqrt{n}}$ and for one marked solution $-\frac{1}{\sqrt{n}}$, it follows

$$A = 2 \cdot P_m \cdot |y\rangle = \frac{2}{n} \cdot \left(n \cdot \frac{1}{\sqrt{n}} - \frac{1}{\sqrt{n}} - \frac{1}{\sqrt{n}} \right) = \frac{2}{n} \cdot \left((n-1) \cdot \frac{1}{\sqrt{n}} - \frac{1}{\sqrt{n}} \right) \tag{10.45}$$

$$A = 2 \cdot P_m \cdot |y\rangle = \frac{2}{\sqrt{n}} \cdot \left(1 - \frac{2}{n} \right) = \frac{2 \cdot n - 4}{n^{\frac{3}{2}}}. \tag{10.46}$$

The amplitude of the state $|\tau\rangle$ indicating the solution in the dimension i is

$$\tau_i = A + \frac{1}{\sqrt{n}} = \frac{3 \cdot n - 4}{n^{\frac{3}{2}}} = \frac{3}{\sqrt{n}} - \frac{4}{n \cdot \sqrt{n}} \tag{10.47}$$

and the non solution in the dimension j with $j \neq i$

$$\tau_j = A - \frac{1}{\sqrt{n}} = \frac{n - 4}{n^{\frac{3}{2}}} = \frac{1}{\sqrt{n}} - \frac{4}{n \cdot \sqrt{n}}. \tag{10.48}$$

For $n = 4$ $\tau_i = 1$ and $\tau_j = 0$, for $n = 2^8$ $\tau_i = 0.186523$ and $\tau_j = 0.0615234$. The probability of measuring the solution depending on the size n is

$$\||\tau_i\rangle\|^2 = \left| \frac{3}{\sqrt{n}} - \frac{4}{n \cdot \sqrt{n}} \right|^2 \tag{10.49}$$

and non solution

$$\||\tau_j\rangle\|^2 = \left| \frac{1}{\sqrt{n}} - \frac{4}{n \cdot \sqrt{n}} \right|^2. \tag{10.50}$$

In the Figure 10.1 we indicated the probability of measuring the solution and non solution for $4 \leq n \leq 16$ and in the Figure 10.2 for $2^8 \leq n \leq 2^{16}$. For more than 4 qubits the probability of measuring a solution will be below 0.5. The probability can be increased by the iterative amplification.

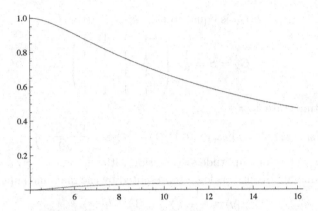

Fig. 10.1 The probability of measuring the solution and non solution for $4 \leq n \leq 16$. The x-axis indicates n and the y-axis the probability. Top curve is the probability of the solution, down curve the probability of the non-solution.

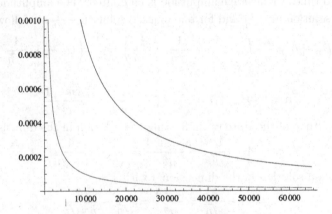

Fig. 10.2 The probability of measuring the solution and non solution for $2^8 \leq n \leq 2^{16}$. The x-axis indicates n and the y-axis the probability. Top curve is the probability of the solution, down curve the probability of the non-solution.

10.3.4 *Iterative amplification*

With the definition

$$\Gamma_m := (G_m \otimes I_1) \cdot U_f \qquad (10.51)$$

the resulting state is $|\tau\rangle$. We describe several amplifications by

$$\left(\prod_{t=1}^{r} \Gamma_m \right) \cdot W_{m+1} \cdot |0^{\oplus m}\rangle |1\rangle = \Gamma_m \cdot \Gamma_m \cdots \cdots \Gamma_m \cdot W_{m+1} \cdot |0^{\oplus m}\rangle |1\rangle =$$

$$= |\tau\rangle \otimes \left(\frac{|0\rangle - |1\rangle}{\sqrt{2}} \right).$$

How many iterations do we need to preform, or what is the suitable value for r? The probability of seeing one solution should be as close as possible to 1 and r should be as small as possible. Suppose that the function $f(x)$ has k solutions with $n \gg k \geq 1$,

$$f_\xi(x) = \begin{cases} 1 & if \quad x = \xi_i \quad i \in \{1, 2, \cdots, k\} \\ 0 & else \end{cases} \tag{10.52}$$

we want to find x for which $f(x) = 1$. All the preceding steps can be easily extended to this more general case. The amplitude for the solution at the iteration t will be indicated by α_t non-solution by β_t. For $t = 0$ before the first iteration of Γ_m

$$\alpha_0 = \frac{1}{\sqrt{n}} \tag{10.53}$$

$$\beta_0 = \frac{1}{\sqrt{n}}. \tag{10.54}$$

In the first iteration Γ_m two times the average amplitude is computed, the amplitude values for non-solution are $\frac{1}{\sqrt{n}}$ and for one marked solution $-\frac{1}{\sqrt{n}}$, it follows

$$A = \frac{2}{n} \cdot \left(n \cdot \frac{1}{\sqrt{n}} - \frac{k}{\sqrt{n}} - \frac{k}{\sqrt{n}} \right) = \frac{2}{n} \cdot \left((n - k) \cdot \frac{1}{\sqrt{n}} - \frac{k}{\sqrt{n}} \right) \tag{10.55}$$

$$A = \frac{2}{n} \cdot ((n - k) \cdot \beta_0 - k \cdot \alpha_0). \tag{10.56}$$

The amplitude of the solution is

$$\alpha_1 = A + \frac{1}{\sqrt{n}} = A + \alpha_0 = \frac{2}{n} \cdot ((n - k) \cdot \beta_0 - k \cdot \alpha_0) + \alpha_0, \tag{10.57}$$

$$\alpha_1 = \frac{1}{n} \cdot (\alpha_0 \cdot (n - 2 \cdot k) + \beta_0 \cdot (2 \cdot n - 2 \cdot k),$$

$$\alpha_1 = \alpha_0 \cdot (1 - \frac{2 \cdot k}{n}) + \beta_0 \cdot (2 - \frac{2 \cdot k}{n}), \tag{10.58}$$

and the non-solution

$$\beta_1 = A - \frac{1}{\sqrt{n}} = A - \beta_0 = \frac{2}{n} \cdot ((n - k) \cdot \beta_0 - k \cdot \alpha_0) - \beta_0, \tag{10.59}$$

$$\beta_1 = -\alpha_0 \cdot \frac{2 \cdot k}{n} + \beta_0 \cdot (1 - \frac{2 \cdot k}{n}). \tag{10.60}$$

We can describe the evolution of the amplitudes in time t by two coupled recurrence equations. They represent a discrete dynamical system of two difference equations

$$\alpha_{t+1} = \alpha_t \cdot \left(1 - \frac{2 \cdot k}{n}\right) + \beta_t \cdot \left(2 - \frac{2 \cdot k}{n}\right) \qquad (10.61)$$

$$\beta_{t+1} = -\alpha_t \cdot \frac{2 \cdot k}{n} + \beta_t \cdot \left(1 - \frac{2 \cdot k}{n}\right). \qquad (10.62)$$

We can indicate the states of a system in three dimensional phase space of α_t, β_t and t with the boundary condition of $\alpha_0 = \beta_0 = \frac{1}{\sqrt{n}}$ (see Figure 10.3). It represents a periodic orbit in time. The projected orbit in the two dimensional subspace α_t, β_t represents an ellipse (see Figure 10.4). The ellipse is determined by the values of n and k (see Figure 10.5). The pro-

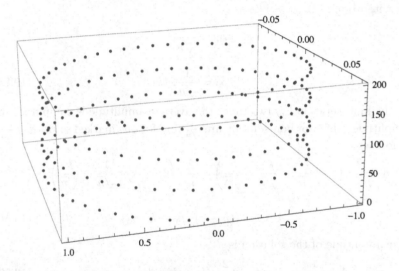

Fig. 10.3 Phase space of α_t, β_t and t with the boundary condition of $\alpha_0 = \beta_0 = \frac{1}{\sqrt{n}}$. The values are $n = 256$, $k = 1$ and $1 \leq t \leq 200$. The x-axis indicates α_t, the y-axis β_t and the z-axis t.

jected orbit in two dimensional subspace of amplitude and time t represents two sine waves, periodic functions described by α_t and β_t (see Figure 10.6). The period is determined by the value of k and n. With $k = 1$ the peak amplitude is one (see Figure 10.7 and Figure 10.5). Such a linear and periodic system is usually described by sine and cosine equations. It should be noted that a cosine wave is a sine wave because of the phase-shift relation

$$\cos(\theta) = \sin\left(\theta + \frac{\pi}{2}\right).$$

The ellipse in a Cartesian system is represented by the equation

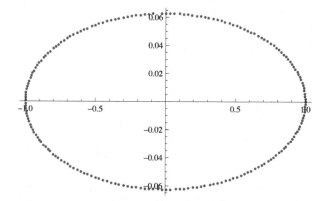

Fig. 10.4 The projected orbit in the two dimensional subspace α_t, β_t with the boundary condition of $\alpha_0 = \beta_0 = \frac{1}{\sqrt{n}}$. The values are $n = 256$, $k = 1$ and $1 \leq t \leq 200$. The x-axis indicates α_t and the y-axis β_t.

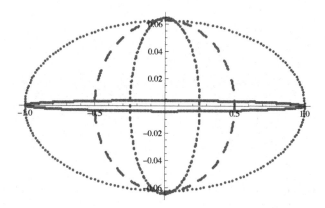

Fig. 10.5 The projected orbit in the two dimensional subspace α_t, β_t with the boundary condition of $\alpha_0 = \beta_0 = \frac{1}{\sqrt{n}}$. The x-axis indicates α_t, the y-axis β_t. The outer ellipse has the values $n = 256$, $k = 1$ as before, the two ellipses with diminishing x-axis radius corresponds to increased k values $k = 4$ and $k = 16$. For all three ellipses with $n = 256$, 200 iterations were done. In the fourth ellipse k is one and $n = 65536 = 2^{16}$, y-axis radius diminish. 1000 iterations were done.

$$\frac{x^2}{a^2} + \frac{y^2}{b^2} = 1. \tag{10.63}$$

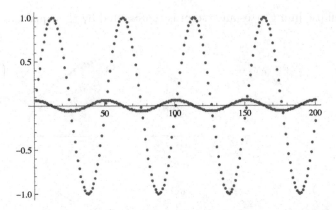

Fig. 10.6 The projected orbit in the two dimensional subspace of amplitude and time t represents a periodic function described by α_t (the dotted curve) and β_t (the continuous curve). The x-axis indicates t and the y-axis the amplitude. The values are $n = 256$, $k = 1$ and $1 \leq t \leq 200$.

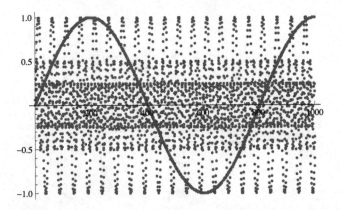

Fig. 10.7 The projected orbit in the two dimensional subspace of amplitude and time t. The x-axis indicates t and the y-axis the amplitude. Four periodic functions represented by α_t with different periods are shown. The period is determined by the value of k and n. With $k = 1$ the peak amplitude is one. The greatest period corresponds to the values $k = 1$ and $n = 65536$. For $n = 256$ the period diminishes, for $k = 4$ and $k = 16$ the peak amplitude diminishes below one and the period diminishes even more. 1000 iterations were done.

Because α_t and β_t are real, following equation representing an ellipse is given by

$$k \cdot \alpha_t^2 + (n - k) \cdot \beta_t^2 = 1. \tag{10.64}$$

Using the the Pythagorean identity

$$\sin^2 \theta + \cos^2 \theta = 1$$

we can rewrite the equation representing the ellipse as

$$k \cdot \left(\sqrt{\frac{1}{k}} \cdot \sin \theta_t \right)^2 + (n - k) \cdot \left(\sqrt{\frac{1}{n - k}} \cdot \cos \theta_t \right)^2 = 1 \qquad (10.65)$$

it follows that

$$\alpha_t = \sqrt{\frac{1}{k}} \cdot \sin \theta_t \quad and \quad \beta_t = \sqrt{\frac{1}{n - k}} \cdot \cos \theta_t \qquad (10.66)$$

and we can rewrite the the two coupled recurrence equations as

$$\sqrt{\frac{1}{k}} \cdot \sin \theta_{t+1} = \sqrt{\frac{1}{k}} \cdot \sin \theta_t \cdot \left(1 - \frac{2 \cdot k}{n} \right) + \sqrt{\frac{1}{n - k}} \cdot \cos \theta_t \cdot \left(2 - \frac{2 \cdot k}{n} \right)$$

$$\sqrt{\frac{1}{n - k}} \cdot \cos \theta_{t+1} = -\sqrt{\frac{1}{k}} \cdot \sin \theta_t \cdot \frac{2 \cdot k}{n} + \sqrt{\frac{1}{n - k}} \cdot \cos \theta_t \cdot \left(1 - \frac{2 \cdot k}{n} \right)$$

simplified as

$$\sin \theta_{t+1} = \sin \theta_t \cdot \left(1 - \frac{2 \cdot k}{n} \right) + \cos \theta_t \cdot \frac{2 \cdot \sqrt{k} \cdot \sqrt{n - k}}{n} \qquad (10.67)$$

$$\cos \theta_{t+1} = -\sin \theta_t \cdot \frac{2 \cdot \sqrt{k} \cdot \sqrt{n - k}}{n} + \cos \theta_t \cdot \left(1 - \frac{2 \cdot k}{n} \right). \qquad (10.68)$$

Trigonometric simplification*

Because

$$-1 \le \left(1 - \frac{2 \cdot k}{n} \right) \le 1$$

we can represent it as

$$\cos \omega = 1 - \frac{2 \cdot k}{n}. \qquad (10.69)$$

Because of the Pythagorean identity

$$\left(1 - \frac{2 \cdot k}{n} \right)^2 + \left(\frac{2 \cdot \sqrt{k} \cdot \sqrt{n - k}}{n} \right)^2 = 1$$

it follows that

$$\sin \omega = \frac{2 \cdot \sqrt{k} \cdot \sqrt{n - k}}{n} \qquad (10.70)$$

and we can rewrite again the the two coupled recurrence equations as

$$\sin\theta_{t+1} = \sin\theta_t \cdot \cos\omega + \cos\theta_t \cdot \sin\omega \tag{10.71}$$

$$\cos\theta_{t+1} = -\sin\theta_t \cdot \sin\omega + \cos\theta_t \cdot \cos\omega \tag{10.72}$$

Because of the trigonometric identities, addition and subtraction theorem, the two coupled recurrence equations with the boundary condition θ_0 are

$$\sin\theta_{t+1} = \sin(\theta_t + \omega) = \sin(\theta_0 + t \cdot \omega + \omega) \tag{10.73}$$

$$\cos\theta_{t+1} = \cos(\theta_t + \omega) = \cos(\theta_0 + t \cdot \omega + \omega) \tag{10.74}$$

and we can rewrite the recurrence equations into two simple equations

$$\alpha_t = \frac{1}{\sqrt{k}} \cdot \sin(\theta_0 + t \cdot \omega) \tag{10.75}$$

$$\beta_t = \frac{1}{\sqrt{n-k}} \cdot \cos(\theta_0 + t \cdot \omega). \tag{10.76}$$

With the boundary condition of $\alpha_0 = \beta_0 = \frac{1}{\sqrt{n}}$ and $\alpha_0 = \sqrt{\frac{1}{k}} \cdot \sin\theta_0$, $\beta_0 = \frac{1}{\sqrt{n-k}} \cdot \cos\theta_0$ it follows that

$$\sin^2\theta_0 = \frac{k}{n} \tag{10.77}$$

and

$$\cos^2\theta_0 = \frac{n-k}{n} = 1 - \frac{k}{n} \tag{10.78}$$

and because of the double angle formula

$$\cos(2 \cdot x) = 2 \cdot \cos^2 x - 1 = 1 - 2 \cdot \sin^2 x$$

and

$$\sin(2 \cdot x) = 2 \cdot \sin x \cdot \cos x$$

it follows that

$$\cos\omega = 1 - \frac{2 \cdot k}{n} = 1 - 2 \cdot \sin^2\theta_0 = \cos(2 \cdot \theta_0). \tag{10.79}$$

$$\sin\omega = \frac{2 \cdot \sqrt{k} \cdot \sqrt{n-k}}{n} = 2\sin\theta_0 \cdot \cos_0\theta_0 = \sin(2 \cdot \theta_0). \tag{10.80}$$

Using the trigonometric identities

$$\alpha_t = \frac{1}{\sqrt{k}} \cdot (\sin\theta_0 \cdot \cos(t \cdot \omega) + \cos\theta_0 \cdot \sin(t \cdot \omega)) \tag{10.81}$$

$$\beta_t = \frac{1}{\sqrt{n-k}} \cdot (-\sin\theta_0 \cdot \sin(t \cdot \omega) + \cos\theta_0 \cdot \cos(t \cdot \omega)) \tag{10.82}$$

the solution for the two difference equations representing the discrete dynamical with the boundary condition $\alpha_0 = \beta_0 = \frac{1}{\sqrt{n}}$ is represented by the two equations

$$\alpha_t = \frac{1}{\sqrt{k}} \cdot \sin(\theta_0 + t \cdot 2 \cdot \theta_0) = \frac{1}{\sqrt{k}} \cdot \sin(\theta_0 \cdot (2 \cdot t + 1)) \tag{10.83}$$

$$\beta_t = \frac{1}{\sqrt{n-k}} \cdot \cos(\theta_0 + t \cdot 2 \cdot \theta_0) = \frac{1}{\sqrt{n-k}} \cdot \cos(\theta_0 \cdot (2 \cdot t + 1)) \tag{10.84}$$

with

$$\theta_0 = \sin^{-1}\left(\sqrt{\frac{k}{n}}\right). \tag{10.85}$$

10.3.5 Number of iterations

The probability of seeing one solution should be as close as possible to 1 and the number of iterations r should be as small as possible. Because there are k solution, the probability of measuring a state that represents a solution is

$$k \cdot \alpha_t^2 = \sin^2(\theta_0 \cdot (2 \cdot t + 1)) = 1 \tag{10.86}$$

$$\theta_0 \cdot (2 \cdot t + 1) = \frac{\pi}{2} \tag{10.87}$$

after t^* iterations the probability of measuring a solution is nearly one

$$t^* := t = \frac{\pi}{4 \cdot \theta_0} - \frac{1}{2} = \frac{\pi}{4} \cdot \sqrt{\frac{n}{k}} - \frac{1}{2} = \frac{\pi}{4} \cdot \sqrt{\frac{2^m}{k}} - \frac{1}{2} \tag{10.88}$$

$$t^* = 0.785398 \cdot \sqrt{\frac{2^m}{k}} - 0.5. \tag{10.89}$$

For $k = 1$ and more than two qubits ($m > 2$, $n = 2^m$) the corresponding value is above the possible lower bound for U_f based search

$$t^* = \sqrt{n} \cdot 0.785398 - 0.5 > \sqrt{n} \cdot 0.324423. \tag{10.90}$$

The number of iterations r

$$\left(\prod_{t=1}^{r} \Gamma_m\right) \cdot W_{m+1} \cdot |0^{\oplus m}\rangle|1\rangle$$

is the largest integer not greater than t^*,

$$r = \lfloor t^* \rfloor = \left\lfloor \frac{\pi}{4} \cdot \sqrt{\frac{2^m}{k}} - \frac{1}{2} \right\rfloor. \tag{10.91}$$

The value of r depends on the relation of n versus k. For $n = 4$ and $k = 1$ we need only one rotation, we need as well only one rotation for

$$\frac{n}{4} = k$$

to find **one** of the k solutions. For 16 qubits and one solution, $k = 1$, $n = 65536 = 2^{16}$, $t^* = 200.562$. In this case we need two hundred rotations. The probability of measuring a state that represents a solution is nearly one. It is possible to adapt the iterations in such a way that the probability of finding a solution is exactly one. One changes θ_0 of the difference equations either in the last step or continuously so that the $r = t^* = \lfloor t^* \rfloor$ as proposed by Brassard [Brassard et al. (2000)], [Brassard et al. (1998)]. The resulting speed up remains quadratic. The iterative amplification algorithm requires the value of k in order to determine the number of iterations. We can determine the value of k by the quantum counting algorithm.

10.3.6   Quantum counting

Quantum counting algorithm is based on the QFT period algorithm to estimate the period of the sin wave period represented by the of the amplitude α_t or β_t [Brassard et al. (1998)]. [Brassard et al. (2000)] (see Figure 10.6). We define t iterations of amplification as

$$\Phi^t = \left(\prod_{t=1}^{t} \Gamma_m \right). \tag{10.92}$$

The state $|\tau\rangle$ has two different amplitudes representing solution and non-solution. They define the two subspaces $|\tau_{solution}\rangle$ and $|\tau_{non}\rangle$ with

$$\Phi^t \cdot W_{m+1}|0^{\otimes m}\rangle|1\rangle = k \cdot \alpha_t \cdot |\tau_{solution}\rangle + (n - k) \cdot \beta_t \cdot |\tau_{non}\rangle \otimes \left(\frac{|0\rangle - |1\rangle}{\sqrt{2}} \right) \tag{10.93}$$

ignoring the auxiliary qubt, or target qubit we can write

$$\Phi^t \cdot W_m|0^{\otimes m}\rangle =$$

$$= \sqrt{k} \cdot \sin(\theta_0 \cdot (2 \cdot t + 1)) \cdot |\tau_{solution}\rangle + \sqrt{(n - k)} \cdot \cos(\theta_0 \cdot (2 \cdot t + 1)) \cdot |\tau_{non}\rangle. \tag{10.94}$$

We define a unitary operator U_Φ that acts on two registers $|t\rangle$ and $|x\rangle$ and one auxiliary qubit,

$$U_\Phi \cdot |t\rangle|x\rangle \otimes \left(\frac{|0\rangle - |1\rangle}{\sqrt{2}}\right) = |t\rangle|\Phi^t|x\rangle \otimes \left(\frac{|0\rangle - |1\rangle}{\sqrt{2}}\right) \qquad (10.95)$$

with

$$U_\Phi \cdot |t\rangle \otimes \left(\frac{1}{\sqrt{2^m}} \sum_{x \in B^m} |x\rangle\right) \otimes \left(\frac{|0\rangle - |1\rangle}{\sqrt{2}}\right)$$

$$= |t\rangle \otimes (k \cdot \alpha_t \cdot |\tau_{solution}\rangle + (n-k) \cdot \beta_t \cdot |\tau_{non}\rangle) \otimes \left(\frac{|0\rangle - |1\rangle}{\sqrt{2}}\right) \qquad (10.96)$$

after the application of U_Ψ the two registers and the auxiliary qubit are entangled. In the first step of the algorithm we build a superposition of m qubits and μ qubits with $T = 2^\mu$ taking into account the auxiliary bit. The value of T can be estimated by the determination of the period of

$$\sin(\theta_0 \cdot (2 \cdot t + 1))$$

assuming $k = 1$. It follows that

$$W_\mu \cdot W_{m+1}|0^{\otimes\mu}\rangle|0^{\otimes m}\rangle|1\rangle =$$

$$= \left(\frac{1}{\sqrt{T}} \sum_{t \in B^\mu} |t\rangle\right) \otimes \left(\frac{1}{\sqrt{n}} \sum_{x \in B^m} |x\rangle\right) \otimes \left(\frac{|0\rangle - |1\rangle}{\sqrt{2}}\right).$$

In the second step we apply the U_Φ operator

$$U_\Phi \left(\frac{1}{\sqrt{T}} \sum_{t \in B^\mu} |t\rangle\right) \otimes \left(\frac{1}{\sqrt{n}} \sum_{x \in B^m} |x\rangle\right) \otimes \left(\frac{|0\rangle - |1\rangle}{\sqrt{2}}\right) =$$

$$\left(\frac{1}{\sqrt{T}} \sum_{t \in B^\mu} |t\rangle\right) \otimes (k \cdot \alpha_t \cdot |\tau_{solution}\rangle + (n-k) \cdot \beta_t \cdot |\tau_{non}\rangle) \otimes \left(\frac{|0\rangle - |1\rangle}{\sqrt{2}}\right).$$

$$(10.97)$$

In the third step we measure the second register of the compound system. As the result the state of the system is projected to the subspace that corresponds to the observed state and the vector representing the state is renormalized to the unit length. The result of the second register is either $f_{solution}(t) = \sin(\theta_0 \cdot (2 \cdot t + 1))$ or $f_{non}(t) = \cos(\theta_0 \cdot (2 \cdot t + 1))$. Both functions have the same period and will be represented as $f(t)$. The new amplitude distribution is normalized and has the same periodic period as $f(t)$. The following steps correspond to the QFT period algorithm as before.

10.4   Circuit Representation

Grover's amplification is based on $G_m = -Q_x$. and can be represented by $O(m)$ quantum gates. The unitary operator Λ_m reverse the sign of $|0\rangle$

$$\Lambda_m \cdot |0\rangle = -|0\rangle$$

and for $|x\rangle \neq |0\rangle$

$$\Lambda_m \cdot |x\rangle = |x\rangle.$$

Λ_m can be implemented efficiently with $f_0(x)$

$$f_0(x) = \begin{cases} 1 & if \quad x = 0 \\ 0 & else \end{cases} \tag{10.98}$$

as

$$\frac{1}{\sqrt{n}} \sum_{x \in B^m} (-1)^{f_0(x)} \cdot |x\rangle \otimes \left(\frac{|0\rangle - |1\rangle}{\sqrt{2}} \right). \tag{10.99}$$

We can write

$$G_m = -Q_x = -I_m + 2 \cdot P_m = 2 \cdot P_m - I_m = -(W_m \cdot \Lambda_m \cdot W_m) \tag{10.100}$$

with the auxiliary qbit for the Λ_m operator representation it becomes

$$G_m = -(W_m \cdot \Lambda_m \cdot W_m) \otimes \left(\frac{|0\rangle - |1\rangle}{\sqrt{2}} \right) \tag{10.101}$$

neglecting the auxiliary qbit it follows that

$$W_m \cdot \Lambda_m \cdot W_m = \begin{pmatrix} 1 - \frac{2}{n} & -\frac{2}{n} & \cdots & -\frac{2}{n} \\ -\frac{2}{n} & 1 - \frac{2}{n} & \cdots & -\frac{2}{n} \\ \vdots & \vdots & \ddots & \vdots \\ -\frac{2}{n} & -\frac{2}{n} & \cdots & 1 - \frac{2}{n} \end{pmatrix}. \tag{10.102}$$

The first row of W_m which is positive and can be represented as

$$\langle w| = \sum_{x \in B^m} \langle x|$$

By the operator Λ_m it becomes negative. $\langle w|$ it multiplies with the first column of W_m

$$|w\rangle = \sum_{x \in B^m} |x\rangle$$

the first column multiplied with the first row results in

$$|w\rangle \langle w| = P_m.$$

This value is subtracted from

$$I_m = W_m \cdot W_m$$

and replaced by $-|w\rangle\langle w|$

$$I_m - |w\rangle\langle w| - |w\rangle\langle w| = I_m - 2 \cdot |w\rangle\langle w| = I_m - 2 \cdot P_m. \qquad (10.103)$$

Because $U_{f(0)}$ that represents $f_0(x)$ can be represented by $O(m)$ gates and all other operators are based on Hadamard operator W_m built by a direct product of m W_1 matrices, G_m can be represented by $O(m)$ quantum gates. Given the fact that the operator U_f is represented by $O(m)$ gates, then Grover's amplification algorithm implements exhaustive search in $O(\sqrt{n})$ steps in n-dimensional Hilbert space H_n.

10.5 Speeding up the Traveling Salesman Problem

A salesman must visit t cities; he must visit each city exactly once and finish at the city where his tour started. We call such a tour a valid tour. The costs of traveling from city i to city j are represented by c_{ij}. The costs do not need to be symmetrical $c_{ij} \neq c_{ji}$. The salesman wishes to conduct a valid tour that costs at most k. The traveling salesman problem (TSP) is the most popular $NP - complete$ problem. An instance (ticket) leads to a "yes" answer in polynomial time. Given a tour, we can verify whether the tour is valid, and the costs are below k in polynomial time.

We search through all possible orderings of the cities and verify, for each ordering, if the tour is valid and the costs are below k. A quantum circuit U_{TSP} with a polynomial number of quantum gates can verify, for a given tour, whether it is a solution. Because we can not reset to the input state, the circuit should recompute the output before applying the amplification step. For t cities, we can represent each city by $\lceil \log_2 t \rceil$ qubits, and a tour by a register of

$$m^* = t \cdot \lceil \log_2 t \rceil$$

qubits. We will examine all of the possible orderings of t cities with repetition for simplicity. Without repetitions, there are $t!$ possible orderings; with repetition,

$$t^t = 2^{t \log_2 t} = 2^m \qquad (10.104)$$

with

$$m = t \cdot \log_2 t \leq m^*.$$

We apply the U_{TSP} operator,

$$\Gamma_m := (G_m \otimes I_1) \cdot U_{TSP} \tag{10.105}$$

determine the value of r by quantum counting

$$\left(\prod_{t=1}^{r} \Gamma_m \right) \cdot W_{m+1} \cdot |0^{\oplus m}\rangle |1\rangle = |\tau\rangle \otimes \left(\frac{|0\rangle - |1\rangle}{\sqrt{2}} \right) \tag{10.106}$$

and and determine the solution by the measurement of the register $|\tau\rangle$. The computing costs are

$$O(t^{\frac{t}{2}}) = O\left(\sqrt{2^m} \right) \tag{10.107}$$

with

$$t! \gg t^{\frac{t}{2}}.$$

Any $NP - complete$ problem can be solved in a similar way.

10.6   The Generate-and-Test Method

The generate-and-test method is a simple AI paradigm. This approach uses a generator and a tester. The generator produces all of the possible solutions, and the tester evaluates each possible solution to see whether it is the expected solution (see Figure 10.8).

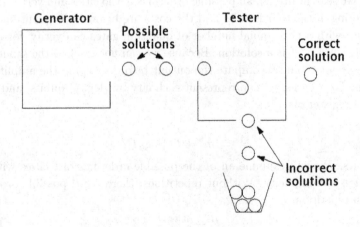

Fig. 10.8   The generate-and-test method.

This approach is mostly used to solve identification problems. The generator produces hypotheses that are tested. For some problems, the possible solutions can be represented by some points in the problem space. For other problems, the possible solutions can be represented by paths in the problem space. We can speed up the generate-and-test method by mapping the generator into a superposition and the tester into an oracle represented by a quantum circuit.

Chapter 11

Quantum Problem-Solving

11.1 Symbols and Quantum Reality

Problem-solving can be modeled by a production system that implements a search algorithm. The search defines a problem space and can be represented as a tree. Because symbols do not by themselves represent any utilizable knowledge, additional heuristic functions are used to speed up the search. Without the use of heuristic functions, real-world problems become intractable because of the exponential growth of the leaves in the tree. A heuristic function is used that rates the value's different states according to how far they are from the desired state. A best-first search is that in which the best rule (according to a heuristic function of the conflict set) is chosen. The better the heuristic measure of the remaining distance to the desired state is, the faster the best-first search [Winston (1992)]. An example for a simple heuristic function is the simple assumption that the distance between the states in the problem space is related to the similarity of the vectors that represent the states. A vector corresponds to a pattern that mirrors the way that the biological sense organs describe the world and is called a sub-symbol. The argument as presented before indicates that the heuristic function results from the Euclidian geometry of the world as experienced by humans. Could physical nature as described by quantum physics also lead to a quantum heuristic? In the relation of sub-symbols to symbols, do quantum-symbols exist?

In quantum computation, there are two known principles to speed up the computation:

- The QFT can determine the period of a wave (periodic function) exponentially faster than any known classical algorithm. QFT is based on the unitary DFT matrix and FFT decomposition.

199

- Grover's algorithm can speed up the search quadratically. Grover's algorithm is based on the unitary Householder reflection, which is represented by a unitary matrix.

In a tree, we search for a leaf ξ. Using Grover's algorithm, we represent the corresponding search tree by a quantum Boolean circuit U_{tree}. What is the speedup in relation to the structure of the represented tree? We will investigate this question starting from classical tree search algorithms, which will lead us to the general model of a quantum computer, the Tarrataca's quantum production system.

11.2   Uninformed Tree Search

In an uninformed search, no additional information about the states is given. The search represented by a search tree is performed from an initial state through the following states until a goal state is reached. A search tree is represented by nodes and edges. Each node represents a state, and each edge represents a transition from one state to the following state. The initial state defines the root of the tree. From each state ν, either B_ν states can be reached or the state is a leaf. B_ν represents the branching factor of the node v. A leaf represents either the goal of the computation or an impasse when no valid transition to a succeeding state exists. In contrast to a real tree in computer science, the root of a tree structure is at the top of the tree and the leaves are at the bottom. Every node besides the root has a unique node from which it was reached, called the parent. The parent is the node above it and is connected by an edge. Each parent ν has B_ν children. The depth of a node ν is the number of edges to the root node. Nodes with the same depth k define the level k. For a tree with a constant branching factor B, each node at each level k has B children, and at each level k, there are $B \cdot k$ nodes [Nilsson (1982)], [Luger and Stubblefield (1993)], [Russell and Norvig (2010)].

Breadth-first search   In a breadth-first search the root node (level $L = 0$) is expanded first. Then each children of the root at the level $L = 1$ are expanded, they become the parents of the children at the level $L = 2$. Then the procedure is repeated for the preceding levels until a goal is reached or all nodes are impasse states (see Figure 11.1). Breadth-first search performs a level wise search. All nodes at level L have to be visited before visiting a node at level $L + 1$. For a constant branching factor B B^m nodes are

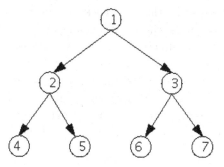

Fig. 11.1   In a breadth-first search the root node (level $L = 0$) is expanded first. Then each children of the root at the level $L = 1$ are expanded, they become the parents of the children at the level $L = 2$.

expanded at level m with $k = 0$ being the root. The total number of nodes at level m is represented by the geometric series

$$1 + B + B^2 + B^3 + \cdots + B^m = \sum_{i=0}^{m} B^i = \frac{1 - B^{m+1}}{1 - B} = O(B^m). \quad (11.1)$$

Every node that is generated has to be represented in memory and the number of nodes grows exponentially. The computing costs and the memory requirements are in worst case $O(B^m)$.

Depth-first search   Progressive depending and local focusing leads to a depth-first search [Newell (1990)]. It always expands the deepest node in the search tree until a goal is reached or all nodes are impasse states (see Figure 11.2). An impasse is present when no valid transition to a

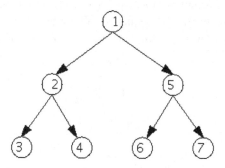

Fig. 11.2   Depth-first search always expands the deepest node in the search tree until a goal is reached or all nodes are impasse states.

succeeding state exists. In this case backtracking to the previous state is done. Another state can be chosen, if possible, or backtracking is repeated. In worst case the same number of nodes are visited as in breadth-first search. Commonly this number is less and the memory requirements are low compared to breadth-first search. Only a path from the root to the current node with the remaining unexpected sibling nodes for each node on the path have to be represented. If m is the maximum depth of the search tree and for a constant branching factor B the memory requirements are

$$B \cdot m + 1 \qquad (11.2)$$

we add a one because the node at the depth m is a leaf or an impasse. The computing costs are in the worst case $O(B^m)$ and the memory requirements $B \cdot m = O(m)$. Depth-first search first search contrary to breadth-first search can fail in the case the maximum depth of the search tree converges to $m \to \infty$. A solution to this problem is the combination of both methods with the benefits of both of them.

Iterative deepening search   In iterative deepening search we gradually increase the limit of the search from one, to two, three, four and continue to do it until a goal is found. For each limit m_k a depth-first search is performed from the root with m_k being the maximum depth of the search tree. During iterative deepening states are generated multiple times [Korf (1985)], [Russell and Norvig (2010)]. The time complexity of iterative deepening search is of the same order of magnitude as breadth-first search [Korf (1985)], as explained by Richard E. Korf: "Since the number of nodes on a given level of the tree grows exponentially with depth, almost all time is spent in the deepest level, even through shallower levels are generated an arithmetically increasing number of times." The paradox can be explained by the arithmetico-geometric sequence. The number of nodes for iterative deepening for each level starting with level zero (for simplicity) is given by

$$1$$

$$1 + B$$

$$1 + B + B^2$$

$$\ldots$$

to level m is given by

$$1 + B + B^2 + B^3 + \cdots + B^m$$

the costs C_m (total number of visited nodes) are represented by the arithmetic-geometric sequence that represent the sum of each iteration

$$C_m = (m+1) \cdot 1 + m \cdot B + (m-1) \cdot B^2 + (m-2) \cdot B^3 + \cdots + 1 \cdot B^m, \quad (11.3)$$

$$C_m = \sum_{i=0}^{m} (m+1-i) \cdot B^i. \quad (11.4)$$

With

$$C_m = \sum_{i=1}^{m+1} (m+1-(i-1)) \cdot B^{i-1}. \quad (11.5)$$

According to Riley [Riley *et al.* (2006)]

$$C_m - C_m \cdot B = C_m \cdot (1-B) = m+1-(2 \cdot m+1) \cdot B^{m+1} + \frac{B \cdot (1-B^m)}{(1-B)}, \quad (11.6)$$

$$C_m = \frac{m+1}{1-B} - \frac{(2 \cdot m+1) \cdot B^{m+1}}{1-B} + \frac{B \cdot (1-B^m)}{(1-B)^2}, \quad (11.7)$$

by simplifying this equation we arrive at

$$C_m = \frac{1+m-B \cdot m - 2 \cdot B^{1+m} \cdot (1+m) + B^{2+m} \cdot (1+2 \cdot m)}{(B-1)^2} = O(B^m). \quad (11.8)$$

The computing costs are in the worst case $O(B^m)$ and the memory requirements $B \cdot m = O(m)$. It follows that we should use depth-first search if the depth of the solution is known, otherwise we should prefer iterative deepening over breadth-first search due to the low memory requirements.

Loops To speed up the search the formation of loops should be prohibited. By comparison with the sequence of carried out states loops can be prevented.

11.3   Heuristic Search

Heuristic search is based on a heuristic function $h(\nu)$ that estimates the cheapest cost from the node ν to the goal.

Greedy best-first search   It expands the node ν that is closest to the goal according to a heuristic function $h(\nu)$. Out of the B children the node ν_i is chosen with

$$\min_{1 \leq i \leq B} (h(\nu_i)). \qquad (11.9)$$

Like depth-first search it follows a single path to the goal. It always expands the deepest node in the search tree according to $h(\nu)$ until a goal is reached or all nodes are impasse states. An impasse is present when no valid transition to a succeeding state exists. In this case backtracking to the previous state is done. Another state can be chosen that is closest to the goal, if possible, or backtracking is repeated. The computing costs are in the worst case $O(B^m)$ and the memory requirements $B \cdot m = O(m)$. However with a good heuristic function $h(\nu)$ the cost can be reduced considerably.

A search   It evaluates the nodes through a function $f(\nu)$ that estimates the cheapest solution that passes through the node ν. The function $f(\nu)$ is composed out of the heuristic function $h(\nu)$ and the function $g(\nu)$ that indicates the cheapest costs of reaching the node ν from the root node representing the initial state.

$$f(\nu) = g(\nu) + h(\nu).$$

As breadth-first search it keeps all evaluated nodes in memory. The computing costs and the memory requirements are in the worst case $O(B^m)$.

A* search A^* search is equivalent to the A search with the constraint that the function $h(\nu)$ is an admissible heuristic, it never overestimates the cost to reach the goal. If $c(\nu)$ are the true cost to reach the goal it follows

$$h(\nu) \leq c(\nu).$$

It follows that the triangle inequality is valid with $c(\zeta, \nu)$ representing the true cost from node ζ to node ν

$$h(\zeta) \leq c(\zeta, \nu) + h(\nu). \qquad (11.10)$$

A^* search is complete and optimal. A solution is found if it exists. A^* search is optimal, no other algorithm is guaranteed to expand fewer nodes. However the number of expanded nodes can grow exponential unless the error of estimates the cheapest cost from the node ν to the goal is extremely small

$$c(\nu) - h(\nu) \leq O(\log c(\nu)). \qquad (11.11)$$

The computing costs and the memory requirements are in worst case $O(B^m)$.

11.3.1 *Heuristic functions*

We will demonstrate the principles of heuristic function $h(\nu)$ on the 8-puzzle example. Two common heuristics for this task are the number of misplaced tiles, and the "city-block distance" [Nilsson (1982); Pearl (1984); Luger and Stubblefield (1998)]. The first heuristic counts the number of misplaced tiles out of place in each state compared to the desired goal. However this heuristic fails to take into account all available information such as the distance the tiles must be moved. The "city-block distance" sums all the distances by which the tiles are out of place, with one count for each square a tile must be moved to reach a position of the desired state. The "city-block distance", also called the "Manhattan distance", is often better than the "number of misplaced tiles" (see Figure 11.3). Both heuristic functions are admissible.

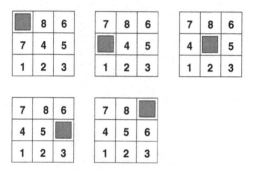

Fig. 11.3 The first pattern (upper left) represents the initial configuration and the last (low right) the desired configuration. The series of moves describe the solution to the problem using the "city-block distance" heuristic function.

11.3.2 *Invention of heuristic functions*

Euclidean geometry of the world The invention process can be inspired by the Euclidean geometry of the world as stated before. The Oksapmin tribe of Papua New Guinea counts by associating a number with the position of the body [Lancy (1983)]. This suggests a representation of numbers by bars at certain positions which can overlap. A bar at a certain position codes the magnitude of the number. The closeness or similarity of different numbers is determined by the overlap of the bar codes [Wichert et al. (2008)] (see Figure 11.4). In the 8-puzzle, each tile is defined by its

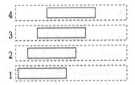

Fig. 11.4   A bar at a certain position codes the magnitude of the number. The closeness or similarity of different numbers is determined by the overlap of the bar codes.

corresponding coordinates. Two numbers can be represented by two bars (see fig 11.5). The amount of overlapping indicates the closeness of different tiles. The resulting function is equivalent to the city-block distance.

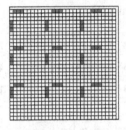

Fig. 11.5   The desired state for the task 8-puzzle and its representation by bars. The associative fields in which the objects are describe have a fixed dimension of ten times ten pixels. Because of this, excessive unused space is present.

The distance between a state and a desired state corresponds to the sum of distance by which the tiles are out of place. The closeness or similarity of a tile to the desired position of the tile is determined by the overlap of the two bar codes representing the tile (see Figure 11.6). The overlap corresponds to the distance by which the tile is out of place. The heuristic function emerged by a reasonable sub-symbolical representation of the states in the 8-puzzle world [Wichert *et al.* (2008)].

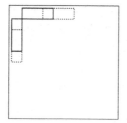

Fig. 11.6   The tile "1" at the position of the tile "6" (shown by dotted bars). The value of the city-block distance is three. The hamming distance between the patterns representing the tile "1" and "6" is also three.

Symbolical problems   Generally the invention of heuristic functions is difficult. In many applications there is no relation to the Euclidean geometry of the world. Examples are chemical structures or mathematical expressions as used in symbolical integration. One way to is to approximate a problem by a relaxed problem with fewer restrictions. For example in the relaxed version of the n-puzzle problem we assume we can move each tile to its position independently of moving the other tiles. The relaxed problem represents an admissible heuristic function of the problem. An optimal solution in the original problem $c(\nu)$ is also a solution in the relaxed problem. By the abolition of present restrictions the cost of the relaxed problem are less or equal to $c(\nu)$. Another way is to decompose the problem into sub-problems and to store all exact solution in a database and to use it to speed up the search using the solution of sub-problems or to extract the heuristic function by machine learning.

11.3.3   *Quality of heuristic*

A frequent used measure is the effective branching factor b. It is independent of the length of the optimal solution. It is related to the costs C_m represented by the number of generated nodes during A^* search [Nilsson (1982)], [Russell and Norvig (2010)]. It is represented by the geometric series (we do not omit level L=0 for simplicity)

$$C_m = 1 + b + b^2 + b^3 + \cdots + b^m = \sum_{i=0}^{m} b^i = \frac{1 - b^{m+1}}{1 - b}. \qquad (11.12)$$

We cannot represent b as a function of m and C_m, however we can plot the values of C_m in dependence of b and m (see Figure 11.7). The exponential grow cost C_m can be only stopped in the case of fully informed search $b = 1$. A heuristic reduces the value of b. By doing so it extends the horizon of

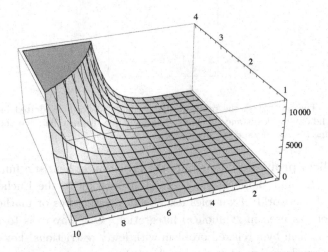

Fig. 11.7   Values of C_m in dependence of branching factor b (1-4) and depth m (1-10).

m of tractable C_m values. No classical universal heuristic function for all domains exist, for each domain a heuristic function has to be invented. This process in general is non-trivial.

11.4   Quantum Tree Search

11.4.1   *Principles of quantum tree search*

There is a simple relation between a tree search and information theory. Suppose that we have a constant branching factor B and the depth of the tree is m. In this case, there are $B^m = n$ leaves. The goal of the search is to visit all of the leaves. The ideal entropy indicates the minimum number of optimal questions that describe the result of an experiment. The experiment represents n leaves of a search tree with equal probabilities $p = (1/n, 1/n..., 1/n)$. The maximal ideal Entropy is

$$H(F) = m = -\sum_i p_i \log_B p_i = \log_B n \qquad (11.13)$$

and corresponds to the depth of the search tree. In the case of $B = 2$, each of the m questions has a reply of either "yes" or "no" and can be represented by a bit (see Figure 11.8). The m answers are represented by

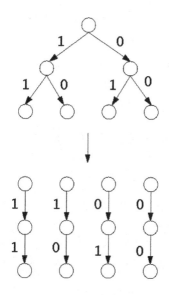

Fig. 11.8 Search tree for $B = 2$ and $m = 2$. Each question can be represented by a bit. Each binary number (11, 10, 01, 00) represents a path from the root to the leaf.

a binary register of length m. There are n different binary registers, which represent all of the possible binary numbers of length m. Each binary number represents a path from the root to a leaf. A path could contain loops, or an impasse could be present before a leaf is reached. However, for each goal, a certain binary number indicates the solution. For a constant branching factor $B > 2$, each question has B possible answers. The m answers can be represented by a base-B number with m digits. For example, with $B = 8$, the number is represented in an octal numeral system. Alternatively, the m answers can be represented by a binary register of length $m \cdot \lceil \log_2 B \rceil$.

Using Grover's algorithm, we search through all possible paths and verify, for each path, whether it leads to the goal state [Tarrataca and Wichert (2011b)]. A quantum circuit U_p with a polynomial number of quantum gates can verify whether each path corresponds to a sequence of productions that lead from the initial state to the goal state. Because we can not reset to the input state, the circuit should recompute the output before applying the amplification step. We apply the U_p operator with,

$$\mu = m \cdot \lceil \log_2 B \rceil \tag{11.14}$$

with the special case $\mu = m$ for constant branching factor $B = 2$, it follows

$$\Gamma_\mu := (G_\mu \otimes I_1) \cdot U_p \tag{11.15}$$

determine the value of r by quantum counting

$$\left(\prod_{t=1}^{r} \Gamma_\mu \right) \cdot W_{\mu+1} \cdot |0^{\oplus \mu}\rangle |1\rangle = |\tau\rangle \otimes \left(\frac{|0\rangle - |1\rangle}{\sqrt{2}} \right) \tag{11.16}$$

and and determine the solution by the measurement of the register $|\tau\rangle$. Because

$$\sqrt{B^m} \approx \sqrt{2^{m \cdot \lceil \log_2 B \rceil}} \tag{11.17}$$

it follows that the computing costs are

$$O\left(\sqrt{B^m} \right) = O\left(\sqrt{2^\mu} \right) = O\left(\sqrt{2^{m \cdot \lceil \log_2 B \rceil}} \right) \tag{11.18}$$

which is much less then uninformed tree search algorithms with

$$O\left(\sqrt{2^{m \cdot \lceil \log_2 B \rceil}} \right) = O\left(\sqrt{B^m} \right) \ll O(B^m) = O\left(2^{m \cdot \lceil \log_2 B \rceil} \right). \tag{11.19}$$

The effective branching factor for quantum tree search b_q is given by the equation

$$C_m = \frac{1 - b^{m+1}}{1 - b} \approx B^{\frac{m}{2}} \tag{11.20}$$

it follows that

$$b_q \approx \sqrt{2^{\lceil \log_2 B \rceil}} \geq \sqrt{B}. \tag{11.21}$$

11.4.2 *Iterative quantum tree search*

The presented algorithm is limited to a search of depth m. This constraint can be overcome by the quantum iterative deepening search. A quantum iterative deepening search is equivalent to the iterative deepening search [Tarrataca and Wichert (2012a)], [Tarrataca and Wichert (2013b)]. We gradually increase the limit of the search from one, to two, three, and four and continue to search until the goal is found. For each limit m, a quantum tree search is performed from the root, with m being the maximum depth of the search tree. The possible solutions are determined by a measurement.

The time complexity of an iterative deepening search has the same order of magnitude as the quantum tree search. With

$$\beta := B^{\frac{1}{2}}$$

the computing costs for each level starting with level zero (for simplicity) are given by

$$O(1)$$

$$O(\beta) = O(B^{\frac{1}{2}})$$

$$O(\beta^2) = O(B^{\frac{2}{2}})$$

$$\cdots$$

to level m is given by

$$O(\beta^m) = O(B^{\frac{m}{2}})$$

the total costs of m_k iterations with m measurments are $O(B^{\frac{m}{2}}) = O\left(\sqrt{B^m}\right)$

$$O(1) + O(B^{\frac{1}{2}}) + O(B^{\frac{2}{2}}) + O(B^{\frac{3}{2}}) + \cdots + O(B^{\frac{m}{2}}) = O(B^{\frac{m}{2}}) = O\left(\sqrt{B^m}\right) \tag{11.22}$$

$$O\left(\sqrt{B^m}\right) = O\left(\sqrt{2^\mu}\right) = O\left(\sqrt{2^{m \cdot \lceil \log_2 B \rceil}}\right)$$

the equation is based on the geometric series

$$1 + \beta + \beta^2 + \beta^3 + \cdots + \beta^m = \sum_{i=0}^{m} \beta^i = \frac{1 - \beta^{m+1}}{1 - \beta} = O(\beta^m) = O(B^{\frac{m}{2}}) \tag{11.23}$$

and the effective branching factor is equal to b_q as for quantum tree search.

11.4.3 *No constant branching factor*

Suppose the branching factor is not constant, in this case the tree search can be described by the effective branching factor. For uninformed tree search for a large number of instances (different initial and goal states) the effective branching factor converge to the averaged branching factor for uninformed tree search [Tarrataca and Wichert (2011b)]. For a not constant branching factor the quantum tree search the maximal branching factor B_{max} has to be used for the quantum tree search. For B_{max} the quantum algorithm using qubit representation is better then the classical tree search described by the effective branching factor b in the case

$$b > b_q. \tag{11.24}$$

If B_{max} is a power of two then

$$b > b_q = \sqrt{2^{\lceil \log_2 B_{max} \rceil}} = \sqrt{B_{max}} \tag{11.25}$$

otherwise

$$b > b_q = \sqrt{2^{\lceil \log_2 B_{max} \rceil}} > \sqrt{B_{max}} \tag{11.26}$$

for example $B_{max} = 9$, then

$$b_q = 4 = \sqrt{2^4} > 3 = \sqrt{9}.$$

and base-9 instead of qubit representation would be more economical. In production systems B_{max} corresponds often to the number of productions. In the 8-puzzle example there are four productions in the long term memory and $B_{max} = 4$ and $b_q = 2$. For blind search the effective branching factor is ≈ 2.8 [Russell and Norvig (2010)], the "city-block distance" heuristic effective branching factor is ≈ 1.24. However one should keep in mind that the invention of heuristic functions is difficult and the 8-puzzle is a well studied problem in the AI community [Nilsson (1982); Pearl (1984); Luger and Stubblefield (1998)]. Heuristic functions can fail. For example in instances of a problem in which one cannot perform the first necessary action without undoing them at a later stage, also called "Sussman anomaly" [Sussman (1975)]. Iterative quantum tree search never fails. This is because during the iterative amplifications of the Grover's algorithm one can adapt the iterations in such a way that the probability of finding a solution is exactly one.

11.5   Quantum Production System

The control structure of a production system (reaction system) can be defined in terms of an iterative quantum tree search [Tarrataca and Wichert (2012b)], [Tarrataca and Wichert (2011a)]. In an iterative quantum tree search, the limit is increased gradually in each step t. For each limit m_t, a quantum tree search is performed from the root, with m_t being the maximum depth of the search tree. With a maximal branching factor B_{max} and using the qubit representation, there are n_t different binary registers, which represent all of the possible binary numbers of length μ_t with

$$n_t = 2^{\mu_t} = 2^{m_t \cdot \lceil \log_2 B_{max} \rceil}. \tag{11.27}$$

The register is called a path descriptor κ_i^t for the iteration step t with $i \in \{1, 2, \cdots, n_t\}$. Each path descriptor κ_i^t represents a possible path from the root to the leaf. A path can be undefined. However, for each goal state, a corresponding κ_i^t exists. The quantum production system is deterministic and reversible because the search is determined by the path descriptor. No conflict resolution is needed. The circuit U_p^t verifies whether each path specified by the path descriptor κ_i^t corresponds to a sequence of productions that leads from the initial state to the goal state. The computation is described by the initial state, the goal state and the long-term memory. The long-term memory is composed of several productions. The productions define the circuit U_p^t. The result of the computation is represented by a path descriptor κ_i^t. After each iterative step t, Grover's algorithm is performed. If no goal at step t was reached, then the resulting path descriptor κ_i^t is randomly chosen. In a case in which the goal state can be reached by only one path at iteration t, the path descriptor κ_i^t is chosen deterministically by Grover's algorithm. The number of possible paths to a goal state can be determined by quantum counting.

11.6 Tarrataca's Quantum Production System

A formal definition of Tarrataca's quantum production system is based on the pure production system [Tarrataca and Wichert (2012b)]. We explain the principles of Tarrataca's quantum production system on a trivial example, the 3-puzzle. In the next step we generalize to n-puzzle and to general quantum production systems. The description is a simplified version of the one presented in [Tarrataca and Wichert (2011a)].

11.6.1 3-puzzle

The 3-puzzle is composed of three numbered movable tiles in a 2×2 frame (see Figure 11.9).

Fig. 11.9   The desired configuration of the 3-puzzle.

One cell of the frame is empty and because of this, tiles can be moved around to form different patterns. The goal is to find a series of moves of tiles into the blank space that changes the board from the initial configuration to a desired configuration). There are twelve possible configurations (see Figure 11.10). For any of this configuration only two movements are possible. The movement of the empty cell are either a clockwise or counterclockwise movement.

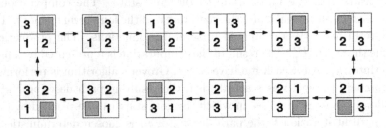

Fig. 11.10   There are twelve possible configurations. For any of this configuration only two movements are possible. The movement of the empty cell are either a clockwise or counter-clockwise movement.

The 3-puzzle is tractable and requires fewer qubits to encode. However the model can be generalized to any n-puzzle. The number of possible solvable configurations of the n-puzzle is

$$\frac{n!}{2}. \tag{11.28}$$

There are $n!$ different configurations, however only $n!/2$ are solvable by moving the empty tile according to the rules. The problem of finding the shortest solution is $NP - complete$.

In our example there are four different objects: 3 cells and one empty cell. Each object can be coded by two qubits (2^2) and a configuration of the four objects can be represented by a register of eight qubits $|x\rangle$. The control function of the quantum production system needs to fulfill two requirements [Tarrataca and Wichert (2011a)]:

- For a given board configuration and a production rule determine the new board configuration.
- To determine if the configuration is the goal configuration.

The function $g(x)$ determines if the configuration is the goal configuration

$$g(x) = g(\underbrace{x_1, x_2, x_3, x_4, x_5, x_6, x_7, x_8}_{board\ configuration}) = \begin{cases} 1 \text{ if goal board configuration} \\ 0 \text{ otherwise.} \end{cases}$$

(11.29)

Function $g(x)$ is represented by a unitary operator T. T acts on the $8 + 1$ qubits with $x \in B^8$ and $c \in B^1$

$$T \cdot |x\rangle|c\rangle = |x\rangle|f(x) \oplus c\rangle.$$

The new board configuration is determined by productions that are represented by the function p. There are four possible positions of the empty cell. The input of the function p is the current board configuration and a bit m that indicates whether the blank cell should perform a clockwise ($m = 1$) or counter-clockwise movement ($m = 0$). Together, there are 8 possible mappings, which are represented by 8 productions. There are four possible positions of the empty cell times two possible moves. For simplicity, we will represent the mappings of the function p by a unitary permutation matrix $L(1)$. For each mapping, the empty tile can have three different neighbors. It follows that, in total, there are $24 = 8 \times 3$ instantiationed rules. They correspond to permutations in the unitary permutation matrix $L(1)$. The matrix acts on the $8 + 1$ qubits with $m \in B^1$ and $x \in B^8$

$$L(1) \cdot |m\rangle|x\rangle = |m\rangle|\gamma\rangle.$$

The $L(1)$ matrix represents the long-term memory of our production system.

Decomposition An important open question is whether the permutation matrix $L(1)$ of dimension $512 = 2^9$ can be decomposed. It is possible to determine if a permutation is tensor decomposable and to chose an efficient tensor decomposition if present [Kolda and Bader (2009)]. An alternative less costly representation of the long-term memory can be realized by a uniformly polynomial circuit. The circuit is based on the truth table that describes the mappings of the function p.

In the case in which the system is not based on an iterative quantum tree search but instead is based on a quantum tree search, we should apply only the move of the blank cell if and only if the input board configuration is not a target board configuration. This process could be performed by including a reference to function g in the new function p's definition and can be described by a unitary operator.

The operator that describes the application of a single production rule for the 3-puzzle and a test condition in order to determine if the final board is a target configuration board is represented in B^{10} as

$$(I_1 \otimes T) \cdot (L(1) \otimes I_1) \cdot |m, x_1, x_2, x_3, x_4, x_5, x_6, x_7, x_8, c\rangle. \qquad (11.30)$$

The operator that describes the application of a two production rules for the 3-puzzle and a test condition in order to determine if the final board is a target configuration board is represented with

$$L(2) \cdot |m_2, m_1\rangle |x\rangle = |m_2, m_1\rangle |\gamma\rangle$$

as

$$(I_2 \otimes T) \cdot (L(2) \otimes I_1) \cdot (L(2) \otimes I_1) \cdot |m_2, m_1, x_1, x_2, x_3, x_4, x_5, x_6, x_7, x_8, c\rangle$$

$$(I_2 \otimes T) \cdot (L(2) \otimes I_1)^2 \cdot |m_2, m_1, x_1, x_2, x_3, x_4, x_5, x_6, x_7, x_8, c\rangle. \qquad (11.31)$$

The operator that describes the application of a t production rules for the 3-puzzle and a test condition in order to determine if the final board is a target configuration board is represented with

$$L(t) \cdot |m_t, \cdots, m_1\rangle |x\rangle = |m_t, \cdots, m_1\rangle |\gamma\rangle$$

and

$$|\kappa^t\rangle = |m_t, \cdots, m_1\rangle$$

as

$$(I_t \otimes T) \cdot (L(t) \otimes I_1)^t \cdot |\kappa^t, x_1, x_2, x_3, x_4, x_5, x_6, x_7, x_8, c\rangle. \qquad (11.32)$$

In quantum computation it is not possible to reset the register $x_1, x_2, x_3, x_4, x_5, x_6, x_7, x_8$ to the pattern representing the initial state. Instead we un-compute the output back to the input before applying the amplification step of the Grover's algorithm. Because of the unitary evolution it follows that

$$(I_t \otimes T)^* \cdot ((L(t) \otimes I_1)^*)^t \cdot (I_t \otimes T) \cdot (L(t) \otimes I_1)^t \cdot \qquad (11.33)$$

$$\cdot |\kappa^t, x_1, x_2, x_3, x_4, x_5, x_6, x_7, x_8, c\rangle = |\kappa^t, x_1, x_2, x_3, x_4, x_5, x_6, x_7, x_8, c\rangle$$

the computation can be undone. The result indicated in the qubit c and can saved into the qubit y by a controlled not gate M_{CNOT}. The computation is defined on B^{10+t} with

$$U_{3-puzzle} := (I_t \otimes T \otimes I_1)^* \cdot ((L(t) \otimes I_2)^*)^t \cdot$$

$$\cdot (I_{(9)+t} \otimes M_{CNOT}) \cdot (I_t \otimes T \otimes I_1) \cdot (L(t) \otimes I_2)^t \qquad (11.34)$$

simplified as

$$U_{3-puzzle} \cdot |\kappa^t, x_1, x_2, x_3, x_4, x_5, x_6, x_7, x_8, c, y\rangle = U_{3-puzzle} \cdot |\kappa^t, x, c, y\rangle.$$
$$(11.35)$$

We apply the $U_{3-puzzle}$ operator,

$$\Gamma_T := (T_t \otimes I_{10}) \cdot U_{3-puzzle} \qquad (11.36)$$

determine the value of r by quantum counting

$$\left(\prod_{t=1}^{r} \Gamma_T \right) \cdot \left((W_t \cdot |0^{\oplus t}\rangle) \otimes |x\rangle \otimes |0\rangle \otimes (W_1 \cdot |1\rangle) \right) = \qquad (11.37)$$

it follows

$$\left(\prod_{t=1}^{r} \Gamma_T \right) \cdot (W_t \otimes I_{10}) \cdot (I_{t+9} \otimes W_1) \cdot |0^{\oplus t}\rangle |x\rangle |0\rangle |1\rangle = |\kappa_i^t\rangle |x\rangle |0\rangle \otimes \left(\frac{|0\rangle - |1\rangle}{\sqrt{2}} \right)$$
$$(11.38)$$

and and determine the solution by the measurement of the register $|\kappa_i^t\rangle$ that represents the path descriptor. The 3-puzzle quantum production system highlighted the principles of quantum production systems. It does not give any true computational speed up due to the simplicity of the problem and due to the naïve implementation of the long term memory by a permutation matrix.

11.6.2 *Extending for any n-puzzle*

For n-puzzle there are $n + 1$ different objects: n cells and one empty cell. Each object can be coded by $\rho = \lceil \log_2 n + 1 \rceil$ qubits and a configuration of $n + 1$ objects can be represented by a register of $z := \rho \cdot (n + 1)$ qubits $|x\rangle$.

The function $g(x)$ is represented a unitary operator T. T acts on the $z + 1$ qubits with $x \in B^z$ and $c \in B^1$

$$T \cdot |x\rangle |c\rangle = |x\rangle |f(x) \oplus c\rangle.$$

The new board configuration is determined by the function p. The input of the function p is the current board configuration and two bits $m = m_1, m_2$ indicating whether the blank cell should perform move up ($m = 0 = |00\rangle$), down ($m = 1 = |01\rangle$), right ($m = 2 = |10\rangle$) or left ($m = 3 = |11\rangle$). The mappings of the function p between states can be described by a truth table and can represented as column permutations.

In the case the empty cell is in the corner only two movements are possible, the other one are not valid. In the case of not valid movement a halt bit flag h represented by one bit is set and no further production is applied. We move the blank cell if and only if the halt bit flag h is not set. The same applies for empty cell on the edge. In this case only three movements are possible. For 8-puzzle $B_{max} = 4$ and $B_{average}$

$$B_{average} = \frac{4 \cdot 1 + 2 \cdot 4 + 3 \cdot 4}{9} = 2.7778. \tag{11.39}$$

With growing value n $B_{average}$ converges to B_{max}.

There are maximal $n + 1$ possible positions of the empty cell. The empty cell can move either up, down, left or right or the halt bit flag is set. Together there $(4 + 1)$ actions and for $n + 1$ positions there are $(n + 1) \cdot 5$ possible mappings represented by $n \cdot 5 + 5$ permutations. In each combination the empty tile can have n different neighbors. It follows that in total there are $(n + 1) \cdot 5 \cdot n = 5 \cdot n^2 + 5 \cdot n$ instantiationed productions. A 8-puzzle there would represented by 360 instantiationed productions.

The instantiationed productions are represented unitary permutation matrix $L(1)$. The matrix acts on the $z + 3$ qubits with $m \in B^2$ and $x \in B^z$ and $h \in B^1$

$$L(1) \cdot |m\rangle |x\rangle |h\rangle = |m\rangle |\gamma\rangle |h'\rangle.$$

11.6.3 *Pure production system*

The pure production system model has no mechanism for recovering from an impasse [Post (1943)]. The system halts if no production can fire. It is composed of the set of productions L (the long term memory) and control system C. A pure production system is a sextuple:

$$(\Sigma, L, W, \gamma_i, \gamma_g, C) \tag{11.40}$$

with

- Σ is a finite alphabet;
- W is the working memory. It represents a state $\gamma \in \Sigma$.
- L is the long term memory. It is the set of B productions. A production p has the form $(precondition, conclusion) \in \Sigma$. The precondition is matched against the contents of the working memory. If the precondition is met then the conclusion is preformed and changes the contents of the working memory;
- $\gamma_i \in \Sigma$ is the initial state. The working memory is initialized with the initial state γ_i;

- $\gamma_g \in \Sigma$ is the goal state;
- δ is the control function of the form $\Sigma \to L \times \Sigma \times h$. It chooses a production and fires it or halts h.

If $C(\gamma) = (p, \gamma', h)$, then the working memory contains symbol γ. It is substituted by the the production p by γ' or the computation halts h. The computation halts if the goal state γ_g is reached or an an impasse is present (no production can be applied).

11.6.4 *Unitary control strategy*

A pure production system can be converted into a quantum production system by mapping the control strategy into a unitary control strategy represented by a unitary operator $L(t)$ on a register $|v_1\rangle$ [Tarrataca and Wichert (2012b)], [Tarrataca and Wichert (2013b)].

$$L(t) \cdot |v_1\rangle = |v_2\rangle.$$

$L(t)$ is used during the iterative quantum tree search to the limit t. The register $|v_1\rangle$ is determined by,

- $\mu = t \cdot \lceil \log_2 B_{max} \rceil$ maximal branching factor represents the path descriptor κ_i^t
- $\alpha = \lceil \log_2 |\Sigma| \rceil$, represents the number of bits required to encode the symbol set
- $\beta = \lceil \log_2 B \rceil$, represents the number of bits required to encode each one of the productions;
- η is a single bit used to encode h

The size of $|v_1\rangle$ is

$$\aleph := \mu + \alpha + \beta + \eta$$

qubits. $2^\aleph$ combinations can be represented. A combination can be represented by a one at a certain position of the vector. The corresponding unitary operator $L(t)$ is represented by a matrix of the dimension $2^\aleph \times 2^\aleph$. The matrix is sparse, it is populated primarily with zeros. It is possible to determine if a permutation is tensor decomposable and to chose an efficient tensor decomposition if present [Kolda and Bader (2009)]. Additionally we need a unitary operator T that determines if the state is the goal state γ_g. As indicated in the 3-puzzle example, the circuit should recompute the output before applying the amplification step of the Grover's algorithm.

11.7   A General Model of a Quantum Computer

In classical models such as the Turing machine, the end of a calculation is indicated by a halt state. An observer must check if the calculation halted. In a quantum Turing machine, a halt flag can be non-trivially implemented due to entanglement and the collapse of the halt qubit after the measurement. A solution to this problem is a universal quantum Turing machine in [Bernstein and Vazirani (1993)], which does not incorporate into its definition the concept on non-termination. Myers in [Myers (1997)] argues that the models presented in [Deutsch (1985)] and [Bernstein and Vazirani (1993)] are not truly universal because they do not allow for non-terminating computation.

A quantum production system represents a general model of computation. This type of system is an alternative approach to the quantum Turing machine and allows an elegant description of the Halting problem through the iterative quantum tree search. It is possible to simulate classical universal models of computation such as the universal Turing machine by a quantum production system as shown in [Tarrataca and Wichert (2013b)]. This model can operate independently of whether the computation terminates or not. The quantum production system also provides the maximal speedup of $\sqrt{n}$ in the case where the Turing machine simulation allows for n multiple computational branches [Tarrataca and Wichert (2013b)].

A quantum computer based on a quantum production system would involve classical artificial intelligence programing languages such as OPS5 [Brownston *et al.* (1985)]. OPS5 programs are executed by matching working memory elements with productions in long-term memory [Forgy (1981)]. Such a programmer does not need to contend with quantum gates, nor is it required to address the principles of quantum computation. However, a strong artificial intelligence background is essential.

11.7.1   *Cognitive architecture*

Unified theories of cognition is a theory that attempts to unify all of the theories of the mind in a single framework. Allen Newell proposed the SOAR cognitive architecture [Laird *et al.* (1987)], [Newell (1990)], [Franklin (1997)]. SOAR is an architecture of the mind: a fixed structure underlying the flexible domain of cognitive processing as well as an architecture for intelligent agents. All of the problem solving activity is formulated as the selection and application of rules to a state to achieve a goal. In SOAR, the domain knowledge is divided into two categories:

- basic problem space knowledge represents legal moves that are represented by productions;
- control knowledge, such as, for example, heuristic functions and other control strategies.

With basic knowledge, SOAR can proceed to perform an unguided search using depth first. Resolving an impasse leads to learning. Impasses are given, for example, when

- two or more productions are chosen to fire;
- no production can fire;
- one chosen production is rejected by another.

The learning mechanism is called chunking. Chunking collapses the results of an impasse into a production that can then be fired if the same, or similar situation occurs again [Laird *et al.* (1986)]. Chunking is a psychological phenomenon that involves the association of expressions and the production of a new, single expression [Newell (1990)]. An extension of the proposed SOAR cognitive architecture by a quantum production system would lead to a hybrid architecture. The quantum production system would be invoked if an impasse were present. Such a hybrid approach would speed up the learning process without a need for domain-specific control knowledge (see Figure 11.11).

11.7.2 *Representation*

The representation of the knowledge is the most important aspect. The unitary operator L that represents the long-term memory with the productions can be represented by a permutation matrix. It is possible to determine whether an abstract permutation is tensor decomposable and to choose an efficient tensor decomposition if present [Kolda and Bader (2009)].

The question of how to decompose L representing a real world problem is related to the question of how to decompose a problem into sub-problems. A problem solving strategy is given by breaking a problem up into a set of subproblems, solving each of the subproblems, and then composing a solution to the original problem from the solutions of the subproblems. How can we decompose a 15-puzzle into an 8-puzzle for example? This

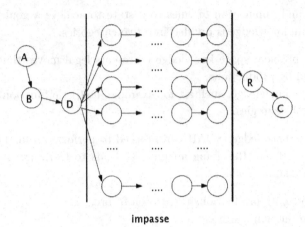

impasse

Fig. 11.11 An extension of the proposed SOAR cognitive architecture by a quantum production system would lead to a hybrid architecture. The quantum production system would be invoked if an impasse is present. Such an hybrid approach would speed up the learning process without the need of domain specific control knowledge.

problem corresponds to the definition of a tensor product and the efficient implementation of a quantum production system to be the decomposition of L,

$$L = \begin{pmatrix} a_{11} \cdot B & a_{12} \cdot B \\ a_{21} \cdot B & a_{22} \cdot B \end{pmatrix} = A \otimes B.$$

Chapter 12

Quantum Cognition

The wave function in quantum mechanics represents a superposition of states. Suppose that an unobservable evolves smoothly and continuously; however, during the measurement, it collapses into a definite state. According to most physical textbooks, the existence of the wave function and its collapse is only present in the microscopic world and is not present in the macroscopic world. More physical experiments indicate that wave functions are present in the macroscopic world [Vedral (2011)]. Physical experiments state that the size does not matter and that a very large number of atoms can be entangled [Ghosh *et al.* (2003)], [Amico *et al.* (2008)]. Clues from psychology indicate that human cognition is based on quantum probability rather than the traditional probability theory as explained by Kolmogorov's axioms [Busemeyer *et al.* (2006)], [Busemeyer and Trueblood (2009)], [Busemeyer *et al.* (2009)], [Busemeyer and Bruza (2012)]. This approach would lead to the conclusion that a wave function can be present at the macro scale of our daily life.

12.1 Quantum Probability

The quantum coin is a system with two states 0 and 1 with the mapping

$$|0\rangle \to \frac{1}{\sqrt{2}} \cdot |0\rangle + \frac{1}{\sqrt{2}} \cdot |1\rangle \tag{12.1}$$

and

$$|1\rangle \to \frac{1}{\sqrt{2}} \cdot |0\rangle - \frac{1}{\sqrt{2}} \cdot |1\rangle \tag{12.2}$$

represented by W_1. If the system starts in state $|0\rangle$ and undergoes the time evolution of two steps the probability of observing 0 becomes 1 due to the fact, of destructive interference. A Markov chain can model a fair coin. In this case the information about the initial state is lost and a fixed distribution is reached. If constantly observed the quantum coin has the same behavior as a fair coin described a Markov chain. Each time the coin is tossed the "random" effect is observed. During the evolution of a not observed quantum coin the information about the initial state is not lost, the system is fully deterministic. For a quantum coin the random effect corresponding to the loss of information occurs only during the measurement. When observed the quantum probabilities correspond to the classical probability theory. If not observed, a complex vector of a length one describes the state of a system. For two state the system is described buy two complex amplitudes ω_1, ω_2 and the probability that the system is in one of the two states is s $|\omega_1|^2$ and $|\omega_2|^2$ with $|\omega_1|^2 + |\omega_2|^2 = 1$. The product of complex number with is conjugate is always a real number

$$\omega^* \cdot \omega = (x - y \cdot i) \cdot (x + y \cdot i) = x^2 + y^2 = |\omega|^2 = \lambda.$$

The quantum probabilities are also called von Neumann probabilities in relation to the von Neumann entropy of a density matrix P

$$P = \lambda_1 \cdot |x_1\rangle\langle x_1| + \lambda_2 \cdot |x_2\rangle\langle x_2| + \cdots + \lambda_n \cdot |x_n\rangle\langle x_n|$$

with the entropy of P

$$E(P) = -\sum_{i=1}^{n} (\lambda_i \cdot \log \lambda_i)$$

and with probabilities λ_i of the presence of a state. They all sum

$$1 = \sum_{i=1}^{n} \lambda_i$$

to one. Two equivalent states represent the same state when a measurement is preformed, but they can have behave differently during the unitary evolution. Two states $|a\rangle$ and $|b\rangle$ are equivalent if

$$|a\rangle = e^{i \cdot \theta} \cdot |b\rangle \tag{12.3}$$

with

$$e^{i \cdot \theta} = \cos \theta + i \cdot \sin \theta. \tag{12.4}$$

For example $|a\rangle$ and $i \cdot |a\rangle$ are two equivalent states for $\theta = \pi/2$. For $\theta = \pi$ two equivalent states are $|a\rangle$ and $-|a\rangle$. The value of θ correspond to an angle. It can take infinite many values corresponding a circle in the complex

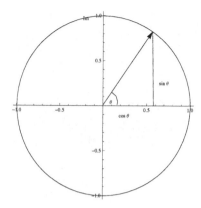

Fig. 12.1   The value of θ correspond to an angle, can take infinite many values describing a circle in the complex number plane of the radius one described by the equation $e^{i \cdot \theta} = \cos \theta + i \cdot \sin \theta$.

number plane. The radius is described by the equation $e^{i \cdot \theta} = \cos \theta + i \cdot \sin \theta$ (see Figure 12.1).

The circle can be extended to a sphere by adding additional third dimension that represents the state of one qubit. This sphere is called the Bloch sphere, it represents the state as well as the amplitude of one qubit. In the Bloch states $|0\rangle$ and $|1\rangle$ are represented by one dimension (see Figure 12.2).

Each proposition a is specified by a belief $\lambda = P(a)$ with $0 \le \lambda \le 1$ and by the phase $\theta \in [0, 2 \cdot \pi)$. The state is either observable $\lambda = P(a)$ or unobservable. An unobservable state is in a superposition that is described by the amplitude. The amplitude is the root of the belief multiplied with the corresponding phase

$$\sqrt{\lambda} \cdot e^{i \cdot \theta}. \tag{12.5}$$

As stated before the numerical degree of belief can result from either from a frequentist approach or be determined from the nature of the universe, like for example the probability of throwing a six in a fair dice. Alternatively it can be seen as a subjective viewpoint. On the other hand it is difficult to attribute any meaning to the phase specified by the angle θ when a proposition with a known belief value a is not observable. The unobservable propositions behave differently, the law of total probability is not valid any more. For mutually exclusive events $b_1, ..., b_n$ with

$$\sum_{i=1}^{n} P(b_i) = 1$$

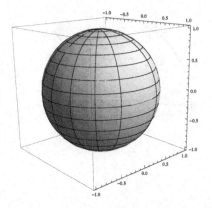

Fig. 12.2 Bloch sphere represents the state as well as the amplitude of one qubit. There are three axis, two represent its phase and one the two states $|0\rangle$ and $|1\rangle$. The representation is not faithful to reality: the states $|0\rangle$ and $|1\rangle$ are not orthogonal in the Bloch sphere representation.

the law of total probability when events $b_1, ..., b_n$ are not observable is not valid,

$$P(a) \neq \left| \sum_{i=1}^{n} e^{i \cdot \theta_{a|b_i}} \cdot \sqrt{P(a|b_i)} \cdot e^{i \cdot \theta_{b_i}} \cdot \sqrt{P(b_i)} \right|^2 ,$$

$$P(a) \neq \left| \sum_{i=1}^{n} e^{i \cdot (\theta_{a|b_i} + \theta_{b_i})} \cdot \sqrt{P(a|b_i)} \cdot \sqrt{P(b_i)} \right|^2 . \qquad (12.6)$$

Humans when making decisions violates the law of total probability, yet it can be explained as a quantum interference effect in a manner similar to the explanation for the results from two-hole experiments in physics.

12.2   Decision Making

Humans when making decisions violate the law of total probability. The violation can be explained as a quantum interference resulting from the phase represented by the angle θ. In an experiment, the violation of the law of total probability was demonstrated by a categorization and decision experiment [Busemeyer *et al.* (2009)]. 26 participants preformed 51 trials per condition. All together there were $26 \cdot 51 = 1326$ observation per condition. During the experiment the participants were shown pictures of faces. They should categorize the person represented on the pictures as good or bad and in the next step decide to act friendly or aggressive. There were two experimental conditions:

- Make a decision without reporting any categorization.
- Make a decision after categorizing a face.

In the second condition the conditional probabilities of categorization images of face were determined

$$P(good|face) = 0.17 \quad P(bad|face) = 0.83$$

mostly the faces were categorized as being bad. Then the conditional probabilities of acting friendly or aggressive were determined,

$$P(aggressive|good) = 0.42 \quad P(friendly|good) = 0.58$$

and

$$P(aggressive|bad) = 0.63 \quad P(friendly|bad) = 0.37.$$

We can represent the experiment by a simple graph with two nodes with the following simplification

$$P(good) = P(good|face) = 0.17$$

$$P(\neg good) = P(bad|face) = 0.83$$

and

$$P(\neg friendly|good) = 0.42 \quad P(friendly|good) = 0.58$$

$$P(\neg friendly|\neg good) = 0.63 \quad P(friendly|\neg good) = 0.37,$$

see Figure 12.3.

For mutually exclusive events

$$P(good) + P(\neg good) = 1$$

the law of total probability is

$$P(Friendly) = \sum_{good} P(Friendly|good) \cdot P(good) \tag{12.7}$$

$$P(Friendly|Good) = P(good) \cdot P(Friendly|good) +$$

$$+ P(\neg good) \cdot P(Friendly|\neg good) \tag{12.8}$$

$$P(friendly) = 0.58 \cdot 0.17 + 0.37 \cdot 0.83 = 0.4057, \tag{12.9}$$

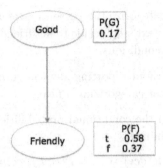

Fig. 12.3   A graph with two nodes and the corresponding conditional probability tables. Each row requires one number p for $P(X) = true$ ($P(X) = false$ is $1 - p$).

$$P(\neg friendly) = 0.42 \cdot 0.17 + 0.63 \cdot 0.83 = 0.5943. \tag{12.10}$$

In the first condition of the experiment a decision without reporting any categorization was determined. The value was

$$P(\neg friendly) = P(aggressive|face) = 0.69.$$

The value is incompatible with the classical probability theory, it does not correspond to the correct value as indicated by the law of total probability

$$0.69 > \sum_{good} P(\neg friendly|good) \cdot P(good) = 0.5943.$$

Why do human violate the law of total probability during decision making? A possible explanation is given by the quantum probabilities. In quantum probabilities the law of total probability is not valid

$$P(\neg friendly) \neq$$

$$\left| \sum_{i=1}^{2} e^{i \cdot \theta_{frendly|good}} \cdot \sqrt{P(\neg firendly|good)} \cdot e^{i \cdot \theta_{good}} \cdot \sqrt{P(good)} \right|^2. \tag{12.11}$$

We will indicate the solution for the Equation 12.11. We simplify the Equation 12.11 to the equivalent equation

$$\left| \sum_{i=1}^{2} e^{i \cdot \theta_{\alpha_i}} \cdot \sqrt{\alpha_i} \cdot e^{i \cdot \theta_{\beta_i}} \cdot \sqrt{\beta_i} \right|^2 = \tag{12.12}$$

$$\left| e^{i \cdot \theta_{\alpha_1}} \cdot \sqrt{\alpha_1} \cdot e^{i \cdot \theta_{\beta_1}} \cdot \sqrt{\beta_1} + e^{i \cdot \theta_{\alpha_2}} \cdot \sqrt{\alpha_2} \cdot e^{i \cdot \theta_{\beta_2}} \cdot \sqrt{\beta_2} \right|^2 =$$

with the complex conjugate representation

$$\left(e^{i\cdot\theta_{\alpha_1}}\cdot\sqrt{\alpha_1}\cdot e^{i\cdot\theta_{\beta_1}}\cdot\sqrt{\beta_1}+e^{i\cdot\theta_{\alpha_2}}\cdot\sqrt{\alpha_2}\cdot e^{i\cdot\theta_{\beta_2}}\cdot\sqrt{\beta_2}\right)\cdot$$

$$\left(e^{i\cdot\theta_{\alpha_1}}\cdot\sqrt{\alpha_1}\cdot e^{i\cdot\theta_{\beta_1}}\cdot\sqrt{\beta_1}+e^{i\cdot\theta_{\alpha_2}}\cdot\sqrt{\alpha_2}\cdot e^{i\cdot\theta_{\beta_2}}\cdot\sqrt{\beta_2}\right)^{*}= \qquad (12.13)$$

$$\left(e^{i\cdot\theta_{\alpha_1}}\cdot\sqrt{\alpha_1}\cdot e^{i\cdot\theta_{\beta_1}}\cdot\sqrt{\beta_1}+e^{i\cdot\theta_{\alpha_2}}\cdot\sqrt{\alpha_2}\cdot e^{i\cdot\theta_{\beta_2}}\cdot\sqrt{\beta_2}\right)\cdot$$

$$\left(e^{-i\cdot\theta_{\alpha_1}}\cdot\sqrt{\alpha_1}\cdot e^{-i\cdot\theta_{\beta_1}}\cdot\sqrt{\beta_1}+e^{-i\cdot\theta_{\alpha_2}}\cdot\sqrt{\alpha_2}\cdot e^{-i\cdot\theta_{\beta_2}}\cdot\sqrt{\beta_2}\right)= \qquad (12.14)$$

$$\alpha_1\cdot\beta_1+\alpha_2\cdot\beta_2+\sqrt{\alpha_1}\cdot\sqrt{\alpha_2}\cdot\sqrt{\beta_1}\cdot\sqrt{\beta_2}\cdot$$

$$(e^{i\cdot(\theta_{\alpha_1}-\theta_{\alpha_2}+\theta_{\beta_1}-\theta_{\beta_2})}+e^{-i\cdot(\theta_{\alpha_1}-\theta_{\alpha_2}+\theta_{\beta_1}-\theta_{\beta_2})})=$$

$$\alpha_1\cdot\beta_1+\alpha_2\cdot\beta_2+\sqrt{\alpha_1}\cdot\sqrt{\alpha_2}\cdot\sqrt{\beta_1}\cdot\sqrt{\beta_2}\cdot2\cdot\cos(\theta_{\alpha_1}-\theta_{\alpha_2}+\theta_{\beta_1}-\theta_{\beta_2}) \quad (12.15)$$

with

$$\theta:=\theta_{\alpha_1}-\theta_{\alpha_2}+\theta_{\beta_1}-\theta_{\beta_2}$$

we can simplify to

$$\alpha_1\cdot\beta_1+\alpha_2\cdot\beta_2+2\cdot\sqrt{\alpha_1}\cdot\sqrt{\alpha_2}\cdot\sqrt{\beta_1}\cdot\sqrt{\beta_2}\cdot\cos(\theta). \qquad (12.16)$$

It should be noted that

$$-1\le\cos(\theta)\le1 \qquad (12.17)$$

and

$$\frac{\alpha_1\cdot\beta_1+\alpha_2\cdot\beta}{2}\ge\sqrt{\alpha_1}\cdot\sqrt{\alpha_2}\cdot\sqrt{\beta_1}\cdot\sqrt{\beta_2}. \qquad (12.18)$$

If

$$0\le\alpha_1\cdot\beta_1+\alpha_2\cdot\beta\le1 \qquad (12.19)$$

then

$$0\le\alpha_1\cdot\beta_1+\alpha_2\cdot\beta_2+2\cdot\sqrt{\alpha_1}\cdot\sqrt{\alpha_2}\cdot\sqrt{\beta_1}\cdot\sqrt{\beta_2}\cdot\cos(\theta)\le2. \qquad (12.20)$$

in the case the value of a query variable has to be determined and some variables are unknown, the probabilities are determined by normalization as described in the section about Bayesian networks.

The solution for the Equation 12.11 is

$$\left| \sum_{i=1}^{2} e^{i \cdot \theta_{frendly|good}} \cdot \sqrt{P(\neg firendly|good)} \cdot e^{i \cdot \theta_{good}} \cdot \sqrt{P(good)} \right|^2 =$$

$$P(\neg firendly|good) \cdot P(good) + P(\neg firendly|\neg good) \cdot P(\neg good) +$$

$$2 \cdot \sqrt{P(\neg firendly|good)} \cdot \sqrt{P(\neg firendly|\neg good)}$$

$$\cdot \sqrt{P(good)} \cdot \sqrt{P(\neg good)} \cdot \cos(\theta). \tag{12.21}$$

The Equation 12.2 is the quantum interpretation of probability. Quantum probabilities obey the law of total probability only in the case

$$\cos(\theta) = 0, \quad \theta = \frac{\pi}{2}$$

in which the interference part is canceled out. In our example with

$$\theta = \theta_{\neg friendly|good} - \theta_{\neg friendly|\neg good} + \theta_{good} - \theta_{\neg good}$$

the quantum probabilities obey the law of total probability in the case

$$\frac{\pi}{2} = \theta_{\neg friendly|good} - \theta_{\neg friendly|\neg good} + \theta_{good} - \theta_{\neg good}.$$

The quantum interpretation of probability can explain the incompatibility with the classical probability theory by the Equation 12.2. The value $P(\neg friendly)$ for a decision without reporting any categorization was 0.69. By Equation 12.2 we can determine the corresponding θ. We add the classical probability 0.5943 the interference term

$$0.69 = 0.42 \cdot 0.17 + 0.63 \cdot 0.83 + 2 \cdot \sqrt{0.42} \cdot \sqrt{0.63} \cdot \sqrt{0.17} \cdot \sqrt{0.83} \cdot \cos(\theta) \tag{12.22}$$

and the value of $\cos(\theta)$ is

$$0.247642 = \frac{0.69. - 0.5943}{0.386446} = \cos(\theta)$$

with

$$\theta = 1.32055 \approx 0.42 \cdot \pi = \frac{21}{50} \cdot \pi.$$

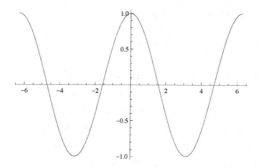

Fig. 12.4   The relation between $\cos(\theta)$ and θ for $-2 \cdot \pi \geq \theta \geq 2 \cdot \pi$.

12.2.1   *Interference*

During hidden inference the interference plays an important part in the quantum interpretation of probability. The interference is determined by the value of $\cos(\theta)$.

- For $\cos(\theta) = 0$ no interference is present.
- For $1 \geq \cos(\theta) > 0$ positive interference is present.
- For $-1 \leq \cos(\theta) < 0$ negative interference is present.

The relation between $\cos(\theta)$ and θ is shown in Figure 12.4 for $-2 \cdot \pi \geq \theta \geq 2 \cdot \pi$. In general

$$\theta := \theta_{\alpha_1} - \theta_{\alpha_2} + \theta_{\beta_1} - \theta_{\beta_2}$$

and in our example

$$\theta = \theta_{\neg friendly|good} - \theta_{\neg friendly|\neg good} + \theta_{good} - \theta_{\neg good}.$$

The interference depends on the phase of each possible state and the corresponding global θ.

- No interference is present in the case

$$\theta = -\frac{3 \cdot \pi}{2}, \quad \theta = -\frac{\pi}{2}, \quad \theta = \frac{\pi}{2}, \quad \theta = \frac{3 \cdot \pi}{2}.$$

- Positive interference is present for

$$\theta \leq -\frac{3 \cdot \pi}{2}, \quad -\frac{\pi}{2} \leq \theta \leq \frac{\pi}{2}, \quad \frac{3 \cdot \pi}{2} \leq \theta.$$

Maximal positive interference is present if the phase of each possible state is equal

$$\theta_{\alpha_1} = \theta_{\alpha_2} = \theta_{\beta_1} = \theta_{\beta_2}.$$

- Negative interference is present for

$$-\frac{3 \cdot \pi}{2} \le \theta \le -\frac{\pi}{2}, \ \frac{\pi}{2} \le \theta \le \frac{3 \cdot \pi}{2}.$$

When performing hidden inference an additional free variable for each state is present according to the quantum interpretation of probability. The free variable corresponds to the phase specified by the angle θ. The probabilities are determined by normalization as introduced in the section about Bayesian networks. We presented an experiment in which positive interference is present. In the next section we present the unpacking effect and the resulting negative interference.

12.3 Unpacking Effects

An event can be described in more or less detail. The unpacking effect is present when the whole is less than the sum of its parts [Boven and Epley (2003)]. With more details the unpacking effects appear. In the experiment by two conditions were present [Busemeyer *et al.* (2011)], [Busemeyer and Bruza (2012)].

- What is the probability that some one died from natural causes? This is the packed condition.
- What is the probability that some one died from cancer? After this what is the probability that some one died from natural causes other than cancer?

see Figure 12.5 for the graph representation. According to classical probability theory

Fig. 12.5 A graph with two nodes.

$$P(Naturally) = \sum_{cancer} P(Naturally|cancer) \cdot P(cancer). \qquad (12.23)$$

It follows that

$$P(naturally) = P(naturally|cancer) \cdot P(cancer)+$$

$$+P(naturally|\neg cancer) \cdot P(\neg cancer). \qquad (12.24)$$

However for packed condition

$$P(naturally) < P(naturally|cancer) \cdot P(cancer)+$$

$$+P(naturally|\neg cancer) \cdot P(\neg cancer). \qquad (12.25)$$

According to the quantum interpretation of probability

$$\left| \sum_{i=1}^{2} e^{i \cdot \theta_{naturally|cancer}} \cdot \sqrt{P(\neg naturally|cancer)} \cdot e^{i \cdot \theta_{cancer}} \cdot \sqrt{P(cancer)} \right|^2$$

$$= P(\neg naturally|cancer) \cdot P(cancer) + P(\neg naturally|\neg cancer)\cdot$$

$$\cdot P(\neg cancer) + 2 \cdot \sqrt{P(\neg naturally|cancer}} \cdot \sqrt{P(\neg naturally|\neg cancer)}$$

$$\cdot \sqrt{P(cancer)} \cdot \sqrt{P(\neg cancer)} \cdot \cos(\theta). \qquad (12.26)$$

with

$$\cos(\theta) < 0.$$

12.4 Conclusion

Quantum cognition uses mathematical quantum theory to model cognitive phenomena. It is assumed that the computation itself is performed on a classical computer and not on a quantum computer. The brain is considered a classical computer in a quantum world. Because the wave function can be present at the macro scale of our daily life, predictions such as, hidden inferences, are based on von Neumann probabilities. Besides probability judgment, other effects, such as emotional judgments or order effects, can be modeled by quantum probabilities and unitary evolution. It is assumed that evolution adapted to the quantum world on the macro scale. According to the quantum cognition assumption, humans violate the law of total probabilities because, under certain conditions, this law is not valid in the real world.

Chapter 13

Related Approaches

13.1 Quantum Walk

Related to Grover's algorithm and the quantum tree search algorithm is the quantum random walk on a graph ([Ambainis (2003)], [Kempe (2003)] and [Ambainis (2004)]). Indeed, Grover's algorithm can also be viewed as a quantum walk algorithm. A quantum random walk is an analog to the random walk. There are two types of random walk, namely, discrete- and continuous-time. We describe the discrete-time random walk on a lattice and the quantum random walk on a graph $G = (V, E)$.

13.1.1 *Random walk*

Randomness could be nature's way to avoid complexity when accomplishing certain tasks. A fly could choose the direction of its flight randomly. The insect flies for a time in a randomly chosen direction. Then, it randomly chooses another direction, and then, another random direction is chosen, and so forth. This process is an example of a random walk in three dimensions. We simplify the model by describing it as a discrete random walk on a three-dimensional lattice [Gaylord and Wellin (1995)]. At each point, the fly can choose to fly in six directions: up, down, north, south, west or east. Each random choice is made after a constant amount of time; the constant flight path intervals are of equal length. In Figure 13.1, we see a simulation of a lattice random walk in dimension three for 1000 steps. A two-dimensional lattice walk is represented in Figure 13.2.

13.1.2 *Quantum insect*

In classical physics, randomness is not present. Suppose that a fly generates randomness by some quantum computing device that simulates the

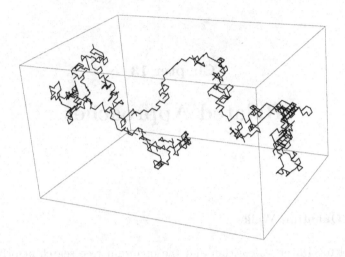

Fig. 13.1   Simulation of a lattice random walk in dimension three for 1000 steps.

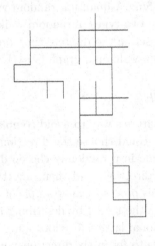

Fig. 13.2   Simulation of a lattice random walk in dimension two for 100 steps.

behavior of a quantum coin. In this case, a true random walk is present. Suppose that the fly is in a closed room and we do not know its position. The fly is evolving into a superposition of several states that can be characterized by its position. Each of the possible positions is associated with a specific probability. The "quantum fly" is in a mixed state. As long as we make no measurements, there are no random effects. The behavior of the system is strictly deterministic. The probability distribution represents the possible positions after several steps, and several measurements of the quantum fly and the classical fly will differ. This difference arises because the randomness in the quantum walk is present only during the measurement.

13.1.3 Quantum walk on a graph

The discrete-time quantum random walk on a graph $G = (V, E)$ can be described by a unitary operator U on Hilbert space

$$H = H_S \otimes H_C.$$

H_S represents the vertex of the graph and H_C describes the destination choice. The destination choice H_C is also called "coin space" [Shenvi *et al.* (2003)] because the choice in one dimension can be described by a quantum coin. U is composed of the operators S and C [Aharonov *et al.* (2001)],

$$U = S \cdot C.$$

A step of the quantum walk is represented by two operations [Childs (2011)]:

- Build a superposition over the neighbor states by operator C;
- Move the state to the new target destination by operator S.

A register represents a state

$$|jk\rangle = |j\rangle|k\rangle \Longleftrightarrow (j, k) \in E.$$

The neighbors of j are represented in the register $|k\rangle$ by the by operator C [Watrous (1998)], [Tarrataca and Wichert (2013a)],

$$C \cdot |j\rangle|k\rangle = |j\rangle \frac{1}{\sqrt{deg(j)}} \sum_{w:(j,w)\in E} |k \oplus w\rangle \qquad (13.1)$$

with $deg(j)$ represents the degree of vertex j and $\sum_{m:(j,m)\in E} \frac{1}{deg(j)} = 1$. After applying the C operator the state of the system is moved from state $|j\rangle$ to state $|k\rangle$ for example by a simple permutation

$$S \cdot |j\rangle|k\rangle = |k\rangle|j\rangle \qquad (13.2)$$

with the effect that the quantum random walk takes places on the edges of the graph.

13.1.4   Quantum walk on one dimensional lattice

The most simple graph is one dimensional lattice. The quantum walk is called the discrete walk on a line. A state is represented by a register

$$|n\rangle|0\rangle, \quad |n\rangle|1\rangle$$

with $n \in Z$ being an integer representing the position on the line and $|0\rangle$ and $|1\rangle$ being the state of the system. A step of the quantum walk is represented by two operations C and S [Ambainis (2003)]. The Hadamard coin is represented by the following unitary matrix

$$C := W_1 = \begin{pmatrix} \frac{1}{\sqrt{2}} & \frac{1}{\sqrt{2}} \\ \frac{1}{\sqrt{2}} & -\frac{1}{\sqrt{2}} \end{pmatrix} = \frac{1}{\sqrt{2}} \cdot \begin{pmatrix} 1 & 1 \\ 1 & -1 \end{pmatrix}. \tag{13.3}$$

The unitary S operator is defined as

$$S \cdot |n\rangle|0\rangle = |n-1\rangle|0\rangle, \quad S \cdot |n\rangle|1\rangle = |n+1\rangle|1\rangle. \tag{13.4}$$

Suppose we start in location $|0\rangle$ and the state $|0\rangle$.

$$S \cdot C \cdot |0\rangle|0\rangle = U \cdot |0\rangle|0\rangle = \frac{|-1\rangle|0\rangle + |1\rangle|1\rangle}{\sqrt{2}} \tag{13.5}$$

after one step the result is similar to classical random walk. After two steps

$$U \cdot U \cdot |0\rangle|0\rangle = \frac{|-2\rangle|0\rangle + |0\rangle1\rangle + |0\rangle|0\rangle - |2\rangle|1\rangle}{2} \tag{13.6}$$

the probability of $n = 1$ is zero contrary to classical random walk. After three steps

$$U \cdot U \cdot U \cdot |0\rangle|0\rangle = \frac{|-3\rangle|0\rangle + |-1\rangle|1\rangle + 2 \cdot |-1\rangle|0\rangle - |1\rangle|0\rangle + |3\rangle|1\rangle}{2 \cdot \sqrt{2}} \tag{13.7}$$

the distribution is biased towards left because of the non-symmetric coin operator W_1. A symmetric unitary coin operator [Ambainis (2003)] would be represented by

$$C := \frac{1}{\sqrt{2}} \cdot \begin{pmatrix} 1 & i \\ i & 1 \end{pmatrix}. \tag{13.8}$$

In Figure 13.3 we see the comparison between the distribution of the classical random walk on a one dimensional lattice line and the quantum random walk with a symmetric coin operator. The quantum random walk propagates quadratically faster to the edges of the graph.

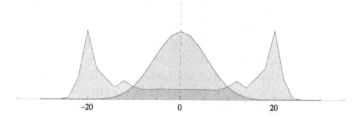

Fig. 13.3   Comparison between the distribution of the classical random walk on a one dimensional lattice and the quantum random walk with a symmetric coin operator after 50 steps [Hogg (2008)]. The walk starts at the origin. The classical walk has a peak near the origin, it corresponds to Gaussian distribution. The probability distribution for the quantum walk is approximately uniform near the origin and maximal near the edges of the graph.

13.1.5   *Quantum walk and search*

In quantum random walk the goal states are marked through an oracle operator as in the Grover's algorithm [Shenvi *et al.* (2003)]. To obtain for goal states with $n = |V|$ the complexity is $O(\sqrt{n})$

With the projection matrix P_m is

$$P_m = |x\rangle\langle x| = \begin{pmatrix} \frac{1}{n} & \frac{1}{n} & \cdots & \frac{1}{n} \\ \frac{1}{n} & \frac{1}{n} & \cdots & \frac{1}{n} \\ \vdots & \vdots & \ddots & \vdots \\ \frac{1}{n} & \frac{1}{n} & \cdots & \frac{1}{n} \end{pmatrix} \tag{13.9}$$

we get Grover's amplification also called Grover's diffusion operator.

$$G_m = 2 \cdot P_m - I_m. \tag{13.10}$$

One can redefine the coin operator in order to perform Grover's diffusion operator [Moore and Russell (2001)]. The reformulated coin operator C is with $m := deg(j)$

$$C \cdot |j\rangle|k\rangle = |j\rangle \cdot \left(\frac{2}{\sqrt{m}} \cdot \sum_{w:(j,w)\in E} |k \oplus w\rangle\langle k| - I_m \right). \tag{13.11}$$

13.1.6   *Quantum walk for formula evaluation*

Quantum random walk can determine the properties of a graph by generating different distributions. Quantum walk algorithms for Boolean formula evaluation can evaluate a Boolean formula quadratically faster than any known classical algorithm. For a Boolean formula $f(x)$ to the input string $x_1, \neg x_1, \cdots, x_m, \neg x_m$. Boolean formula is $f(x) = 1$ otherwise $f(x) = 0$ [Farhi and Gutmann (1998)], [Childs *et al.* (2007)], [Ambainis (2007)], [Ambainis *et al.* (2007)]. However one should not neglect the cost of building the coin operators that represent the instanced formula. For example to speed up alpha-beta search by evaluating AND-OR formulas as used in games [Farhi *et al.* (2008)], [Cleve *et al.* (2008)], the instantationed graph has to be determined dynamically during the performed search.

"We conclude by mentioning some open problems. Our algorithm needs to know the full structure of the formula beforehand to determine the coin's bias at each internal vertex...", cited from [Ambainis *et al.* (2007)].

13.2 Adiabatic Computation

Adiabatic quantum computation is an alternative approach to quantum computation. It is based on time evolution of a quantum system. The energy of a system can be described by a function [Farhi *et al.* (2000)], [Farhi *et al.* (2009)].

The lowest energy that the system can assume is called the ground state and corresponds to the global minima of the function. If the energy is dependent on two variables it can be represented by a two dimensional function (see Figure 13.4). A ball that is left on the slope will descend until it reaches the lowest point in the valley and will stay there. The corresponding point is stationary. If the function describing the energy of the system is changed very slowly the ball will be resting in a location which is the minimum point of the new equation. If one starts with a solution to the first simple function one will end up the process with a solution to a complicated function. The Hamiltonian H, which is the operator that is responsible for the time evolution of the state vector $\mathbf{x}(t)$. In quantum physics H is represented by the Schrödinger equation. The equation describes a linear superposition of different states at time t represented by the vector $\mathbf{x}(t)$

$$i \cdot h \cdot \frac{d}{dt}\mathbf{x}(t) = H \cdot \mathbf{x}(t) \tag{13.12}$$

with $i = \sqrt{-1}$ and h being the Planck's constant. The Hamiltonian operator H is related to the total energy of the system. The initial Hamiltonian H_{init} is in the ground state that corresponds to the solution of the initial simple problem. Then the initial Hamiltonian is changed very slowly until

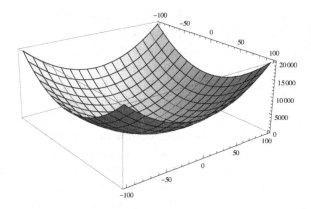

Fig. 13.4   The energy of a system can be described by a function. The lowest energy that the system can assume is called the ground state and corresponds to the global minima of the function. If the energy is dependent on two variables it can be represented by a two dimensional function.

it becomes the final Hamiltonian H_{final}.

$$H_{iniu} \overset{slowly}{\longrightarrow} H_{final}. \tag{13.13}$$

As the Hamiltonian is slowly changed multiple qubits are close to a point representing to the ground state. Adding a slight amount of energy by slowly changing the Hamiltonian keeps the system in the ground state. If we change the Hamiltonian to fast the system could go out of the ground state. It is not clear if the adiabatic computation is more or less efficient than a computation on a classical computer. For some problems, its efficiency could be better than the efficiency of classical computers.

13.2.1   *Quantum annealing*

Quantum annealing is a method for finding the global minimum of a function [Brooke *et al.* (1999)], [Johnson *et al.* (2011)]. A minimum of a function can be determined by gradient descent. Gradient descent starts at a random point of the function and moves down in the direction of steepest descent. It continues until it cannot proceed downward anymore. Often, a local (not necessarily global) minimum is found. Gradient descent is the basis of many learning and optimization algorithms, such as the back-propagation algorithm [Hertz *et al.* (1991)]. Quantum annealing attempts to avoid local minima by means of a quantum fluctuation parameter that replaces a state by a randomly selected neighboring state. In simulated annealing [Hertz *et al.* (1991)], the temperature plays a role that is related to quantum fluctuation. In simulated annealing, the neighborhood stays the same throughout the search. The temperature determines the probability of moving out of a local minimum. At the beginning, the temperature is high, and the probability of moving out of a minimum is high. Then, it is slowly reduced until the probability of moving out of a minimum is zero.

In quantum annealing, the quantum fluctuation parameter replaces a local minimum state with a randomly selected neighboring state in some fixed radius. The neighborhood extends over the whole search space at the beginning, and then, it is slowly reduced until the neighborhood shrinks to those few states that differ minimally from the current states. In a quantum system, the quantum fluctuation can be performed directly by an adiabatic process rather than needing to be simulated. These processes are based on quantum tunneling. The Heisenberg's uncertainty principle is given by

$$\Delta(G)\Delta(K) \geq \frac{|\langle x|[G, K] \cdot x\rangle|}{2}. \tag{13.14}$$

The principle is applied to the momentum and location of moving particles and is represented by

$$\Delta(x)\Delta(p) \geq \frac{h}{2} \tag{13.15}$$

where x is the position and p the momentum of a particle and h the Planck constant. It represents the relation between

$$\Delta(x)\Delta(p) \approx h \tag{13.16}$$

the position uncertainty times the momentum uncertainty. This relation is also valid for energy E and time t

$$\Delta(E)\Delta(t) \approx h. \tag{13.17}$$

This arrangement contradicts the first law of thermodynamics, which is the conservation of energy, where the sum of the amount of energy of a system remains constant. In quantum physics, there is uncertainty between the energy E and the time t.

$$\Delta(E) \approx \frac{h}{\Delta(t)}. \tag{13.18}$$

This uncertainty means that some energy can be borrowed, to overcome some mountain and go out of a minimum as long as we repay it in the time interval [Hey and Walters (2003)]

$$\Delta(t) \approx \frac{h}{\Delta(E)}. \tag{13.19}$$

Quantum tunneling is based on the Heisenberg uncertainty principle, as shown, and the wave-particle duality of matter represented by the wave propagation.

Quantum annealing can speed up some machine learning tasks that are based on a gradient descent method, such as the back-propagation algorithm that is used in artificial neural networks. It is an alternative to the simulated annealing that is used in the learning and optimization tasks. Adiabatic quantum computers based on quantum annealing do not correspond to a universal Turing machine. Rather, they are related to analog computers.

13.3 Quantum Neural Computation

Neuroimaging indicates how information processing is implemented in the brain and when specific structures and processes are invoked. For example, fMRI measures local properties of the cerebral blood flow and is based on blood oxygen level dependence. Changes of activity associated with various stimulus conditions are correlated with brain activity. However: "It is unclear that we will come to a better understanding of mental processes simply by observing which neural loci are active while subjects perform a task ", [Kosslyn (1999)]. In this section, we will describe the relationship between three quantum computation principles that speed up the computation and the human brain.

Human vision is based on information integration and is non-reversible. Hubel and Wiesel's discoveries provided a large amount of influence on the ways that neuroscientists think about the brain [Hubel (1988)]. They have inspired several models for pattern recognition. In these models, the neural units have a local view, unlike the common fully-connected networks [Fukushima (1980)], [Wichert (1993)], [Riesenhuber and Poggio (1999)], [Fukushima (1989)], [Cardoso and Wichert (2010)]. They gradually reduce the information from the input layer through the output layer. This task is accomplished by integrating local features into more global features in sequential transformations. Its purpose is to classify topological data by gradually reducing the information from the input layer through the output layer. Each of these transformations is composed of two different steps. The first step reduces the information by representing it with previously learned templates. The second step blurs the information to allow positional shifts,

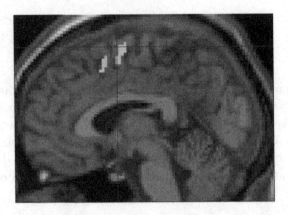

Fig. 13.5   Changes of activity associated with various stimulus conditions are correlated with the brain activity. A cluster indicates a brain activity during an experiment
[Wichert *et al.* (2002)].

giving the model some invariance under shifts and distortions. A quantum
neural model should perform a reversible computation. Neurons do not
perform a reversible computation, neither do neural networks. Associative
memory, as introduced in this book, is non-reversible.

A quantum associative memory should be represented by an operator W
and the Grover's algorithm to recall the patterns. For a question pattern,
a superposition of all possible stored answer patterns would be generated
by the operator W, which acts as an oracle [Tay *et al.* (2010)]. The operator W indicates the solution. In the next step, the Grover's algorithm
performs the phase amplification. Quantum computation is based on two
principles that are the basis of quantum algorithms. The resulting quantum
algorithms are capable of performing a quadratic computation faster than
a classical algorithm. The corresponding principles can be integrated into
the unified theories of human cognition, such as SOAR.

A non-computable process involves the possibility of generating true randomness [Penrose (1991)]. Classical physics leads to the paradox of free
will in a deterministic world. The question concerning randomness is highly
metaphysical. In classical physics, randomness does not exist; in quantum
physics, it cannot be explained. Besides randomness, quantum computation
cannot offer any non-computable schema such as that claimed by the quantum mind or the quantum consciousness hypothesis [Nunn *et al.* (1994)].

On the other hand, quantum cognition assumes that the brain is a classical computer in a quantum world. Because a wave function can be present at the macro scale, predictions such as the hidden inference are based on von Neumann probabilities and not on classical probability theory.

13.4 Epilogue

Quantum computation is based on two principles to speed up the computation:

- The QFT can determine the period of a wave.
- Grover's algorithm can speed up the search quadratically for a given number of possible solutions.

These two principles can be combined together in a quantum counting algorithm to estimate the number of possible solutions. It appears that in some domains of artificial intelligence, such as neural associative memories, diagnostic reasoning or sub-symbolic problem solving quantum algorithms other than quantum annealing are less useful. However, a symbolical artificial intelligence framework allows an elegant description of a possible universal quantum computer model that is capable of faster execution of programs.

The geometrical structure of the world can be used to speed up problem solving. This structure is present in simple Euclidian geometry as experienced by humans. It is also present in the geometrical structure of the world, as described by the quantum physics results with Grover's algorithm, which is based on the Householder reflection.

Bibliography

Aharonov, D. (1999). *Noisy Quantum Computation*, Ph.D. thesis, Hebrew University.

Aharonov, D., Ambainis, A., Kempe, J. and Vazirani, U. (2001). Quantum walks on graphs, in *Proceedings of ACM Symposium on Theory of Computation (STOC'01)*, pp. 50–59.

Aikins, J. (1986). Prototypical knowledge for expert systems, *Artificial Intelligence* **20**, pp. 163–210.

Ambainis, A. (2003). Quantum walks and their algorithmic applications, *International Journal of Quantum Information* **1**, p. 507, URL http://www.citebase.org/abstract?id=oai:arXiv.org:quant-ph/0403120.

Ambainis, A. (2004). Quantum search algorithms, *SIGACT News* **35**, 2, pp. 22–35, doi:http://doi.acm.org/10.1145/992287.992296.

Ambainis, A. (2007). A nearly optimal discrete query quantum algorithm for evaluating NAND formulas, *ArXiv e-prints* .

Ambainis, A., Childs, A. and Reichardt, B. (2007). Any and-or formula of size n can be evaluated in time $n^{\frac{1}{2}+o(1)}$ on a quantum computer, in *Foundations of Computer Science, 2007. FOCS '07. 48th Annual IEEE Symposium on*, pp. 363 –372, doi:10.1109/FOCS.2007.57.

Amico, L., Fazio, R., Osterloh, A. and Vedral, V. (2008). Entanglement in many-body systems, *Reviews of Modern Physics* **80**, 2, pp. 517–576.

Anderson, J. (1983). *The Architecture of Cognition* (Harvard University Press).

Anderson, J. A. (1995a). *An Introduction to Neural Networks* (The MIT Press).

Anderson, J. R. (1995b). *Cognitive Psychology and its Implications*, 4th edn. (W. H. Freeman and Company).

Aspray, W. (1990). *John von Neumann and the origins of modern computing*, History of computing (MIT Press), ISBN 9780262011211.

Ballard, D. H. (1997). *An Introduction to Natural Computation* (The MIT Press).

Bennett, C. (1973). Logical reversibility of computation, *IBM Journal of Research and Development* **17**, pp. 525–532.

Bennett, C. H. (1982). The thermodynamics of computation–a review, *International Journal of Theoretical Physics* **21**, 12, pp. 905–940.

Bennett, C. H. (1988). Notes on the history of reversible computation, *IBM J. Res. Dev.* **32**, 1, pp. 16–23.

Bennett, C. H. (1989). Time/space trade-offs for reversible computation, *SIAM Journal on Computing* **18**, 4, pp. 766–776, doi:10.1137/0218053, URL http://link.aip.org/link/?SMJ/18/766/1.

Bennett, C. H. (2003). Notes on landauer's principle, reversible computation, and maxwell's demon, *Studies In History and Philosophy of Science Part B: Studies In History and Philosophy of Modern Physics* **34**, 3, pp. 501 – 510, doi:DOI:10.1016/S1355-2198(03)00039-X.

Bennett, C. H., Bernstein, E., Brassard, G. and Vazirani, U. (1997). Strengths and weaknesses of quantum computing, URL http://www.citebase.org/abstract?id=oai:arXiv.org:quant-ph/9701001.

Bennett, C. H., Brassard, G., Crépeau, C., Jozsa, R., Peres, A. and Wootters, W. K. (1993). Teleporting an unknown quantum state via dual classical and einstein-podolsky-rosen channels, *Phys. Rev. Lett.* **70**, 13, pp. 1895–1899, doi:10.1103/PhysRevLett.70.1895.

Bentz, H. J., Hagstroem, M. and Palm, G. (1989). Information storage and effective data retrieval in sparse matrices, *Neural Networks* **2**, 4, pp. 289–293.

Bernstein, E. and Vazirani, U. (1993). Quantum complexity theory, in *STOC '93: Proceedings of the twenty-fifth annual ACM symposium on Theory of computing* (ACM, New York, NY, USA), ISBN 0-89791-591-7, pp. 11–20, doi:http://doi.acm.org/10.1145/167088.167097.

Biederman, I. and Ju, G. (1988). Surface vs. edge-based determinants of visual recognition, *Cognitive Psychology* **20**, pp. 38–6.

Boltzman, L. (1995). *Lectures on Gas Theory* (Dover Books on Physics).

Boven, L. V. and Epley, N. (2003). The unpacking effect in evaluative judgments: When the whole is less than the sum of its parts, *Journal of Experimental Social Psychology* **39**, pp. 263–269.

Boyer, M., Brassard, G., Hoeyer, P. and Tapp, A. (1998). Tight bounds on quantum searching, *Fortschritte der Physik* **46**, p. 493, URL http://www.citebase.org/abstract?id=oai:arXiv.org:quant-ph/9605034.

Brassard, G., Hoyer, P., Mosca, M. and Tapp, A. (2000). Quantum Amplitude Amplification and Estimation, *eprint arXiv:quant-ph/0005055* .

Brassard, G., Hoyer, P. and Tapp, A. (1998). Quantum counting, URL http://www.citebase.org/abstract?id=oai:arXiv.org:quant-ph/9805082.

Brooke, J., Bitko, D., Rosenbaum, T. and Aeppli, G. (1999). Quantum annealing of a disordered magnet, *Science* **284**, 5415, pp. 779–781.

Brownston, L., Farell, R., Kant, E. and Martin, N. (1985). *Programming Expert Systems in OPS5: An Introduction to Rule-Based Programming* (Addison-Wesley).

Brunak, S. and Lautrup, B. (1990). *Neural Networks Computers with Intuition* (World Scientific).

Busemeyer, J. R. and Bruza, P. D. (2012). *Quantum Models of Cognition and Decision* (Cambridge University Press).

Busemeyer, J. R., R., E. M. P., Franco and Trueblood, J. S. (2011). A quantum theoretical explanation for probability judgment errors, *Psychological Review* **118**, 2, pp. 193–218.

Busemeyer, J. R. and Trueblood, J. (2009). Comparison of quantum and bayesian inference models, in P. Bruza, D. Sofge, W. Lawless, K. van Rijsbergen and M. Klusch (eds.), *Quantum Interaction, Lecture Notes in Computer Science*, Vol. 5494 (Springer Berlin / Heidelberg), pp. 29–43, URL http://dx.doi.org/10.1007/978-3-642-00834-4-5.

Busemeyer, J. R., Wang, Z. and Lambert-Mogiliansky, A. (2009). Empirical comparison of markov and quantum models of decision making, *Journal of Mathematical Psychology* **53**, 5, pp. 423 – 433, doi:DOI:10.1016/j.jmp.2009.03.002.

Busemeyer, J. R., Wang, Z. and Townsend, J. T. (2006). Quantum dynamics of human decision-making, *Journal of Mathematical Psychology* **50**, 3, pp. 220 – 241, doi:DOI:10.1016/j.jmp.2006.01.003.

Byrne, P. (2007). The many worlds of hugh everett, *Scientific American Magazine* , pp. 98–105.

Cardoso, A. and Wichert, A. (2010). Neocognitron and the map transformation cascade, *Neural Networks* **23**, 1, pp. 74–88.

Childs, A. M. (2011). *LECTURE 14: Discrete-time quantum walk*, University of Waterloo, URL http://www.math.uwaterloo.ca/~amchilds/teaching/w11/l14.pdf.

Childs, A. M., Reichardt, B. W., Spalek, R. and Zhang, S. (2007). Every NAND formula of size N can be evaluated in time $N^{\frac{1}{2}+o(1)}$ on a quantum computer, *eprint arXiv:quant-ph/0703015* .

Church, A. (1936a). A note on the entscheidungsproblem, *Journal of Symbolic Logic* **1**, 1, pp. 40–41.

Church, A. (1936b). An unsolvable problem of elementary number theory, *American Journal of Mathematics* **58**, 2, pp. 345–363.

Church, A. (1941). *The Calculi of Lambda-Conversion*, Annals of Mathematics Studies (Princeton University Press, Princeton, New Jersey, USA).

Churchland, P. S. and Sejnowski, T. J. (1994). *The Computational Brain* (The MIT Press).

Cleve, R., Gavinsky, D. and Yonge-Mallo, D. (2008). Quantum algorithms for evaluating min-max trees, in Y. Kawano and M. Mosca (eds.), *Proceedings of Theory of Quantum Computation, Communication, and Cryptography (TQC 2008)*, Vol. 5106 (Springer Berlin / Heidelberg), pp. 11–15.

Cooper, G. and Herskovits, E. (1990). Determination of the entropy of a belief network is np-hard, Tech. rep., Medical Computer Science, Stanford University.

Cormen, T. H., Leiserson, C. E., Rivest, R. L. and Stein, C. (2001). *Introduction to Algorithms, 2/e* (MIT Press).

Deutsch, D. (1985). Quantum theory, the church-turing principle and the universal quantum computer, in *Proceedings of the Royal Society of London-Series A, Mathematical and Physical Sciences*, Vol. 400, pp. 97–117.

Deutsch, D. (1997). *The Fabric of Reality* (Penguin Group).

Deutsch, D. and Jozsa, R. (1992). Rapid Solution of Problems by Quantum Computation, *Royal Society of London Proceedings Series A* **439**, pp. 553–558.

Everett, H. (1959). "relative state" formulation of quantum mechanics, *Reviews of Modern Physics* **29**, pp. 454–462.

Farhi, E., Goldstone, J., Gosset, D., Gutmann, S., Meyer, H. B. and Shor, P. (2009). Quantum adiabatic algorithms, small gaps, and different paths, URL http://www.citebase.org/abstract?id=oai:arXiv.org:0909.4766.

Farhi, E., Goldstone, J. and Gutmann, S. (2008). A quantum algorithm for the hamiltonian nand tree, *Theory of Computing* **4**, 1, pp. 169–190, doi:10.4086/toc.2008.v004a008.

Farhi, E., Goldstone, J., Gutmann, S. and Sipser, M. (2000). Quantum Computation by Adiabatic Evolution, *ArXiv Quantum Physics e-prints* .

Farhi, E. and Gutmann, S. (1998). Quantum computation and decision trees, *Phys. Rev. A* **58**, 2, pp. 915–928, doi:10.1103/PhysRevA.58.915.

Feldman, J. (1985). Four frames suffice: A provisional model of vision and space, *Behavioral and Brain Sciences* **8**, pp. 265–289.

Fikes, R. E. and Nilsson, N. J. (1971). Strips: A new approach to the application of theorem proving, *Artificial Intelligence* **2**.

Forgy, C. (1981). Ops5 user's manual cmu-cs-81-135, Tech. rep., Computer Science Department, Carnegie-Mellon University, Pittsburgh, Pensilvania USA.

Franklin, S. (1997). *Artificial Minds* (MIT Press).

Freeman, J. A. (1994). *Simulating Neural Networks with Mathematica* (Addison-Wesley).

Fukushima, K. (1980). Neocognitron: a self organizing neural network model for a mechanism of pattern recognition unaffected by shift in position. *Biol Cybern* **36**, 4, pp. 193–202.

Fukushima, K. (1989). Analisys of the process of visual pattern recognition by the neocognitron, *Neural Networks* **2**, pp. 413–420.

Fuster, J. (1995). *Memory in the Cerebral Cortex* (The MIT Press).

Gardner, M. (1979). Mathematical games: Mathematical games: The random number omega bids fair to hold the mzsteries of the universe, *Scientific American* , pp. 20–30.

Gaylord, R. J. and Wellin, P. R. (1995). *Computer Simulations with Mathematica* (Spriner Verlag).

Ghosh, S., Rosenbaum, T. F., Aeppli, G. and Coppersmith, S. N. (2003). Entangled quantum state of magnetic dipoles, *Nature* **425**, pp. 48–51.

Gilovich, T. (1999). Tversky, in *The MIT Encyclopedia of the Cognitive Sciences* (The MIT Press), pp. 849–850.

Givan, R. and Dean, T. (1997). Model minimization, regression, and propositional strips planning, in *15th International Joint Conference on Artificial Intelligence*, pp. 1163–8.

Goldstone, R. (1999). Similarity, in *The MIT Encyclopedia of the Cognitive Sciences* (The MIT Press), pp. 763–765.

Grover, L. K. (1996). A fast quantum mechanical algorithm for database search, in *STOC '96: Proceedings of the twenty-eighth annual ACM symposium on Theory of computing* (ACM, New York, NY, USA), ISBN 0-89791-785-5, pp. 212–219, doi:http://doi.acm.org/10.1145/237814.237866.

Grover, L. K. (1997). Quantum mechanics helps in searching for a needle in a haystack, *Physical Review Letters* **79**, p. 325, URL doi:10.1103/ PhysRevLett.79.325.

Grover, L. K. (1998a). A framework for fast quantum mechanical algorithms, in *STOC '98: Proceedings of the thirtieth annual ACM symposium on Theory of computing* (ACM, New York, NY, USA), ISBN 0-89791-962-9, pp. 53–62, doi:http://doi.acm.org/10.1145/276698.276712.

Grover, L. K. (1998b). Quantum computers can search rapidly by using almost any transformation, *Phys. Rev. Lett.* **80**, 19, pp. 4329–4332, doi:10.1103/ PhysRevLett.80.4329.

Haines, T. (1999). *Walking with Dinosaurs - a Natural History* (BBC Worldwide Limited).

Hecht-Nielsen, R. (1989). *Neurocomputing* (Addison-Wesley).

Heisenberg, W. (1949). *The Physical Principles of the Quantum Theory* (Courier Dover Publications).

Hertz, J., Krogh, A. and Palmer, R. G. (1991). *Introduction to the Theory of Neural Computation* (Addison-Wesley).

Hey, A. and Walters, P. (2003). *The New Quantum Universe* (Cambridge University Press).

Hirvensalo, M. (2004). *Quantum Computing* (Springer-Verlag, Berlin Heidelberg).

Hogg, T. (2008). Quantum random walk from the wolfram demonstrations project, http://demonstrations.wolfram.com/QuantumRandomWalk/.

Hubel, D. H. (1988). *Eye, Brain, and Vision* (Scientific Ammerican Library, Oxford, England).

Hummel, J. (1999). Binding problem, in R. A. Wilson and F. C. Keil (eds.), *The MIT Encyclopedia of the Cognitive Sciences* (The MIT Press), pp. 85–86.

Hyman, A. (1985). *Charles Babbage: Pioneer of the Computer* (Princeton University Press).

Jackson, P. (1999). *Introduction to Expert Systems*, 3rd edn. (Addison-Wesley).

Johnson, M. W., Amin, M. H. S., Gildert, S., Lanting, T., Hamze, F., Dickson, N., Harris, R., Berkley, A. J., Johansson, J., Bunyk, P., Chapple, E. M., Enderud, C., Hilton, J. P., Karimi, K., Ladizinsky, E., Ladizinsky, N., Oh, T., Perminov, I., Rich, C., Thom, M. C., Tolkacheva, E., Truncik, C. J. S., Uchaikin, S., Wang, J., Wilson, B. and Rose, G. (2011). Quantum annealing with manufactured spins, *Nature* **473**, 7346, pp. 194–198, URL http://dx.doi.org/10.1038/nature10012.

Kahn, G., Kepner, A. and Pepper, J. (1987). Test: a model-driven application shell, in *National Conference on Artificial Intelligence*, pp. 814–18.

Kaye, P. R., Laflamme, R. and Mosca, M. (2007). *An Introduction to Quantum Computing* (Oxford University Press, USA).

Kempe, J. (2003). Quantum random walks - an introductory overview, *Contemporary Physics* **44**, pp. 307–327, URL http://www.citebase.org/abstract? id=oai:arXiv.org:quant-ph/0303081.

Kitaev, A. (1996). Quantum measurements and the abelian stabilizer problem, *Electronic Colloquium on Computational Complexity* **3**, TR96-003.

Klahr, P. and Waterman, D. (1986). *Expert Systems: Techniques, Tools and Applications* (Addison-Wesley).

Knoblauch, A., Palm, G. and Sommer, F. (2010). Memory capacities for synaptic and structural plasticity, *Neural Computation* **22**, pp. 289–341.

Kohonen, T. (1989). *Self-Organization and Associative Memory*, 3rd edn. (Springer-Verlag).

Kolda, T. G. and Bader, B. W. (2009). Tensor decompositions and applications, *SIAM Review* **51**, 3, pp. 455–500.

Kolmogorov, A. (1933). *Grundbegriffe der Wahrscheinlichkeitsrechnung* (Springer-Verlag).

Korf, R. E. (1985). Depth-first iterative-deepening : An optimal admissible tree search, *Artificial Intelligence* **27**, 1, pp. 97 – 109, doi:DOI:10.1016/0004-3702(85)90084-0.

Kosslyn, S. M. (1999). If neuroimaging is the answer, what is the question? *Philosophical Transactions of the Royal Society of London B Biological Sciences* **354**, pp. 1283–1294.

Kropff, E. and Treves, A. (2005). The storage capacity of potts models for semantic memory retrieval, *Journal of Statistical Mechanics: Theory and Experiment* .

Kurbat, M., Smith, E. and Medin, D. (1994). Categorization, typicality, and shape similarity, in A. Ram and K. Eiselt (eds.), *Proceedings of the Cognitive Science Meeting* (Atlanta, GA), pp. 520–530.

Kurfess, F. J. (1997). Neural networks and structured knowledge, in C. Hermann, F. Reine and A. Strohmaier (eds.), *Knowledge in Neural Networks* (Logos Verlag, Berlin), pp. 5–22.

Kurzweil, R. (1990). *The Age of Intelligent Machines* (The MIT Press).

Laird, J. E., Rosenbloom, P. S. and Newell, A. (1986). Chunking in soar: The anatomy of a general learning mechanism, *Machine Learning* **1**, 1, pp. 11–46.

Laird, J. F., Newell, A. and Rosenbloom, P. S. (1987). SOAR: An architecture for general intelligence, *Artificial Intelligence* **40**.

Lakeoff, G. (1987). *Women, Fire, and Dangerous Things* (The University of Chicago Press).

Lambert, D. (1983). *Collins Guide to Dinosaurs* (Diagram Visual Information Ltd).

Lambert, D. (1993). *The Ultimate Dinosaur Book* (Dorling Kindersley).

Lancy, D. (1983). *Cross-Cultural Studies in Cognition and Mathematics* (Academic Press, New York).

Landauer, R. (1961). Irreversibility and heat generation in the computing process, *IBM Journal of Research and Development* **5**, pp. 183–191.

Landauer, R. (1992). Information is physical, in *Physics and Computation, 1992. PhysComp '92., Workshop on*, pp. 1–4.

Lewis, H. R. and Papadimitriou, C. H. (1981). *Elements of the Theory of Computation* (Prentice Hall PTR, Upper Saddle River, NJ, USA), ISBN 0132624788.

Luger, G. F. and Stubblefield, W. A. (1993). *Artificial Intelligence: Structures and Strategies for Complex Problem Solving: Second Edition* (The Benjamin/Cummings Publishing Company, Inc, Menlo Park, CA, USA).

Luger, G. F. and Stubblefield, W. A. (1998). *Artificial Intelligence, Structures and Strategies for Complex Problem Solving*, 3rd edn. (Addison-Wesley).

Marcinowski, M. (1987). *Codierungsprobleme beim Assoziativen Speichern*, Master's thesis, Fakultät für Physik der Eberhard-Karls-Universität Tübingen.

Markov, A. (1954). *The theory of algorithms* (National Academy of Sciences, USSR).

Maxwell, J. C. (2001). *Theory of Heat (9ed)* (Courier Dover Publications).

McClelland, J. and Kawamoto, A. (1986). Mechanisms of sentence processing: Assigning roles to constituents of sentences, in J. McClelland and D. Rumelhart (eds.), *Parallel Distributed Processing* (The MIT Press), pp. 272–325.

McClelland, J. and Rumelhart, D. (1985). Distributed memory and the representation of general and specific memory, *Journal of Experimental Psychology: General* **114**, pp. 159–188.

Miikkulainen, R. (1993). *Subsymbolic Natural Language Processing: An Integrated Model of Scripts, Lexicon and Memory* (The MIT Press).

Minsky, M. (1975). A framework for representing knowledge, in P. Winston (ed.), *The Psychology of Computer Vision* (McGraw-Hill, New York), pp. 211–77.

Minsky, M. (1986). *The Society of Mind* (Simon and Schuster, New York).

Mitchell, T. (1997). *Machine Learning* (McGraw-Hill).

Moore, C. and Russell, A. (2001). Quantum Walks on the Hypercube, *eprint arXiv:quant-ph/0104137* .

Murphy, G. and Brownell, H. (1985). Category differentiation in object recognition: Typicality constraints on the basic category advantage, *Journal of Experimental Psychology* **11**, p. 70ff.

Myers, J. M. (1997). Can a universal quantum computer be fully quantum? *Phys. Rev. Lett.* **78**, 9, pp. 1823–1824, doi:10.1103/PhysRevLett.78.1823.

Newell, A. (1990). *Unified Theories of Cognition* (Harvard University Press).

Newell, A. and Simon, H. (1972). *Human Problem Solving* (Prentice-Hall).

Newell, A. and Simon, H. (1976). Computer science as empirical inquiry: symbols and search. *Communication of the ACM* **19**, 3, pp. 113–126.

Nielsen, M. A. and Chuang, I. L. (2000). *Quantum Computation and Quantum Information* (Cambridge University Press, Cambridge, MA, USA).

Nilsson, N. J. (1982). *Principles of Artificial Intelligence* (Springer-Verlag).

Nunn, C. M., Clarke, C. and Blott, B. (1994). Collapse of a quantum field may affect brain function, *Journal of Consciousness Studies* **1**, 1, pp. 127–139.

OFTA (1991). *Les Réseaux de Neurones* (Masson).

Opwis, K. and Plötzner, R. (1996). *Kognitive Psychologie mit dem Computer* (Spektrum Akademischer Verlag, Heidelberg Berlin Oxford).

Osherson, D. N. (1987). New axioms for the contrast model of similarity, *Journal of Mathematical Psychology* **31**, pp. 93–103.

Osherson, D. N. (1995). Probability judgment, in E. E. Smith and D. N. Osherson (eds.), *Thinking*, Vol. 3, 2nd edn., chap. two (MIT Press), pp. 35–75.

Palm, G. (1982). *Neural Assemblies, an Alternative Approach to Artificial Intelligence* (Springer-Verlag).

Palm, G. (1990). Assoziatives Gedächtnis und Gehirntheorie, in *Gehirn und Kognition* (Spektrum der Wissenschaft), pp. 164–174.

Palm, G., Schwenker, F. and Bibbig, A. (1992). Theorie Neuronaler Netze 1, Skript zur Vorlesung, university of Ulm, Department of Neural Information Processing.

Pearl, J. (1984). *Heuristics: Intelligent Strategies for Computer Problem Solving* (Addison-Wesley).

Pearl, J. (1989). *Probabilistic Reasoning in Intelligent Systems: Networks of Plausible Inference* (Morgan Kaufmann, Palo Alto, CA).

Penrose, R. (1991). *The Emperor's New Mind* (Penguin).

Post, E. (1943). Formal reductions of the general combinatorial problem, *American Journal of Mathematics* **65**, pp. 197–268.

Quillian, R. (1968). Semantic memory, in M. Minsky (ed.), *Semantic Information Processing* (MIT Press), pp. 227–270.

Reid, C. (1996). *Hilbert* (Spriner Verlag).

Resnikoff, H. L. (1989). *The Illusion of Reality* (Springer-Verlag).

Rieffel, E. and Polak, W. (2011). *Quantum Computing - A Gentle Introduction* (The MIT Press).

Riesenhuber, M. and Poggio, T. (1999). Hierarchical models of object recognition in cortex, *Nature Neuroscience* **2**, pp. 1019–1025.

Riley, K. F., Hobson, M. P. and Bence, S. J. (2006). *Mathematical methods for physics and engineering* (Cambridge University Press).

Ross, S. M. (2009). *Introduction to probability and statistics for engineers and scientists*, 4th edn. (Academic Press).

Rumelhart, D. and McClelland (1986). On learning the past tense of english verbs, in J. McClelland and D. Rumelhart (eds.), *Parallel Distributed Processing* (MIT Press), pp. 216–271.

Russell, S. and Norvig, P. (2010). *Artificial intelligence: a modern approach*, Prentice Hall series in artificial intelligence (Prentice Hall), ISBN 9780136042594, URL http://books.google.pt/books?id=8jZBksh-bUMC.

Russell, S. J. and Norvig, P. (1995). *Artificial intelligemce: a modern approach* (Prentice-Hall).

Schrödinger, E. (1935). Die gegenwärtige situation in der quantenmechanik, *Naturwissenschaften* **23**, 807.

Schwenker, F. (1996). Küntliche Neuronale Netze: Ein Überblick über die theoretischen Grundlagen, in G. Bol, G. Nakhaeizadeh and K. Vollmer (eds.), *Finanzmarktanalyse und -prognose mit innovativen und quantitativen Verfahren* (Physica-Verlag), pp. 1–14.

Shannon, C. E. (1948). A mathematical theory of communication, *Bell System Technical Journal* , pp. 1–54.

Shannon, C. E. (1953). Computers and automata, *Proceedings of the I.R.E.* **41**, pp. 1253–1241.

Shastri, L. (1988). *Semantic Networks: An Evidential Formulation and its Connectionistic Realization* (Morgan Kaufmann, London).

Shenvi, N., Kempe, J. and Whaley, K. B. (2003). Quantum random-walk search algorithm, *Phys. Rev. A* **67**, 5, p. 052307, doi:10.1103/PhysRevA.67.052307.

Shim, G. M., Kim, D. and Choi, M. Y. (1990). Statistical-mechanical formulation of the wiiishaw model with local inhibition, *Physical Review A A* **43**, 12, pp. 7012–7018.

Shor, P. (1994). Algorithms for quantum computation: discrete logarithms and factoring, in *Proceedings 35th Annual Symposium on Foundations of Computer Science*, pp. 124–134, doi:10.1109/SFCS.1994.365700.

Shor, P. W. (1995). Polynomial-Time Algorithms for Prime Factorization and Discrete Logarithms on a Quantum Computer, *ArXiv Quantum Physics e-prints* .

Simon, H. A. (1991). *Models of my Life* (Basic Books, New York).

Smith, E., Balzano, G. and Walker, J. (1978). Nominal, perceptual, and semantic codes in picture categorization, in J. Cotton and R. Klatzky (eds.), *Semantic factors in cognition* (Hillsdale, NJ: Erlbaum Associates), pp. 137–168.

Smith, E. and Sloman, S. (1994). Similarity vs. rule-based categorization, *Memory Cognition* **22**, pp. 377–386.

Smith, E. E. (1995). Concepts and categorization, in E. E. Smith and D. N. Osherson (eds.), *Thinking*, Vol. 3, 2nd edn., chap. one (MIT Press), pp. 3–33.

Sommer, F. T. (1993). *Theorie neuronaler Assoziativspeicher*, Ph.D. thesis, Heinrich-Heine-Universität Düsseldorf, Düsseldorf.

Squire, L. R. and Kandel, E. R. (1999). *Memory. From Mind to Moleculus* (Scientific American Library).

Steinbuch, K. (1961). Die Lernmatrix, *Kybernetik* **1**, pp. 36–45.

Steinbuch, K. (1971). *Automat und Mensch*, 4th edn. (Springer-Verlag).

Stonier, T. (1990). *Information and the Internal Structure of Universe* (Springer-Verlag).

Sun, R. (1995). A two-level hybrid architecture for structuring knowledge for commonsense reasoning, in R. Sun and L. A. Bookman (eds.), *Computational Architectures Integrating Neural and Symbolic Processing*, chap. 8 (Kluwer Academic Publishers), pp. 247–182.

Sussman, G. (1975). *A Computer Model of Skill Acquisition* (MIT, Cambridge).

Szilárd, L. (1929). Über die entropieverminderung in einem thermodynamischen system bei eingriffen intelligenter wesen, *Zeitschrift für Physik* **53**, pp. 840–856.

Tarrataca, L. and Wichert, A. (2011a). Problem-solving and quantum computation, *Cognitive Computation* **3**, pp. 510–524, URL http://dx.doi.org/10.1007/s12559-011-9103-6.

Tarrataca, L. and Wichert, A. (2011b). Tree search and quantum computation, *Quantum Information Processing* **10**, 4, pp. 475–500, 10.1007/s11128-010-0212-z.

Tarrataca, L. and Wichert, A. (2012a). Iterative quantum tree search, CiE 2012 - How the World Computes, 2012.

Tarrataca, L. and Wichert, A. (2012b). A quantum production model, *Quantum Information Processing* **11**, 1, pp. 189–209, URL http://dx.doi.org/10.1007/s11128-011-0241-2, 10.1007/s11128-011-0231-4.

Tarrataca, L. and Wichert, A. (2013a). Intricacies of quantum computational paths, *Quantum Information Processing* **12**, pp. 1365–1378, doi:10.1007/ s11128-012-0475-7.

Tarrataca, L. and Wichert, A. (2013b). Quantum iterative deepening with an application to the halting problem, *PLOS ONE* **8**, 3.

Tarski, A. (1944). The semantic conception of truth and foundations of semantics, *Philos. and Phenom. Res.* **4**, pp. 241–376.

Tarski, A. (1956). *Logic, Semantics,Metamathematics* (Oxford University Press, London).

Tarski, A. (1995). *Pisma logiczno-filozoficzne. Prawda*, Vol. 1 (Wydawnictwo Naukowe PWN, Warszawa).

Tay, N., Loo, C. and Perus, M. (2010). Face recognition with quantum associative networks using overcomplete gabor wavelet, *Cognitive Computation* , pp. 1– 6URL http://dx.doi.org/10.1007/s12559-010-9047-2, 10.1007/s12559-010-9047-2.

Toffoli, T. (1980a). Reversible computing, in *Proceedings of the 7th Colloquium on Automata, Languages and Programming* (Springer-Verlag, London, UK), ISBN 3-540-10003-2, pp. 632–644.

Toffoli, T. (1980b). Reversible computing, Tech. rep., Massschusetts Institute of Technology, Laboratory for Computer Science, Massachusetts, MA, USA.

Toffoli, T. (1980c). Reversible computing, in J. de Bakker and J. van Leeuwen (eds.), *Automata, Languages and Programming, Lecture Notes in Computer Science*, Vol. 85 (Springer Berlin / Heidelberg), pp. 632–644, URL http://dx.doi.org/10.1007/3-540-10003-2$_$104.

Topsoe, F. (1974). *Informationstheorie* (Teubner Sudienbucher).

Turing, A. (1936). On computable numbers, with an application to the entscheidungsproblem, in *Proceedings of the London Mathematical Society*, Vol. 2, pp. 260–265.

Turing, A. M. (1950). Computing machinery and intelligence, *Mind* **59**.

Tversky, A. (1977). Feature of similarity, *Psychological Review* **84**, pp. 327–352.

Vedral, V. (2011). Living in a quantum world, *Scientific American* **304**, 6, pp. 38–43.

von Neumann, J. (1945). First draft of a report on the edvac, Tech. rep., University of Pennsylvania.

Watrous, J. (1998). Quantum simulations of classical random walks and undirected graph connectivity, *CoRR* **cs.CC/9812012**.

Wennekers, T. (1999). *Synchronisation und Assoziation in Neuronalen Netzen* (Shaker Verlag, Aachen).

Wichert, A. (1993). MTCn-nets, in *Proceedings World Congres on Neural Networks* (Lawrence Erlbaum), pp. 59–62.

Wichert, A. (1998). Hierarchical categorization, in M. W. Evens (ed.), *Ninth Midwest Artificial Intelligence and Cognitive Science Conference* (AAAI Press), pp. 141–148.

Wichert, A. (2000). A categorical expert system "jurassic", *Expert Systems with Application* **19**, 3, pp. 149–158.

Wichert, A. (2001). Pictorial reasoning with cell assemblies, *Connection Science* **13**, 1.

Wichert, A. (2004). Categorial expert systems, *Expert Systems* **21**, 1, pp. 34–47.

Wichert, A. (2005a). Associative computer: a hybrid connectionistic production system, *Cognitive Systems Research* **6**, 2, pp. 111–144.

Wichert, A. (2005b). Associative diagnose, *Expert Systems* **22**, 1, pp. 26–39.

Wichert, A. (2006). Cell assemblies for diagnostic problem-solving, *Neurocomputing* **69**, 7-9, pp. 810–824.

Wichert, A. (2009). Sub-symbols and icons, *Cognitive Computation* **1**, 4, pp. 342–347.

Wichert, A. (2011). The role of attention in the context of associative memory, *Cognitive Computation* **3**, 1.

Wichert, A. (2012). Inference, ontologies and the pump of though, in E. Davelaar (ed.), *Connectionist Models of Neurocognition and Emergent Behavior* (World Scientific), pp. 227 –224.

Wichert, A. (2013). Proto logic and neural subsymbolic reasoning, *Journal of Logic and Computation* **23**, 3, pp. 627–643.

Wichert, A., Abler, B., Grothe, J., Walter, H. and Sommer, F. T. (2002). Exploratory analysis of event-related fmri demonstrated in a working memory study, in F. Sommer and A. Wichert (eds.), *Exploratory analysis and data modeling in functional neuroimaging*, chap. 5 (MIT Press, Boston, MA), pp. 77–108.

Wichert, A., Pereira, J. D. and Carreira, P. (2008). Visual search light model for mental problem solving, *Neurocomputing* **71**, 13-15, pp. 2806–2822.

Wickelgren, W. A. (1969). Context-sensitive coding, associative memory, and serial order in (speech)behavior, *Psychological Review* **76**, pp. 1–15.

Wickelgren, W. A. (1977). *Cognitive Psychology* (Prentice-Hall).

Williams, C. P. and Clearwatter, S. H. (1997). *Explorations in Quantum Computing* (Springer-Verlag).

Willshaw, D., Buneman, O. and Longuet-Higgins, H. (1969). Nonholgraphic associative memory, *Nature* **222**, pp. 960–962.

Winston, P. H. (1992). *Artificial Intelligence*, 3rd edn. (Addison-Wesley).

Zalka, C. (1999). Grover's quantum searching algorithm is optimal, *Physical Review A* **60**, p. 2746, URL http://www.citebase.org/abstract?id=oai:arXiv.org:quant-ph/9711070.

Index